The Flip Side of Free

The Flip Side of Free

Understanding the Economics of the Internet

Michael Kende

The MIT Press
Cambridge, Massachusetts
London, England

This book was set in Stone Serif and Stone Sans by Westchester Publishing Services. Printed and bound in the United States of America.

Library of Congress Cataloging-in-Publication Data

Names: Kende, M. (Michael), author.
Title: The flip side of free : understanding the economics of the internet / Michael Kende.
Description: Cambridge, Massachusetts : The MIT Press, [2021] | Includes bibliographical references and index.
Identifiers: LCCN 2020020604 | ISBN 9780262045650 (hardcover)
Subjects: LCSH: Internet--Economic aspects. | Information technology--Economic aspects. | Technological innovations--Economic aspects. | Internet--Security measures.
Classification: LCC HC79.I55 K45 2021 | DDC 384.3/1--dc23
LC record available at https://lccn.loc.gov/2020020604

10 9 8 7 6 5 4 3 2 1

Contents

I The Upside of Free

    1 Introduction 3

    2 The Global Standard 21

    3 Why Is Wi-Fi Free? 39

    4 Something for Nothing 63

II The Downside of Free

    5 Did We Give Away Our Privacy? 83

    6 Is Our Data Secure? 107

    7 Platform Power 121

    8 The Digital Divide 149

III The Future of Free

    9 Trust the Future 175

    10 The Need for Change 191

Acknowledgments 201

Notes 203

Bibliography 221

Index 237

I The Upside of Free

1   Introduction

The first lesson of economics is scarcity: there is never enough of anything to fully satisfy all those who want it. The first lesson of politics is to disregard the first lesson of economics.

—Thomas Sowell

Sitting in a Starbucks recently, I logged on to the free Wi-Fi to check my email and catch up on the news. I also had to make a call overseas and used FaceTime. As my call was ringing, I noticed people coming in and going to a side counter to pick up their coffee, which they had ordered and paid for using the Starbucks app. I then had a quick flashback to life before the Internet and thought how different this would have been before.

Earlier, Starbucks may have provided a few free newspapers, or I would have brought my own. I would have had to make my call from a payphone, if I had enough change. And the line for coffee would have been longer, with some anxiously checking their watches so they would make it on time to work. My earlier self would have been amazed to see what a telephone could do. But as my current self began to download the Starbucks app to try it, I wondered if it was just a bit too free and easy.

Had everyone rushing in to pick up their ready coffee actually read the terms of use when they downloaded the app? Or, like most people, did they just click their acceptance? You would have to read the Starbucks Rewards terms, the Starbucks Card terms, and the application terms, which took you to a privacy statement. At a total of around twenty-two thousand words, the app would have to save a lot of time waiting for coffee to make up for the time needed to read the entire terms of use.

But without reading the privacy statement, how would you know that Starbucks "may allow third parties to collect device and usage information and location information across your different devices through mobile software development kits, cookies, web beacons and other similar technologies"?[1] I assume most people know by now that these are no-cal, hi-spy cookies, but what is a "web beacon"? And who are the third parties and what are they doing with the data?

So much for privacy—so what about security? Using the app to pay for a coffee is convenient, but it requires a link to a credit card. Well, sure enough, hackers have figured out how to load money from other people's credit cards and spend it using their apps. And unless a user has opted out of the arbitration procedure within thirty days of agreeing to the terms of use, they have given up many legal rights, including the right to join a class action proceeding. And you can't opt out online: you have to mail a traditional letter.

Starbucks is just one example of the trade-offs we are making every day. If you want to linger, they provide free Wi-Fi, and if you want to rush in and pick up your coffee, there is a free app for that, at least in the United States. But free has a flip side, and we are beginning to grapple with it.

Economics is often called the *study of scarcity*: there is a limit on the natural resources that can be extracted, products that can be produced, and services that can be delivered. At the same time, government often embodies the saying that if you have a hammer, everything looks like a nail. In the physical world, economics examines how markets allocate resources and when they fail, while governments oversee or regulate markets. However, on the Internet, there is no scarcity tied to streaming one more perfect copy of a song or view of a video, and typically online taxes have not been imposed, mergers not challenged, and content not regulated.

Because there is no scarcity, there seems to be no constraint. We went from being wired to our desks using slow, beige computers to having ubiquitous mobile access over shiny new devices. We went from buying media in stores to streaming it for free, from paying for phone calls by the minute to free video calls. There is no end to the free services and content that we can access, and when we access more, whether at home, on the road, or at a hotspot, we generally don't pay for the extra data we use. And everything is becoming "smart"—that is, online: phones, TVs, watches, speakers, earphones, even refrigerators, with seemingly insatiable demand for more.

But then it all began to change. It is hard to pinpoint one turning point. Was it the Snowden revelations? Cambridge Analytica? Russian election interference? The WannaCry attack? Christchurch? Was there a distinct turning point, or was it just a slow accumulation that finally reached its limits? Whatever it was, the techlash started, and governments have taken notice.[2] The techlash led to the techno caveat "I love my smart speaker," which is now often followed by "but I wonder if it is listening all the time?"

I have worked on Internet issues for most of my career, and I am overwhelmingly optimistic about the benefits of the Internet. I started as an academic economist working on the benefits of networks, and the Internet is one of the largest, and certainly most useful, networks imaginable. I worked as a US regulator at the Federal Communications Commission (FCC), as broadband began to emerge and Internet providers began to merge. At the Internet Society, and as a consultant, I have advised governments and international organizations around the world on policy and regulation as Internet access came to be seen as increasingly important to a country's economy.

At the same time, I am also an enthusiastic user. I can remember the first internal email I sent when I worked in the Information Technology group at Procter & Gamble after college; the first external email I sent to my father when I started studying graduate economics at MIT; installing the earliest Mosaic browser when I taught at INSEAD business school; and moving from AOL to cable broadband when I worked for the FCC. I am also an enthusiastic early adopter and upgrader of all gadgets digital; what I cannot pass down to my daughters piles up in a closet.

And regardless of from which angle I look, I remain hopeful about the future of the Internet. The response to the COVID-19 crisis demonstrated conclusively the value of the Internet and its economics, albeit in drastic and unwanted circumstances. Under conditions of lockdown, many were able to continue to work so that governments, businesses, and schools were able to provide services. Students were able to keep up with their studies, telemedicine was available, families and friends could communicate, health researchers could share data, and we could also settle back for some well-deserved entertainment. Free services alleviated concerns with tightening budgets, and usage skyrocketed with little slowdown.

But one must also be realistic about the gathering challenges, which were also highlighted during the pandemic. Cyberattacks increased, both because of the increased usage and also because fearful users were lured into clicking the wrong links. At the same time, privacy concerns multiplied, particularly with the contract tracing apps meant to alert users that they had been in physical proximity to someone who learned they were infected. And finally, the largest Internet companies became larger as a result of the increased usage.

How did we get to this point? Within the space of several generations, the Internet evolved from its roots as a research network to an essential platform in many countries for our social lives, politics, employment, and government, with attendant concern about any threats. In part, it is a result of design, as a network that can be everything to everyone, allowing anyone to go online, find content, create services, and, unfortunately, import all the foibles and crimes of human behavior along with the overwhelming good.

It is also because of the unique economics of the Internet. Open Internet standards are freely embedded in the range of devices we can use to go online, creating a globally interconnected network. Once online, we can access a host of free services, allowing us to interact with our family and friends, entertain ourselves, search for work, and conduct our jobs. And increasingly our data plans are unlimited or offer enough data that we do not have to worry about the cost of checking email or falling into a YouTube spiral.

But, of course, there is a flip side to this, starting with the standard objection that online services are not free—that we exchange them for our personal data. As a stylistic point, there is sometimes a desire to highlight the trade-off in every instance by emphasizing that the services are "free"—the quotations signaling that there is in fact a payment, in this case in the form of personal data. As this point is underscored in the very title of this book, there is no need to highlight it with every occurrence. I will call the services free, not "free," and explain the flip side.

Indeed, the flip side of many features of the Internet has emerged as almost an online version of Newton's third law of motion, that every action has an equal and opposite reaction. The Internet fosters competition, allowing anyone to start a website and begin selling, but it is now hard to compete with Amazon. The Internet is good for democracy, by allowing campaigns to reach voters with less cost than television, but it also allows outsiders the same freedom to meddle in elections. The Internet is good for social interaction, by allowing us to keep in touch, but it also creates feelings of envy and facilitates bullying.

The solutions to these issues are not proving to be easy, and sometimes even the solutions have a flip side. Platforms are under fire for the size of some of the providers, the content they sometimes carry, and impact on privacy. Some have argued that the companies should be broken up, but even if that was possible, it would entail throwing away the baby with the bathwater. Much of the value of the social media, for instance, comes from the size of the networks of users. Some have also argued that the platforms should be responsible for any content uploaded, but the cost of such filters and the risks of failure would also prohibit new and innovative companies from entering and growing.

The book will examine why much of the Internet is free, what the economic implications are, and present policy solutions to the emerging challenges. The Internet is increasingly important in our lives, our economies, and our societies. It is increasingly important for our livelihoods, social life, entertainment, interaction with government, politics, and so much more. The most valuable companies in the world are now Internet companies, built on data often exchanged for free content and services, which in turn is fueling the development of new advanced services that are coming our way.

The result is a series of paradoxes. Many of us know the impact of Internet services on our privacy, but we use the services anyway. And even when our trust is violated, there seems to be little impact on usage. In terms of companies, the Internet lowers barriers to entering markets, but it is hard to compete with the largest providers. And while we complain about companies having too much data, developing countries that do not have widespread Internet usage may suffer from the opposite problem: not enough data being gathered to develop new advanced services in these countries, worsening the digital divide between developed and developing countries. Privacy, trust, market power, data gathering—all are impacted by free, which turns out to have a price. This book is meant to help make sense of these paradoxes and discuss what we can do about them.

First, the basics. What is the Internet, what are the relevant economics, and how is the Internet governed today?

Introduction to the Internet

There are many angles from which one can explain the Internet, from a technical, commercial, or policy perspective. I will take a very practical perspective, to follow the traffic.[3] Following this path will then allow us to, as the saying goes, follow the money.

To go online, a user needs a device. This could be a traditional desktop or laptop computer, a smartphone, a tablet, a game console, or even a television.

It says a lot about the success of the Internet standards that any computer, anything "smart," anything starting with a lone *i* or *e* will access the Internet without further having to configure the settings or install any additional software. This is a result of the universal availability and adoption of Internet standards, covered in chapter 2.

Once we have our device, we need a way to go online. Typically, that is through an Internet service provider (ISP). At home or in the office, we can plug our computers in using an Ethernet cable. We may also have a Wi-Fi router that we can use to access the Internet without a cable. From the Ethernet or Wi-Fi router, the ISP may carry our traffic over the telephone network, over the cable television network, or over newer and faster fiber-optic networks. We can also access the Internet using a mobile technology such as 3G or 4G, particularly when we are outside the home or office.

While we do pay our ISP for access, generally that is a monthly fee; once we have paid, there is often no additional charge for the amount of data that we use, whether we look at one website or hundreds. That is why we can typically use Wi-Fi for free in a café or other hotspot: the owner is not paying more if more people use the Wi-Fi. This is covered more in chapter 3.

With our Internet access established, to surf a website on our device we will open a web browser, which we downloaded for free. While the World Wide Web seems interchangeable with the Internet, it is in fact a service sitting on top of the Internet—a wildly successful service, to be sure, which makes it easy to access almost anything by following links, and which significantly helped popularize the Internet. Within the browser, we may use a search engine such as Google to find the website we are looking for. The search results are provided for free in exchange for showing some ads relevant to our search. Likewise, the content of the website itself is likely to be free, for reasons explored in chapter 4.

To go to our website, we can type in or click the domain name, such as www.example.com. The famous *.com* is the top-level domain name, *example* is the secondary domain name corresponding to the organization, and *www* is the host server—in this case, a web server. This name must be unique so that there is no confusion. There are also possibly corresponding email addresses, such as Michael@example.com, where Michael refers to a specific user, separated from the domain name by the indelible @ symbol.

Domain names are meant to make things easy for us to remember, however, and are not used to direct traffic to its destination. Instead, domain names correspond with unique Internet protocol (IP) addresses, which can look something like this: 192.0.2.1.[4] The conversion from the domain name to the IP address is done by the domain name system (DNS), which matches each domain name with a corresponding IP address. Each domain name, each IP address, and the correspondence must be unique, and these identifiers are managed by an organization called ICANN (the Internet Corporation for Assigned Names and Numbers).[5] ICANN was set up as a nonprofit by the US government to manage and administer Internet names and addresses.

So, when your ISP receives your request for a website, it resolves the IP address and forwards the request. If the website belongs to a customer of the same ISP, the request will be routed quickly to the destination. However, with billions of users and millions of websites, there is a good chance that your request is going outside your ISP to one or more additional providers that create connectivity. That is, in fact, the fundamental design of the Internet, to enable *internetworking* and create the network of networks that is the Internet.

This internetworking leads to an oddity: the notion of *location* is a bit blurry online, as opposed to what we are familiar with in the physical world. We used to know exactly where a letter was going or a television show was being broadcast. Now, an email may be picked up anywhere. And that video from a vacation may have been uploaded from an airport in Europe to a website based in California, but downloaded from a data center in your city—no matter where you live.

That leads to a quick note on geography. The Internet is, intrinsically, borderless. Bits fly back and forth without regard to borders. But that is not to say that borders do not matter. They do, in practical terms, quite a bit. The bits can only travel across borders where there is Internet infrastructure, and each country sets its own infrastructure policies and has its own ISPs. Even if there is infrastructure, the bits could form content that is not permissible in a country based on copyright or legal restrictions.

So statements here that apply to a user in the United States, with a new iPhone, a 4G mobile subscription with unlimited usage, and access to iTunes for content, do not yet make much sense for a user in Zambia with a basic phone, a 2.5G prepaid connection, and no or limited mobile app stores.

The United States, as both the historical home of the Internet and the current home of many of the largest Internet companies, must by nature feature strongly in any discussion of the Internet past and present. The Internet in

Europe developed soon after, and together the United States and European Union have developed many of the earliest policies addressing the Internet space. Of course, the Internet has spread everywhere, with a number of the largest companies now coming from China.

Unfortunately, however, the digital divide with emerging countries is still strong, based on general demographics and specific policies. Income levels, education, and geography all play a role in the availability and adoption of Internet, but these can be somewhat mitigated or overcome with strong policies that facilitate the deployment of broadband networks, make access affordable, and provide training. As a result, countries can, and have, leapfrogged to new technologies—notably mobile broadband access—and they can, and hopefully will, identify the best digital policies to adopt and leapfrog to those. This is further discussed in chapter 8, with a focus on sub-Saharan Africa, the region with the lowest average Internet usage and where, not coincidentally, I have done much of my policy work.

Ultimately, however, in every country, the networks needed to provide Internet access cost money to build, and it costs money to develop and deliver the content. It also costs money to develop the Internet standards upon which we rely. But as we will see, costs are distributed in such a way that the content is generally free, we do not pay for additional usage of data, and the underlying standards are openly available. In many ways, free access and usage have driven the success of the Internet. To understand how, let's spend a few minutes on the economics.

Applying Economics to the Internet

Everything in the physical world effectively has a limited supply: that is true for natural resources, and it is true for the products made from natural resources. That is also true for services, the providers of which have limited amounts of time available. On the other hand, there may be little or no intrinsic limit on demand. So how are these resources allocated? In a market system, they are allocated based on price.

In his popular physics book, *A Brief History of Time*, Stephen Hawking notes that he was warned that every equation would cost him half his readers, but he puts in Einstein's famous $E = MC^2$ anyway.[6] I don't know if the same is true for graphs in an economics book, but I would modestly propose

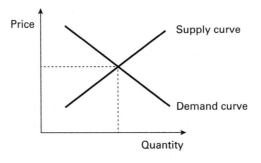

Figure 1.1
Supply and demand.

that the graph in figure 1.1 is the equivalent touchstone, showing the market supply and demand for a product or service.

The curves show how, at a low price, demand for a product is high, while the willingness to supply the product is low. As price rises, demand will decrease, as shown along the demand curve, while the supply will rise as price rises, as shown along the supply curve. When price is too low, there is excess demand for the product, and if price is too high, there is excess supply. Where the two curves intersect, there is an equilibrium where the price is just right: that is the price where the amount demanded just equals the amount supplied.

This outcome is known as the result of perfect competition. Perfect competition only holds under a number of strict assumptions: that what is being sold is not differentiated, that there are many buyers and sellers, and that customers have perfect information. As we will see throughout this book, perfect competition is rarely attained. Companies try to differentiate their products to increase demand, there may be few suppliers because it costs a lot to enter a market, and customers often do not have information about all of their options. Internet markets, like other markets before them, are often populated by only a few companies. However, when that happens offline, the companies tend to raise prices; online, free services remain free.

While the supply and demand curve equilibrium holds for everything made of atoms, how does it work for everything consisting of digital bits? A hardback book costs money to print, it costs money to ship to stores, and it costs money to sell to a customer. Setting aside, only for the sake of this example, of course, the royalties to the author and the costs for the publisher, the physical costs of the book must be recovered. But if the book is digitized, the cost of creating another copy, or a million copies, all perfect, is effectively nothing. Online copies can be effectively distributed for free, with or without the consent of the author or publisher.

Of course, to make the first copy of the book costs money. The same is true for all online services: developing Google Search, Facebook, Twitter—all cost a lot of money. But most of the cost does not depend on the number of users; it is fixed. So the companies must come up with a way of covering those fixed costs, and, as we will see in chapter 4, that is through advertising. In the meantime, to maximize the number of users and their usage, the price for us is free.

Free is in many ways a special price.[7] First, of course, demand is unconstrained, but that does not mean it is limitless. It is impacted by our own tastes, and it is constrained by other factors that do have limits, such as our attention. Broadcast television can be viewed without charge, but we could not watch more than twenty-four hours a day, and even within the day we have other limits such as work, sleep, family, sport, and our sanity. Our going to a movie might be limited by the cost of tickets, but even with access to free online movies, we might watch more, but not all the movies available.

But free does seem different. In recent years, economics has recognized that humans are not always rational economic actors; we also bring a number of psychological aspects to our decision-making. A new field of economics—behavioral economics—was born, which has enriched our understanding of much of economics. For instance, what *free* means, often using experiments to test theories. In one such experiment, a stand was set up offering passers by two types of chocolate—a fine Lindt truffle from Switzerland, for fifteen cents apiece, or a plain Hershey's Kiss for one cent apiece. Subjects recognized the quality of the Swiss truffles, and more than two-thirds bought one even at the higher price.

Then, the price of both was dropped by one cent. Because the difference between the prices remained at fourteen cents, there should be no difference in relative demand, if consumers were rational. But now the Hershey Kisses were free, while the Swiss truffles were fourteen cents—and the ratio of demand switched to more than two-thirds preferring the Hershey's Kisses.[8]

We can put ourselves in the shoes of the subjects and may have our own theories about the relative preferences. But overall, the reasons for the switch include not having to take out any money and potentially wait for change, and also not having to feel like making any kind of commitment to the choice. There may also be deeper evolutionary traits at play.

For our purposes, we can see the benefits of free playing out every day with our Internet use. We arrive at a foreign airport and quickly want to check email: rather than taking out a credit card to buy online access, we can sign up quickly for a free blast of Wi-Fi. Someone recommends a new fitness app: no need to do a lot of research—simply download it and try it out yourself. Your circle of Facebook friends increases? No need to worry about the additional cost of following their stories.

If someone begins to charge for something that was free, we can imagine the opposite reaction to the one greeting the free price for Hershey's chocolate. In fact, the reaction may be even more disproportionate. We associate the American Red Cross with blood drives, first aid training, disaster relief, and support for soldiers, their families, and veterans. So, it might surprise you to hear that some veterans interviewed not so long ago spoke out very strongly against the Red Cross for something that had happened seventy years earlier. The backstory is that during World War II, the American Red Cross set up service stations across Europe for US soldiers, where they could get food and coffee, including free doughnuts. And then the Red Cross briefly began to charge a nominal amount for doughnuts, a shameful disgrace in the view of the veterans interviewed, all of whom admitted that they had not themselves actually paid for a doughnut.[9]

Why did the Red Cross start charging soldiers for doughnuts? Was it a need to cover costs? Simply a lapse of judgment? Well, they were actually asked to raise prices by the US government. The US allies also had service stations, but their countries were much more war-torn and could not afford to give away food and coffee. This created resentment toward the newcomers, so the US Secretary of War asked the Red Cross to remove the disparity by charging for the doughnuts. The Red Cross was opposed, but went along—and despite efforts to correct the record, they have been unsuccessful in removing the stain.

So why the long-standing animosity? First, of course, no one likes a price increase under the best of circumstances, much less in a war zone, and people become very attached to the familiar price, particularly if it is free. But further, this price increase may evoke even stronger reactions than any other increase of price because people would view it as a change in category—from something free to something charged.[10] While the issue of doughnuts in war is thankfully distant, think how people might have reacted if the Lindt experiment reversed, and formerly free chocolate was charged for—or if Google asked for a credit card the next time you typed in a search query.

Free things surround us. Almost every Swiss village has a water fountain in the town, providing an endless stream of cold, free, drinkable water. It is common to see children stopping for a sip, runners for a gulp, and bikers filling up their water bottles. All appreciate the free service. But no one is coming by to fill a tank for household use, even though it is free.

One reason is that running water is provided by a utility, and in countries such as Switzerland where I live, we are lucky that it is low price and potable. But what if the utility was turned into a for profit company? Water is life, and the price could be set very high. This would be an example of an economic *market failure*, since we would pay much more for water, and we would use less than we may need.

By definition, a market failure cannot be corrected by the market alone, or it would not arise. Instead, a third party must intervene, and typically that is the government. There is typically not room for more than one water utility in a market, given the costs needed to build the network to deliver the water to every household and building. So, it is typically provided by a government agency or a private company regulated by the government to sell water at an affordable price. That is a market control that could only be provided by a government.

Spring water is also more expensive than tap water from the utility, not to mention free water from the fountain. Take the extreme case of Svalbarði glacier water from Norway, which is "as fresh as the day it fell as snow up to 4,000 years previously" because it is "gently melted" from an iceberg in Kongsfjorden to create "an epicurean product, which is redefining the very notion of pure drinking water."[11] A case of six bottles—with gift tubes, of course—is available for EUR 389.70 ($436.81), which is redefining the very notion of conspicuous consumption.

Of course, it is not always the case that every high price is a market failure. In the case of the glacier water, product differentiation is a constant feature of market economies. The water is targeted at those on the upper part of the demand curve, and there are plenty of brands of spring water pricing below the glacier water on the demand curve. As long as there is no artificial barrier to entry and consumers are informed, it is up to the market, not governments, to decide whether it is a "fair" price or not.

Of course, if the Norwegian glacier water was actually filtered tap water from New Jersey, that would be important information. There is absolutely no reason to think that is the case, and while New Jersey tap water is no doubt excellent, it may not justify the price commanded by Svalbarði— even if it tastes the same. The buyers of glacier water would clearly feel that they overspent on the water. In these cases, where the seller was keeping information from the buyer, and it was not possible for the buyer to verify the information, there is a market failure that could require government intervention.

Finally, the discussion here took one point for granted, and that was that markets are contingent on property rights. After all, you can only sell something that you own, and you would only buy something to own it. Usually, in most countries, and for most products and services, there is no ambiguity, as long as the government has a legal framework for establishing and enforcing property rights. Where there is ambiguity, however, there are problems. Think about the air around you. Do we own the air, with the right to breathe cleanly, or do factories own the air, with the right to pollute?[12]

Not only is the assignment of the rights important, but so are the transaction costs for exercising those rights. Say that the citizens of a city had the absolute right to clean air. Well, we also buy what comes out of the factories, and we may work at those factories, so we might be willing to effectively sell the right to pollute the air a bit to the factories. But the transaction cost of negotiating with each citizen would be prohibitive—and what if one citizen holds out? Turned the other way, what if the factories had the right to pollute, but we could pay them to pollute less? The transaction costs of negotiating among the citizens and with the factories would again be prohibitive: for instance, some citizens might prefer others to pay so they can still enjoy the clean air, while others will resent this attempt at free riding.

The government has a crucial role to play here. Not necessarily in assigning the property rights; we have seen that would not solve the problem, even if it was possible. But rather, in mediating a solution for eliminating toxic pollutants, like lead, and reducing others, including carbon emissions. Which brings us back to the Internet and the central role of personal data—which, like clean air, has no clear property rights today and, also like clean air, needs some level of government intervention.

We will see through the course of this book how public policy can impact the issues that have arisen in the context of the Internet. Sometimes the Internet raises traditional challenges with existing government policies, sometimes it raises new challenges, and often the remedies must be adapted to the realities of the Internet. This brings us to Internet governance.

Internet Governance

Like any other endeavor involving people and their activities, governance has always been a key feature in the development and growth of the Internet. Governance is a difficult concept to define; for one broad definition, the Institute on Governance defines it as "how society or groups within it, organize to make decisions."[13] Note that though governance and government share the same root word, they are not synonymous; governance can take place with varying or no levels of government involvement.

In fact, governments were slow to govern the Internet, whether because of a shallow understanding of the Internet or a deep understanding of the risks of regulating a fast-moving online world. To keep this distinction between governance and government, one can think of *Internet governance* in two parts—governance of the Internet and governance on the Internet.

Governance of the Internet covers the issues needed to develop the Internet itself and keep it functioning. It is a relatively narrow definition covering technical issues and coordination. How are Internet standards developed? Once developed, are they imposed or adopted? What about domain names, such as www.example.com? While a number of companies can take the name Ford, there can be only one Ford.com. Who gives out the name Ford.com? This is part of the governance of the issues that keeps the Internet running. It has been remarkably successful and somewhat unique. This is covered further in chapter 2.

Governance on the Internet is another matter. It is a much broader and more fraught definition, which covers issues relating to content and online activities, some of which might be traditional and some new. It covers topics including spam, copyright, market power, and child pornography, and it raises issues of sovereignty and cross-border enforcement. Sometimes the issues result from technology, and sometimes the issues are resolved by technology. As we will see further in this book, as the Internet increases in its impact, governments have increasingly begun to assert their same role online as they have traditionally taken offline.

Take one early famous case decided in the year 2000. People were selling Nazi memorabilia on Yahoo!. In the United States, that activity is protected under the First Amendment rights to free speech, but in France there are laws against it. Yahoo! was taken to court in France and argued that it was a US company enabling an activity that is legal in the United States. When the French court learned more about the technology and determined that Yahoo! could determine when a user was in France, they required Yahoo! to block French users from the banned content. This is an existing law applied to new challenges.

On the other hand, the *right to be forgotten* is a new regulation applied to new challenges. The concept is relatively simple. Embarrassing public information about people's past—arrests, convictions, bankruptcies, and so on—has always been kept in archives (government or newspaper), but pre-Internet it was hard to systematically find such information. Online, with Google, they are all easy to find, making it difficult for an individual to turn a new page. In 2014, the European Court of Justice upheld a right to be forgotten that requires Google to remove links to information that is out-dated, irrelevant, or not in the public interest—not the underlying content, just the links to that content. But, of course, without Google, that content is part of a dusty digital archive that is again difficult to find.

Before the economic and social impact of the Internet was fully felt, a role for government in the governance of the Internet was not always exercised, acknowledged, or welcomed. In one iconic expression of online freedom, John Perry Barlow, who cofounded the Electronic Frontier Foundation, wrote *A Declaration of the Independence of Cyberspace* in 1996. Its first lines were these: "Governments of the Industrial World, you weary giants of flesh and steel, I come from Cyberspace, the new home of Mind. On behalf of the future, I ask you of the past to leave us alone. You are not welcome among us. You have no sovereignty where we gather."[14]

It is safe to say that governments could not, and did not, heed this heartfelt plea after millions, then billions of users began interacting online, bringing with them their offline habits and adding a few new ones. At the same time, the Internet sector (broadly defined) grew to 10 percent or more of some countries' GDPs. However, government interaction with the

Internet did in a sense keep with the spirit of the declaration, if not the letter, at least in the West.

The Internet began to increase in scope and scale. In recognition of the
benefits of ICT and the need to address the growing digital divide, the United
Nations General Assembly, at the invitation of the International Telecommunication Union (ITU), convened the World Summit on the Information
Society, under the patronage of then UN Secretary General Kofi Annan.[15] A
separate Working Group on Internet Governance (WGIG) was established
as part of the World Summit on the Information Society[16] and provided the
following definition of Internet governance in 2005: "Internet governance
is the development and application by Governments, the private sector
and civil society, in their respective roles, of shared principles, norms, rules,
decision-making procedures, and programmes that shape the evolution
and use of the Internet."[17]

Written just nine years after the Declaration of Independence of Cyberspace, this definition is a world apart in tone and impart. However, rather
than paving the way for a government take-over of governance, it sets out
a *multistakeholder* model of governance, which endures through today.
Government is one of the many stakeholders, and its respective role is
to represent states, which have sovereign rights for "policy authority for
Internet-related public policy issues."[18]

A few years later, at a G8 conference in 2011, French President Nicolas
Sarkozy delivered a more pointed statement to the tech world: "The universe that you represent, is not a parallel universe which is free of rules of
law or ethics or of any of the fundamental principles that must govern and
do govern the social lives of our democratic states."[19] More succinctly, as
Internet scholar Jovan Kurbalija notes, "If you commit a cybercrime, you
don't go to cyberjail—you go to real jail."[20]

Nonetheless, in many ways, government-led governance of the Internet
is different than what could have been. Where I live in Geneva, the home
of many international organizations, there is a World Health Organization
(WHO), a World Trade Organization (WTO), the International Telecommunication Union (ITU), the International Labor Organization (ILO), and the
World Intellectual Property Organization (WIPO), among others. These organizations have taken on Internet-related issues to varying degrees, but it is fair
to say that there is no equivalent of an "International Internet Organization."
The ITU, established first to regulate interconnection between international

telegraph operators, and then telephone operators, plays a significant role in the Internet, working on connectivity and ICT access. Although some countries have pushed for the ITU to have a greater role in Internet governance, this has been opposed by countries that did not want to alter the status quo by giving control over parts of the Internet to a multilateral government body.

Likewise, despite the growing size and importance of the Internet, most countries do not have any dedicated Internet agency—although, in light of the growing size and importance of the Internet, regulating aspects of the Internet is high on the agenda of many countries. But different agencies take on different roles at both the national and international levels, which can at times lead to a fragmented or even contradictory approach.

Western countries generally accept not regulating the Internet unless needed. My own interest in the area was piqued when I worked at the US Federal Communications Commission in the late 1990s. It was a time when many countries, including the United States, were introducing or strengthening competition in telecommunications. To create a level playing field, telecom regulators developed detailed rules regarding the terms and rates at which telecom operators interconnected and enabled customers to make phone calls across networks.

Many of the same telecommunications companies also carried Internet traffic, using the same infrastructure as they did for telecommunications, but with no regulation whatsoever. They negotiated their own interconnection arrangements, with effectively no government involvement.[21] Despite a range of mergers and changes in business models, this lack of regulation has largely persisted through today.

The US government set up the nonprofit ICANN around the same time, in 1998, to make sure that the domain name system functions. While some governments pushed for more government control of this function, the United States government slowly relinquished control until 2016, when it transitioned all oversight over names and numbers to ICANN and the global Internet community. ICANN is a symbol of multistakeholder governance: governments do play an advisory role, but so do other commercial and noncommercial constituencies, and no one group has primacy.

Governance of the Internet is crucial: standards need to be developed, adopted, and adapted over time; domain names and IP addresses must be managed; and security must be increased, among a host of issues. Governance on the Internet is receiving yet more attention these days, as attention focuses on the tragic use of social media in the Christchurch shooting, which was broadcast on Facebook Live; foreign meddling in elections; market power; digital trade; and other issues. As we will see, the current laissez-faire role of the government in these issues on the Internet may be untenable.

Conclusion

The book is developed in three parts. The first part examines in what ways the Internet is free and why. It shows how Internet standards were developed and why they are free or freely available to use. It looks at why usage is generally not metered, and it looks at why Internet services and content are often free and the trade-off that we make to get those.

The second part examines the flip side of the economics of the Internet. It looks at privacy, it looks at cybersecurity, and it looks at the market power that has developed in the Internet space. The book notes that many of these problems are developed-world problems. There is still a digital divide that must be bridged to bring the rest of the world online—hopefully learning from the challenges exposed elsewhere and addressing these problems up front.

Finally, the third part presents some thoughts about the future and how data, and its governance, may become the leading issue going forward. A key thread running through this book is data. Free is, indeed, a special price, and we will see how it drives uptake and usage of free services and applications with unmetered access. And there is nothing wrong with free services and usage. The result, however, is an accumulation of personal data, and this data underpins the flip side of free.

Data is the price of free service and the new currency of the Internet age. Data contains our private information, and data is the target of cybersecurity threats. We worry that some companies have too much data and that some countries are generating too little. And it is clearly the path to the future of artificial intelligence and machine learning. Thoughts on the roles and responsibilities of companies, governments, and users close the book.

2 The Global Standard

In pioneer days they used oxen for heavy pulling, and when one ox couldn't budge a log, they didn't try to grow a larger ox. We shouldn't be trying for bigger computers, but for more systems of computers.

—Admiral Grace Hopper, pioneer computer scientist

The electronic era is littered—literally—with changes in standards that leave many of us with drawers full of obsolete devices, software, cables, discs, battery packs, tapes, and adapters. Sometimes, we make the wrong choice and buy a Betamax only to see the VHS standard prevail. Other times, we buy a new device and can't use the same charger or need an adapter for our headphones. Then, once bitten, twice shy.

But not with the Internet. No one shopping for a new computer has to ask if it will work with their Wi-Fi router or has to switch ISPs when they get home and setup the computer. Switching between a PC and a Mac means getting new software and transferring—and possibly reformatting—documents and files, but there is no change in getting access to favorite websites or posting a blog. No adapters are needed, no conversion is required.

That is not just in our homes and offices. When we travel, we may have to change money on arrival, remember to drive on the other side of the road, bring adapters to be able to plug in our computers, and arrange roaming on our cell phones. But wherever we go, the Internet works.[1] We can turn on our devices and connect to Wi-Fi, open our browser, and use all our services, without disruption.

To discuss Internet standards, it is important first to consider the definition of the Internet.[2] That is easier said than done, because the Internet keeps changing, and the definition depends on who is asking the question and why. An engineer developing technologies may have a different definition than a policy maker seeking to regulate the Internet, which may differ again from the definition of a user seeking to use the Internet, if they even think about the question at all.

At the most basic level, the Internet is a network of networks, and the networks are connected using the transmission-control protocol/Internet protocol (TCP/IP) suite of protocols. This set of protocols basically acts to route the traffic we send and receive and makes sure it arrives as it was sent.[3] However, we will also consider the standards that enable users to access the Internet, such as Wi-Fi, and the standards behind the web browsers that we use once online. Strictly speaking, these are not part of the Internet, but together we will consider all of them as Internet standards because their availability is a key factor in the global success of the Internet.

All of these Internet standards have in common that they are open: they are freely available to anyone to adopt, and many of them are free to use. This represents a shift in the way that standards were traditionally set and one of the key reasons for the adoption and success of the Internet. And though most users might not be aware of them, the open standards have contributed to the ethos of free that has carried over to online services and content.

Standard Setting

Standards are an important hallmark of civilization—for measuring distances, trading goods, keeping time. The earliest standards, though imprecise, derive from a human measurement—notably, the foot for measuring length—or from nature, such as the weight of a grain of wheat. The hand, like the foot, was traditionally used as a measurement and today is still used to measure the height of a horse in the United States and other English-speaking countries (although both the hand and the foot have been given standard measurements in inches now).

For buying and selling, in particular, it is important to have a standard for weight and volume. Over time, as trade expanded, the need for agreed upon standards grew, along with the ability to set them more precisely. This resulted in the nearly global metric system, alongside the holdout imperial system notably used in the United States.

Standards also played a significant role in the industrial revolution. Originally, cars were made using craft production. Each part was made by hand by a craftsperson and then fitted together. This process was slow, and the resulting cars could differ from each other based on how the parts were fitted together. Mass production of automobiles was introduced by the Ford Motor Company with its assembly line. The assembly line, however, was made possible by the standardization of interchangeable parts, enabling each worker to perform the same task quickly as cars moved by.

The electronic age then introduced networks, which are firmly based on standards. Telephone standards ultimately led to a global network in which any caller using a fixed or mobile phone can call any other. Broadcast standards ensure that viewers or listeners can receive programming transmitted by the broadcaster through any television or radio. The information age then introduced computer standards, to connect peripherals such as memory devices or printers and to be able to run software.

In economic terms, among other benefits, standards deliver *network effects*. These arise when the value of a product or service depends on the number of other users of the same product or service. There are both direct and indirect network effects. *Direct network effects* arise for services that are used to communicate between people: the more users on the same network, the more beneficial it is to join the network. *Indirect network effects* arise for complementary services such as software: we indirectly benefit from more users of the same computer standard because more software will be available.

For most things we buy, we probably do not worry about how many other buyers there are or what is compatible. Go through a department store: you don't have to make sure that a new spatula is compatible with your old frying pan, check whether your new training shoes are supported by your treadmill, or find out how many people bought the same suit. For some things, we might even prefer if they are unique or rare.

If I am shopping for a new smartphone, on the other hand, it matters very much to me how many owners there are of a smartphone using the same standards. If it could not be used to call other brands of smartphones, it would have little value. Likewise, if there were few apps available, it would have little value. The fact that any smartphone today can be used to call any other phone—smart or not—and that it likely has millions of apps available, is a result of standards that deliver overwhelming network effects.

What we call information and communications technology (ICT) is made up of two main parts—telecommunications and computers. Although telecommunications and computers eventually merged and morphed into the open Internet, they were originally provided as separate proprietary systems: *proprietary* in that they were developed, owned, and delivered by one company exclusively or under license; *systems* in that they encompassed a combination of the components needed to deliver the service.

In the United States, which had a pioneering role in developing and commercializing ICT, these proprietary systems were provided by AT&T and IBM, respectively. In its prime, AT&T's Bell System did not just provide the lines and services connecting subscribers, but also the switches connecting the lines and the equipment in the house or business. Likewise, IBM did not just provide the mainframe computers, but also the operating system, services, and all peripherals. Both eventually defended antitrust cases over their unwillingness to open their systems to competition for components of the system.

The Bell System and IBM were in some ways at the opposite ends of the spectrum with respect to network effects. At one end of the spectrum, telecommunications is purely dependent on direct network effects. A phone without anyone to call is just a fancy paperweight. Interconnection between operators was critical. In the early days of telephony in the United States, there were a number of operators who did not interconnect, so subscribers may have needed multiple phones and lines to reach different users. There are pictures of the multiple wires crisscrossing streets to generate these redundant connections, until they were effectively brought under the control of the Bell System. Between countries, and later between competitors, interconnection was based on agreed upon standards to ensure a unified network.

At the other end of the spectrum were mainframe computers, which were initially standalone devices. In the early days, there were few, if any, network effects. Computers were not interconnected. Indeed, one of the early objectives of the Internet was to enable computer resources to be shared and different systems to interoperate. In addition, peripherals, software, and support were all provided by the same company, so there was relatively little benefit (other than economies of scale) from the number of other purchasers of the same system.

Most systems fall inside this spectrum: they can be used as standalone devices, but there are also some network effects, and thus benefits from standards. For instance, a video cassette recorder (VCR) was used on its own to tape television shows, which just depended on having compatible blank tapes, or to watch prerecorded movies, which depended on the studios making their movies available on that standard, a decision based on the number of owners of compatible VCRs.

Overall, standards can be *de facto*—that is, market-driven—or they can be *de jure*—officially ratified by a standards body. De facto standards can arise organically and can coexist, and they can also be adopted as de jure standards. Traditionally, there were four ways that any type of standard could be developed and adopted:[4]

1. *Standards war.* Multiple companies or groups of companies may each develop their own standard and battle it out in the marketplace. One of the earliest and most famous examples is the Betamax versus VHS battle for VCRs. Although the Sony Betamax was generally acknowledged as the better technology, the VHS group first identified the eager market for compatible prerecorded movies and won that war. In other cases, multiple standards persist and coexist—including Apple versus the Microsoft operating system for personal computers and, more recently, Apple's iOS and Google's Android standards for smart devices. These are all de facto standards.

2. *Standards-developing organization.* In some cases, to ensure that there is no standards war, companies may group together into a standards-developing organization (SDO) to pool together and create a standard, which by definition is de jure. For instance, to prevent the VCR war from recurring, major electronics companies came together to agree on a format for its replacement, the DVD, forming the DVD Forum for steering the development. This lowers the risk of developing the next obsolete standard such as Betamax but may also lower the return from developing a widespread standard because it has to be shared with others in the SDO.

3. *Prescriptive.* In some cases, the government can set a de jure standard. That is the case, for instance, with television standards such as those for

high-definition television. This enables the government to determine certain characteristics of the standard while also ensuring that there is just one standard for the country. In other cases, a large buyer—which could be the government or a large company such as Walmart—can effectively set a standard through its procurement choices. The standard chosen in this fashion could be developed by an SDO, or it could be a de facto standard.

4. *Converter or adapter.* Finally, if no single standard is set or emerges, a converter or adapter may allow adopters of one standard access to the other standard, although they may vary in cost or efficiency. This is true for electrical plugs, headphone jacks, chargers, and a variety of otherwise incompatible standards. Alternatively, where this doesn't work, in certain cases customers can *multihome*, simply adopting more than one standard, which could be as easy as having separate charging cords for iPhones and Android devices.

The development of the Internet—with its open standards—in some ways touched on all four methods of standard setting while in the end introducing a new way of setting standards.

First, the Internet was not the only networking technology over time. The International Organisation for Standardisation (ISO) created its own standard, the Open Systems Interconnection (OSI) model, which was mandated by the US government at one point. In addition, there were several proprietary options—including the IBM Systems Network Architecture (SNA) and the Digital Equipment Company DecNET standard. The Internet eventually emerged based on a number of aspects of its development and intrinsic characteristics described ahead.[5]

Second, the US government not only initiated the development of the Internet but also mandated usage for defense and education networks.[6] The government also took actions to help promote the adoption of Internet technology. For instance, it supported the inclusion of TCP/IP into the Unix operating system so that as Unix spread among universities, more researchers became familiar with TCP/IP. It also set up a $20 million fund to help computer manufacturers integrate TCP/IP.[7] As a result, by 1990 it was estimated that TCP/IP was available for almost every computer system available in the United States.

Third, one of the drivers behind the government support for the Internet was to enable resource sharing and interoperability of existing networks, which led to some important characteristics of the Internet. In particular, as noted, the Internet is a network of networks. Each network could have its own standard and connect devices from vendors using different operating systems. As such, the Internet itself effectively acted as an adapter to allow existing computers and local networks to interoperate.[8] This lowered the barriers to adopting the Internet because it did not depend on the choice of devices or local area networks (LANs).

Finally, the developers of the Internet developed open standards, accommodating inputs from anyone and outputs for all to use, created by new open standards organizations. These organizations did not just help develop and adapt Internet standards over time, but also, through their openness— and the resulting network effects—essentially removed the need to develop any competing standard over the long run.

Internet Development

The history of the development of the Internet is long and colorful and has been told at length elsewhere.[9] In a nutshell, the US government, via the Defense Advanced Research Projects Agency (DARPA), initiated the work to develop its ARPANET network in the 1960s. A significant driver of the development of ARPANET was to enable resource sharing—to enable users to access large and expensive computers when they were not in the same location. As other defense networks were introduced, including radio and satellite networks, they were also connected to ARPANET to enable internetworking.

The ARPANET network was first tested in 1969 and first presented to the public in 1972. In that year, email was first developed—including the iconic choice by its developer, Ray Tomlinson, of the @ symbol to separate the name of the user from the name of the machine they were using. Email became the first Internet "killer app" by allowing easy communication between researchers, but it also established a pattern that has driven the development of the Internet through today. The developers were also users, not customers, and developed and refined tools that they themselves wanted to use—often, as with email, with no aim to sell the result.

As other networks were connected, the fundamental TCP/IP protocols were developed by Vint Cerf and Bob Kahn to implement internetworking. The protocols were developed in 1973 and increasingly implemented through 1983, when the ARPANET switched to TCP/IP, and then through 1985, when the US National Science Foundation developed the NSFNET using TCP/IP for serving higher education. As noted earlier, by 1990 essentially every computer system sold in the US supported TCP/IP.

Internet usage was thus spreading as a result of the increased use of PCs and workstations that were Internet-enabled and LANs, notably using Ethernet, that were connecting the workstations to each other and then to the Internet. If you have not heard of TCP/IP, it is because it is already installed in any device you are using to interact with the Internet and as a rule does not require any modification or updating from us. It just works.

The way that work on the Internet protocols continued and spread had a significant impact on its growth. Ultimately, it is also the end product itself that determined success, not just the means of development.

Internet Hourglass

A number of important characteristics have contributed to the Internet's adoption and success.[10] As noted, it was designed as a network of networks, to allow existing or future networks to interoperate regardless of the technology used in each network. To accommodate all of the individual networks and their specific purposes, it had to be a general-purpose network—one that could support applications that its founders could foresee at the time and those that we may still not conceive of today.

To help visualize this, the Internet is sometimes described as an hourglass.[11] The top part is the endless number of applications that can run over the Internet, including the World Wide Web, and the bottom part is the variety of networks the Internet connects, including the mobile network. In this model, the narrow waist is the IP that is responsible for sending and receiving traffic from the applications across the networks. Another way to describe it is *everything over IP, IP over everything*: all applications work on IP, and IP works on all networks.

In practical terms, this describes how—unlike traditional telephony or cable TV—the applications can be separated from the networks. When you pay for TV service over a coax cable or fiber-optic network, the pay TV provider supplies not just the connection, but all of the TV content; likewise, for telephony, the operator traditionally provides the network connection and the service. That is not the case for the Internet; in fact, the ISP may not necessarily provide any of the applications for a user.

One principle resulting from this separation is sometimes called *permissionless innovation*, meaning that not only does the Internet support new applications, but no one has to ask permission to develop and use those applications. The benefits were quickly highlighted, as we already have seen with the development of email, which did not result from any commercial decision or committee discussion. As stated by the developer, Ray Tomlinson, he invented it "mostly because it seemed like a neat idea. There was no directive to 'go forth and invent email.'"[12] From this modest start, it changed communications and became one of the defining features of the Internet age.

Permissionless innovation also enabled Tim Berners-Lee to develop the World Wide Web while working at CERN, the European physics lab, in Geneva. Where a driver of the Internet was to enable users to share access to computers, the World Wide Web was initiated as an easy way to enable researchers to share the information sitting on those computers by clicking on links rather than typing in any underlying code. As with email, it was not the result of an official mandate; in fact, Berners-Lee's boss at the time famously wrote "Vague, but exciting…" on his initial proposal and gave him time to work on it without ever making it an official project of CERN. The web eventually helped popularize the Internet to the extent that many think the web *is* the Internet, rather than being one of many Internet applications.

While this concept may seem obvious or intuitive today, it was fairly radical at the time. To return to telephony, telephone networks such as the Bell System were not just proprietary systems, but telephony was a completely centralized network—meaning in the first instance that operators such as the Bell System kept a tight control over the whole system. The Bell System did not just make all telephones; they did not want anything else connected to the telephones. The beginning of the end of this control in the United States came with the Hush-A-Phone, which solved a problem that seems very quaint today. At that time, every phone was connected to the wall with a (short) cord, and it was difficult to get privacy. The Hush-A-Phone device attached to the telephone mouthpiece to prevent the speaker from being overheard. Although there was nothing electronic or mechanical about it, the Bell System objected to this use of their phones as degrading the quality of service, and the US regulator (the FCC) backed the complaint—but in 1957 the Supreme Court finally weighed in on the side of Hush-A-Phone.

It was not until 1968, though, that "any lawful device" was allowed to be connected to the phone system, and this quickly unleashed significant innovation—including, most importantly for our story, the dial-up modem that allowed online connections that paved the way to Internet access for anyone with a phone line. In Europe, the opening was even slower: in 1994, when I lived in France, I brought a small modem back from the United States, and it was confiscated by customs because it was not on the list of modems allowed by France Telecom. I was given three months to pick it up and take it out of France or it would be destroyed.

However, being allowed to attach your own device to the telephone network was just part of the story. Subscribers were still completely limited to the few features that could be built into a device such as a phone or fax machine—for instance, memory dialing. Most features such as call waiting, call forwarding, and others first needed to be installed by the phone company in their central switches, and then customers had to sign up—and pay—for those features. This centralization of telephony remains true today, including for mobile telephony. It is also true of other communication networks, such as television and radio, which broadcast content from the center to traditionally "dumb" televisions and radios.

The Internet is not centralized. Instead, the Internet is based on the *end-to-end principle*, whereby the intelligence of the network is distributed to the end points. This is a key implication of being a network of networks: while any individual network could be centralized, the network of networks could not because there is no obvious center where one could put the intelligence.[13] The key result is that a new application can be installed at the end points—devices—and does not require any changes in the network so long as it uses Internet protocols. There is no need to ask anyone for permission to do so—and no one to ask, in any case.

The result of these principles defines how we use the Internet today. Innovators can develop new services and applications. Users can then access these on devices such as mobile phones and laptop computers. Going full circle, in some cases these services are substitutes for traditional centralized services—Skype instead of phone calls, WhatsApp instead of text messages, and YouTube instead of pay TV. These all can be used for free, and alongside paid models such as Spotify and Netflix, users have a number of choices that reduce their use of traditional communication services.

This ultimately defines the value of the hourglass model. On top of a controlled and centralized telephone network, as well as cable television networks, mobile telephony, and others, a decentralized permissionless environment was built and thrived. Although this has not always been tension-free, the vast investments in networks have increased the Internet bandwidth available to keep up with, and propel, all the new content and services that continue to be made available today.

Open Standards

A key driver for the end result of the Internet was the means to the ends. The Internet was, and is, developed by academics, researchers, corporate engineers, and others, working together to find the best solution and the best way to find solutions. The result was not just the development of the Internet, but also the development of the Internet using open standards, which are open in two important respects—open to everyone to provide input into the development of standards, and open to everyone to use the resulting standards, typically at no cost.

Key to the development of the Internet is what happened when it began to expand beyond its roots in academia, research, and government—that is to say, what happened when commercial vendors became involved. Dan Lynch and other Internet developers began a series of workshops for vendors, culminating in the Interop conferences. The 1988 conference had 5,529 attendees and featured a Show and Tel-Net, or ShowNet, that enabled more than fifty vendors to link together and show that their equipment was interoperable while also initiating cooperation among the vendors to make the demonstrations.[14]

As part of this process, the vendors began to contribute and cooperate in the development of the TCP/IP protocols, rather than co-opt or override the process.[15] They contributed engineers, ideas, and sometimes existing intellectual property under patent to be put into standards that for the most part became available to others at no cost. Of particular note, the vendors who had their own networking standard and sold their own computers, notably IBM and Digital, might not have wished to compete with their own network standard and, in particular, not work with the Internet, which enabled connections between different computer brands. Vint Cerf explained to me that to avoid this issue, he "went to the research departments of IBM, HP and Digital, not to their commercial sales and engineering department. The research teams got the excitement of the Internet and implemented the protocols."[16]

The contributions of the vendors were channeled through new forms of standards organizations that emerged, notably the Internet Engineering Task Force (IETF).[17] The IETF set an important example not just in providing open standards, but in showing how the open standards are set. It emphasizes and extends the role of users in setting standards; it does not require membership, just participation; and though vendors continue to participate, their engineers do so as individuals. The emphasis is on demonstrating a new standard before it is adopted and finding the best standard.[18]

The ethos was captured by one of the pioneers of the Internet, David Clark, who stated in an early IETF plenary presentation that "we reject: kings, presidents, and voting. We believe in: rough consensus and running code."[19] *Rough consensus* is sometimes measured by asking a working group to hum rather than vote, which enables the chair to take the temperature of the group without providing the impression that a vote is taking place.[20]

Early on, before there was even a way to distribute them online, the first Request for Comment (RFC) was written in 1969 by Steve Crocker. The RFCs began as a way to share ideas and developed into a means to develop and present new and updated standards. As the IETF developed, it adopted the RFCs, and today they can all be accessed free on the web. Again, as with email, the tools of the Internet were developed and used by those continuing to work on the Internet and its standards.

After Tim Berners-Lee developed the World Wide Web at CERN, he encouraged CERN to make it freely available, which it did in April 1993. He also bypassed the opportunity to commercialize the standard himself, leaving it open for others—including, most famously, Marc Andreessen and the researchers who created Mosaic and then went on to start Netscape, which released the first commercial browser. Instead, Berners-Lee initiated the World Wide Web Consortium (W3C), which took charge of developing the key web standards as open standards.

The standards developed by IETF extend well beyond the core TCP/IP protocols today. For instance, the WebRTC standard allows real-time communications (RTC)—such as video calls—directly from browsers without plug-ins. It is embedded in most browsers—fixed and mobile—and enables websites to offer real-time communications with no extra cost to them or effort on the part of users. As with IETF, the W3C standards extend beyond the basic web standards, including work on WebRTC. As a result, instead of reinventing the wheel trying to develop video capabilities, for instance, an entrepreneur can simply implement the WebRTC standards and instead focus on their core business.

Key standards for connectivity to the Internet—namely, Ethernet and Wi-Fi—are developed by the Institute of Electrical and Electronics Engineers (IEEE). Ethernet, which is known more formally as the IEEE 802.3 standards, was first developed at Xerox by a team including Robert Metcalfe. While Metcalfe left to start 3Com to commercialize Ethernet in 1979, the so-called DIX group (Digital Equipment Corporation, Intel, and Xerox) submitted Ethernet to IEEE as a candidate for a LAN standard, which was approved in 1982. The wireless equivalent is Wi-Fi, which was developed and patented in Australia and then became the IEEE 802.11 standard in 1999.

These three organizations develop the standards for physical Internet connectivity (IEEE), end-to-end Internet interoperability (IETF), and the World Wide Web (W3C). They all develop open standards, and together with the Internet Society (ISOC) and the Internet Architecture Board (IAB), they created the OpenStand movement in 2012.[21] ISOC is the organizational home of the IETF, among other roles. The IAB provides long-term technical direction for the development of the Internet and is both a committee of the IETF and an advisory body of ISOC.

OpenStand adopted core principles for open standards development, including cooperation between the different organizations, due process and broad consensus in the development of standards, a choice based on technical merit, global accessibility to the standards specifications that are broadly affordable, and voluntary adoption of the results.

It is worth briefly focusing on one specific principle relevant to the topic of this book—namely, "ensuring a broad affordability of the outcome of the standardization process." While TCP/IP and the key web standards were developed by researchers who ensured that they are available at no cost, as companies began to get involved in the standards process for the Internet, they began to contribute their intellectual property, which was typically patented. This is true for Ethernet and Wi-Fi, but also other standards at IETF and W3C. During this process, two issues became relevant, which are fairly common to standard setting.

First, when contributing their intellectual property, vendors did not always disclose all of the relevant patents. This created a risk that once the patents were embedded in the standard, the patent holder could charge a high rate for the license. Second, even with disclosure, there was a risk that the cost of the patents, stacked together, could be significant.[22]

The modern smartphone is a notable example of patent stacking. According to one study, the patent royalties in a $400 smartphone cost at least $120—and that does not include the cost of the components, which cost about the same as their royalties.[23] Of that, it is estimated that the cost of the Wi-Fi patents was $50, based on rates that have been requested or awarded by courts; the ultimate rates paid are confidential and unknown.[24] These royalties paid understate the true costs of the patents: a running series of lawsuits among smartphone companies have been waged over patent infringement claims, involving a fortune in legal fees, time, and damages.[25]

To combat these issues, Internet standards organizations have imposed conditions on patents. First, all patents must be disclosed prior to entry into the standards development process. This is to ensure that there is no holdup afterward, particularly for the standard-essential patents (SEPs) that could not be avoided with the resulting standard. Likewise, to prevent stacking, patent owners must agree to fair, reasonable, and nondiscriminatory (FRAND) rates for their patents. In the case of IETF and W3C, the norms are for royalty-free licensing of patents.[26]

As a result, open standards are not always free, but the standards developers know the patents embedded into competing standards candidates and can work on the basis of developing affordable standards. Overall, as a general rule, patents in software standards—such as those underlying browsers—are free, as is the resulting software; patents in hardware—Ethernet and Wi-Fi—are not free, and neither is the resulting hardware.

FRAND is in the eye of the beholder, however. Negotiations over royalties are typically between the patent holder and someone wishing to use it, and they are confidential, so they do not provide any benchmarks. If negotiations break down, they can go to court, and different courts in the same country or different countries come up with different resolutions.[27]

The free cost for TCP/IP certainly helps explain the widespread use of the Internet, just as free access to web standards helps explain the widespread use of the web. Although the connectivity standards are not free, they are freely available to be embedded in an ever-increasing array of devices able to go online and provide Internet access, the prices of which continue to fall.

Open Source

Alongside the rise of open standards came the rise of open-source software. Open-source software literally means that the source code is openly available to anyone to be studied, altered, and distributed. More broadly, however, it allows for the collaborative development, testing, and use of software. Just as Wikipedia is the result of an amazing amount of volunteer work and collaboration, so too is open-source software.

Although typically associated with volunteers and often resulting in software that can be used free of charge, the open-source movement has been aligned with software companies from its early days. The origins of the open-source movement came from the free software movement promoted by the Free Software Foundation. In 1998, the term *open source* was introduced by a group wishing to bring the benefits of the movement to the commercial software industry, and the Open Software Initiative was created. A key difference between the groups is philosophical, with the free software movement opposed to the concept of proprietary software.[28]

Indeed, one motivation for the open software movement came when Netscape released the source code for its Netscape Navigator browser. Other prominent examples include the Linux operating system and Android for smartphones, which is based on Linux. Linux is free and open-source software (FOSS), meant to encompass both the free software movement and the open-source movement while neutral on their differences.[29]

Open source is closely intertwined with the development of the Internet. Although AT&T's Bell Labs created Unix, for a number of years it was effectively available as open source, leading to the development of the Berkeley Software Distribution (BSD) version of Unix, to which DARPA funded the inclusion of TCP/IP. As this version was widely distributed among researchers, it enabled them to easily join the Internet and is credited as one of the reasons that the Internet quickly grew in popularity at the expense of other networking standards.

In the next phase of the Internet, as noted, Tim Berners-Lee did not attempt to patent or commercialize the World Wide Web, and CERN put the software in the public domain.[30] These decisions allowed the World Wide Web building blocks to become open source, which led to the early browsers being developed and commercialized by others, starting with Netscape. In turn, one of the leading browsers today, Firefox from Mozilla, is based on the open-source release of the Netscape browser and itself remains open source.

Netscape was an early proponent of open source in the Internet space. In addition to its browser release, it released Secure Sockets Layer (SSL) as open source, allowing for secure encrypted interactions, such as e-commerce trans-actions, and it also was an early adopter of other open technologies.[31] Other examples of key open-source software important to the Internet include the Apache Web Server software, Google Chromium, Drupal, OpenSSL, and others, including a number of open source media formats for audio and video streaming and playing. There is now a movement to incorporate open-source software more closely into open standards development.

Open source has a number of significant benefits. First, the software benefits from the wisdom of crowds in developing something that meets a broad range of needs for a broad range of users. In addition, many argue that it is more secure and reliable because of the chance to review the source code and find bugs and make edits. There is a flip side, however: the development resources can slip through the cracks and in at least one case resulted in a major Internet vulnerability, as discussed further in chapter 6.

Conclusion

It is hard to determine the impact of free standards on the widespread adoption and usage of the Internet, in part because it is so closely intertwined with the general freedom associated with Internet development, adoption, and use. For instance, it was not just that Tim Berners-Lee and CERN allowed the web protocols to be used for free, but that they were freely available to anyone who wanted to develop their own browser.

These free standards helped create an ethos of free around the Internet—but the free standards were mostly seen by other developers, who could incorporate them into their own products and services. The public largely was, and likely still is, unaware of the open standards that underpin their use of the Internet and the web. The results are clear for users, given the marrying of fast innovation with global connectivity and network effects, but most do not likely associate that with the upsides of free in the way that free content and services are recognized.

Today, the Internet is so widespread and embedded in our lives that one could imagine, as a thought experiment, that a lot could be charged for access to Internet standards. A top-end smartphone can cost upward of a thousand dollars today, and a lot of the difference between that and a basic twenty-five-dollar mobile phone lies in the features enabling Internet access. We spend billions online for content, for services, and to order products; would we not pay a lot for the browser that provides access to that? In surveys, a surprising number of people will confess to preferring the Internet over their own body parts, a dream job, true love, sex, and even chocolate![32]

However, the flip side of that question is, would the Internet be the global standard worth paying for today if we had to pay from the start? Much early adoption in academia and research came because it was already on an available version of Unix; then it was made available on workstations, and eventually PCs, with no extra charge. Likewise, the ability to use browsers at no cost from the beginning enabled the explosive growth of the web.

In addition, free access to the standards was intrinsically a part of broader freedoms: the freedom to contribute to the development of the Internet rather than developing a competing network protocol, along with the freedom to use the results; likewise, the freedom to develop a browser based on an existing standard rather than developing a new one, and to develop websites based on those standards; and the freedom to include Ethernet and Wi-Fi in all manner of devices without license restrictions, albeit not for free.

One must look no further than the rest of a smartphone to see a glimpse of the counterfactual. First, the costs of the patent stack themselves are significant, keeping the cost high and out of reach of many. Second, the patents for proprietary standards lend themselves to competitive tensions, such that the major manufacturers are suing and being sued and sometimes not able to offer phones in certain markets. Such competitive pressures and resulting costs would have had a significant impact on the success of the Internet if they arose over components of all the key standards.

And finally, the smartphone introduced mobile apps and app stores, which themselves are a standard, but not standardized across all the mobile operating systems. Specifically, an app written for Apple's iOS is not compatible with Google's Android system. Users switching systems have to redownload the apps, and developers have to implement their apps in each store. This creates a standards standoff somewhat similar to that of the computer operating systems—Windows and Mac OS—that preceded them. Both smartphone systems operate over the Internet, however, ensuring that apps can interact across systems and with online services.

So intrinsic are the open standards to the Internet as it is today that, though this book concerns itself with exploring the flip side of free Internet, there is not really any flip side to open standards. Yes, the development of standards might be faster if the process was not open, but would it be complete? Would the standards meet such a broad range of needs? Yes, security might have been better in a proprietary standard, but plenty of proprietary products are filled with bugs.[33] Any flaw, any setback, is vastly outweighed by the benefits of the global Internet and the development of a new form of standards development.

3 Why Is Wi-Fi Free?

Free Wi-Fi for Everyone. Now at Starbucks.
—Starbucks

Using the free Wi-Fi at Starbucks, it is possible to make a free FaceTime call. But if you ask the barista to use the store phone to make an international call, they would say no. Amazingly, you would likely be using the same network for the calls: the phone and Wi-Fi may plug into the same line and be offered by the same network operator, and the calls basically follow the same path to the same destination.

Why is Wi-Fi free to use? Of course, Wi-Fi is not free for Starbucks; it has to pay a monthly fee. But unlike a phone line, once the coffee shop pays for Wi-Fi, it can typically use it as much as it wants for no extra charge. So the coffee shop can offer free Wi-Fi to its customers to attract and keep them, the same way that it may have offered newspapers in the past, at no extra cost per reader. At home, we enjoy the same benefits: once we pay for our broadband, there are typically no usage charges, unlike with our telephones.

The differences in pricing ultimately come from a difference in the underlying technology. Take the highway system: The telephone network is like driving down the road and having your own lane reserved for you for the duration of the drive. The only way to allow more cars is to build more lanes, which is expensive. The Internet, on the other hand, mimics the way roads are used today. It allows many cars to share the same lanes. They may slow down during peak times, but ultimately everyone gets through.

The technology in turn impacts the pricing, but is not determinative; after all, even with road systems, different countries have different ways to charge for use, or not charge. To understand how the technology translates to the pricing of Internet access, it is important to understand the history of how the Internet was offered and how prices are set. The Internet was built on the phone network, and it took a phone call to get online initially using dial-up access, so we start with telephone pricing.

Telephony

Internet access shares the same network as telephony, often offered by the same company. That was true with fixed, or wired, telephony since the Internet was first introduced and is also true for mobile, or wireless, telephony, which came later. This chapter starts with fixed telephony, explaining why each phone call is charged by time and destination.

In the fixed network, to make a phone call, the phone of the caller must have an uninterrupted connection by wire to the phone of the receiver of the call, whether that call goes next door, to the next town, or around the world. Each subscriber has its own phone line, and within a geographic area all phone lines go to the same location, called an *exchange*. Within an exchange, all lines cannot all be connected to each other at all times; they are connected for the duration of a call through a switch.

In the early days, the caller would tell the switchboard operator who they were calling, and then the operator would manually plug a cable from the caller's line into the receiver's line to make the connection. The automatic switch was then born out of commercial necessity. An undertaker in the US Midwest was married to a switchboard operator who conveniently routed all calls about funerals his way. A competitor by the name of Almon Brown Strowger soon realized why he was losing business and invented the automatic telephone switch in 1889. This was an early foreshadowing of the ability of an intermediary—in this case, the switchboard operator; later, Internet platforms—to influence commercial decisions.

Operators were still required for long-distance calls, as direct dialing for these calls took many more years to be implemented. To make calls between towns, trunk lines were installed between exchanges, and the call would be switched from the local exchange through the trunk to the local exchange at the other end. As these trunks were expensive, there was not always enough room for all the calls, and the long-distance operator would complete the call when space opened. As technology improved, the switches were made more efficient and the lines had more capacity, but the basics never changed.

Every time you make a phone call, a part of the network—from the caller to the receiver—is reserved for that call. It is the same if you talk, if you don't talk, if you play loud music or whisper sweet nothings. No one else can use that slice of the network. Technically speaking, a *circuit* is created (traditional telephony is said to be *circuit-switched*), and at any time, there are a limited number of circuits that can be created—a large number, but not unlimited.

We pay for the call to reserve this capacity for our use. That is mainly to help cover the cost of the technology, but there is also an opportunity cost: when we use that circuit, no one else can use it. The price we pay must cover these costs, but also ultimately depends on the structure of the market.

How to Set Prices

To understand the pricing of Internet access, or anything else for that matter, the boundaries of the price are set by the underlying cost and the consumer valuation. If something costs money to create, at a minimum that cost must be recovered to stay in business. That sets out the lower boundary for price. Of course, the value to consumers may be more than the cost—think of the Norwegian glacier water—which represents the upper bound for price that companies are keen to try to reach.

Where the price falls between producer cost and consumer valuation depends on the market structure. In a monopoly—in which, by definition, a company does not face any competition—that company is a *price setter*. The monopoly can keep raising its price until doing so lowers its profits by costing more in sales than the increase in price brings. At the other end of the spectrum, in the case of perfect competition, companies are called *price takers* because they can only accept the price the market will bear and are unable to set their own prices. In the case of perfect competition, prices are set at cost. Both monopoly and perfect competition are very special cases.

Not surprisingly, most markets are somewhere in the middle. For example, car companies compete essentially in the same categories of cars but try to differentiate themselves through styling, features, safety, and branding to appeal to a certain demand and avoid head-on price competition with competitors. At the same time, there is a limit on the number of companies that can manufacture cars because of the cost of developing and producing cars, which further serves to restrict the number of sellers. That is also largely true for mobile phone service: operators try to compete not just on price, but on the price of the phone and the services that are included, while again there are limits on the number of companies that can invest to develop a competing network.

As a result, typically prices are somewhere between the monopoly price and the price that would exist under perfect competition. The prices are based on value but tempered by competition, and the sellers are said to have a degree of market power. We see this in smartphones, for instance, where the Apple standard competes with the Android standard. Apple builds the only phones using the Apple standard and is able to largely maintain prices at the higher end, while Android phone makers compete among themselves, largely at lower prices, which has also taken market share away from Apple. We will examine the cases of Internet companies and market power in chapter 7.

One common way to extract value is based on usage. Sellers would love to charge more to someone who will use their product more—in economics, this is known as *price discrimination*—but it is not possible for most products. If you look around your house, almost everything you see has a one-time price. Your clothes, furniture, electronics, decorations—all are bought at one price. You might say, and even believe, that you are going to use your new treadmill a lot, but even if the salesperson believes you, there is no way to charge more.

The exception is anything that requires a refill—printers, SodaStream, and Nespresso coffee, for instance. Here, the manufacturer can easily determine the usage level, by the demand for the refills. In these cases, the refills can be charged above cost so that the vendor profits from use over time. Often, in return, the base unit—the printer, for instance—is priced low, possibly even below cost, in order to increase demand. This model works, of course, only so long as no competitors are able to provide compatible refills, which would reduce or eliminate the ability to charge an above-cost price for the refills.

Usage-based pricing is driven in good part by costs. Think of anything that runs through pipes or sockets into the house—water, electricity, gas, and the telephone. You could not imagine paying a one-time price for electricity, or even a monthly fixed fee; your usage has costs to the utility, they are able to accurately meter your usage, and you pay for it. The same is true for water and for gas, and as we will see, for telephony, but not for broadband, for which a monthly fixed fee is common.

While the term *price discrimination* has the negative connotation of discrimination, that is in the eye of the beholder. Another form of price discrimination relates to the willingness, or ability, to pay, with different prices charged for the same thing. We generally do not begrudge children cheaper prices at the movies, particularly if we have our own, even though they take up the same space (at the same cost) as an adult. Likewise for senior discounts, student rates, and happy hour at the bar. Such forms of price discrimination only work if the recipient of the discount is able to prove they are in the targeted group and cannot easily resell the discounted good or service to the general public.

The phone company has enough information to price discriminate in all these ways. By dialing the phone, the customer is not just initiating the call but also telling the system where the call is going. In the old days, when we just used fixed phones, a telephone number conveyed information about location, including the country, the area, and even the local phone exchange to which each line is connected. The local exchanges used to have names preceding the number, such as MUrray Hill 5-9975, a number on the show *I Love Lucy*. The phone company also knows what time you made the call and how long the call lasted.

So the phone company can differentiate calls based on a significant amount of information. But do they have the market power to impose those prices on the market? Indeed they do, or at least they did.

In terms of market structure, the traditional telephone network is a *natural monopoly*, given the cost of the network. A natural monopoly is a prime example of a market failure—in this case, due to a barrier to entry—a situation in which regulation is often justified to avoid monopoly prices. In many countries, the government typically built, owned, and operated the telephone network, as part of the postal, telegraph, and telephone (PTT) service. In the few countries where the telephone company was private, such as in the United States with AT&T's Bell System, the company was regulated.

In both cases, the prices were set by the government or the telephone regulator, based on several constraints. First, it was key to make sure that the operator was able to cover its costs (including a return on investment), but not reap more than those costs. Second, within that constraint, prices were typically set with social goals in mind. The goal was to benefit from the cost efficiencies of the natural monopoly by only having one network while minimizing the impact of the market failure on prices.

Regulators generally price discriminated, setting different rates for different calls. On the theory that international and even long-distance calls were for business or more of a luxury for individuals, they were charged above cost. Likewise, calls during business hours were charged more than those on nights and weekends. This generated a cross subsidy for expanding networks to higher-cost areas, and to enable local calls, seen as more of an everyday necessity, to be charged below cost, with the overall rates balanced so that all costs were covered.

Although calls were generally charged per minute, in the United States local calls were not metered, with only a monthly charge. On the other hand, in Europe local calls were metered. Our phone in Switzerland around 1980 had a counter, like an electricity meter, and each unit had a cost: it turned faster for an international call than a local call, but it always turned. Using the phone in the hallway, fixed to the wall with a painfully short cord, with the money spinning by, made a call to a friend a pressure-filled experience for a teenager. One that my own teenage daughters—who now tease me as old-fashioned for still using email!—could hardly begin to appreciate.

Over time, the model for telephony changed. In many countries, competition was introduced, and competitors immediately targeted the higher-priced international and long-distance calls, for which there was a greater margin over cost, and the rates began to rebalance. Then, mobile telephony entered, in which competition was often present from the beginning, and the pricing models changed further. Soon competition, rather than regulation, served to lower prices.

Although the Internet uses the same network as telephony, it uses a different technology for communication, leading to a different pricing model.

Internet Technology

The Internet is not just priced differently than telephony: it is priced differently because the telephony model inspired a basic difference in how to use the telephone network.

Packet Switching

The tragic events of 9/11 provided an unwanted illustration of the difference between the technology of the Internet and the telephone network. My sister worked within sight of the World Trade Center, and at the time

I lived in Washington, DC. Because all the lines were blocked, it took several hours of calling to find out that she was thankfully okay.

While some of the lines were blocked because of the destruction of one of Verizon's exchanges adjacent to the World Trade Center, and some because they were reserved for emergency use, the underlying issue is that the telephone system was not built to handle the volume of attempted calls from relatives and friends seeking news. The total number of telephone connections in the exchanges available was based on the statistical average usage of the network, and that day was anything but average.

At the same time, the Internet was also experiencing unusually high traffic volume, of course—but the result was that it was slower, but still worked. Again, the system was optimized for far less usage, so it led to congestion, but traffic went through. To help ease the load, websites such as CNN's simplified the graphics on their pages to create less traffic.

Today, sadly, we have much more experience with tragedies and disasters in the Internet age, and we tend not to turn just to calls or texts, relying instead on online messaging services such as WhatsApp and new applications such as Facebook's Safety Check, which creates a virtual bulletin board on which someone, with one message, can let all their friends and family know they are safe in an emergency. Again, these services may slow down, but as long as the network is available, they will not be blocked like a phone call would when there is too much usage.

The question therefore is why on that day, the Internet slowed while the phone system effectively stopped. As noted, the Internet uses the same basic network infrastructure, but uses it much differently. The phone system reserves one line, or circuit, per call, while the Internet shares the lines. It can share the lines because it does not send a continual transmission. A common analogy is instead of sending a heavy book as a whole, the Internet basically rips the book into pages, gives them an address, mails them separately, and then puts them back together at the other end in the right order.

So for the Internet, instead of creating a circuit, as with telephony, everything you do is broken down into little *packets* (the Internet is called *packet-switched*), addressed, and routed over the Internet, then put back together at the other end. Just as the pages of the book may go their separate way through the mail system to arrive at the destination, the packets can be separated and directed at the links with the least traffic.

Indeed, the wasteful way the telephone network uses capacity helped inspire the more efficient way underlying the Internet. Donald Davies, a computer scientist at the British National Physical Laboratory (NPL), visited the Massachusetts Institute of Technology in 1965, where he saw an early time-sharing system in which one computer was shared among multiple users.[1] He noted that each of the users' communications with the computer were "bursty"—that is, coming in waves—but that they were reserving expensive telephone circuits even when there was no traffic. He conceived of packet switching as a way computer networks could share those phone lines, in order to lower the costs of connecting to the computer. Packet switching was soon adopted for ARPANET and then the Internet.

The other inventor of packet switching was Paul Baran, working at the RAND Corporation in the United States, who introduced the concept in 1964—although he called the units of communications *message blocks*; Donald Davies coined the term *packets*. It took several years to discover that both had independently come up with the same concept. Had the Internet already been functioning, they would have found each other's work much earlier, of course. Nevertheless, today their independent research is readily acknowledged, along with that of Leonard Kleinrock.

The result is that the packets mix with other packets like the cars on the highway; there is no reserved space for any users or services. Without a dedicated circuit over which to send the transmission, ISPs only commit to use their best efforts to deliver the packets. The more users, and the more they are doing, the more packets, and the longer they may take to arrive (even if that delay is essentially imperceptible).

Again, think of the road system. Going back to 9/11, while I was calling my sister, I was driving home. A trip that would normally take twenty minutes at that time of day took more than two hours, as the entire city effectively evacuated in the alarm and confusion of the events. That was a severely exaggerated time, but all road trips are impacted by congestion at certain times of the day and on certain days of the week.

There are a few ways to fix congestion on the roads: reduce the number of cars by charging a toll or prohibiting certain vehicles at certain times; build more lanes; or create a dedicated fast lane for some vehicles, such as buses, taxis, or other high-occupancy vehicles. In the Internet space, these solutions have all been explored in some fashion or another. One hopes that the ultimate solution is to build more lanes—more capacity—to increase the overall speed and promote usage. The new capacity has a one-time cost to build, which is passed on in monthly fees, but then the usage does not create additional costs. These differences are also reflected in the way the Internet is interconnected.

Internet Interconnection

Now we have to spend a few minutes discussing how the Internet is interconnected—how the network of networks is built and held together—and in particular how packets get from one point in the Internet to another. Broadly speaking, there are two sets of actors. The ISPs, which provide access for users, and backbones, which take traffic from the ISPs and exchange it to bring it to the final destination.

It is necessary for your ISP to get access to the rest of the Internet. After all, an ISP may sell access to a lot of your neighbors, but how do you get access to users in a neighboring country? In figure 3.1, ISP 1 can exchange traffic among its own users. But each ISP must connect directly or indirectly to every other ISP in order to deliver and receive its customers' traffic.

Traditionally, you could think of the Internet as a hierarchy, in which you as a user sit at the bottom, underneath your ISP. The ISPs at the bottom buy *transit* from a backbone, which sits above them in the hierarchy. In a transit relationship, the backbone will exchange all of the traffic to and from the ISP with the rest of the Internet. The backbone can exchange the traffic directly with its other ISP customers, but again, that will not cover much of the global Internet. Backbone 1 can directly exchange traffic between ISPs 1 and 2, for instance.

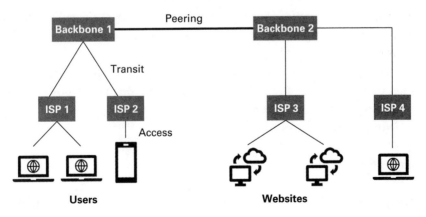

Figure 3.1
Internet hierarchy. *Source:* Michael Kende, 2020.

At the other end of a request, websites can be developed and made available by users through their own ISP connections, at the bottom of the hierarchy. Often websites are hosted by a specialized company, or small companies can buy their own servers to hold the traffic. They would also have to buy transit from an ISP or backbone, such as ISP 3, in order to deliver their web content or services to users and thereby move traffic up the hierarchy.

At the top of the hierarchy, the backbones are so large that there is no entity larger from which to buy transit. Instead, backbones enter into *peering* relationships with other backbones of similar size. This is the case for backbones 1 and 2 in the diagram, and it is what allows users of ISP 1 to access the websites connected to ISP 3. Typically, peering is done without exchanging any payments—that is, for free—because, as alluded to by the name, peering is agreed upon between peers, which exchange roughly the same amount of traffic with each other.

This concept of peering arose in the early days of the Internet, when engineers were trying to find a way to exchange traffic among the pioneer ISPs. Each recognized that the Internet had to be interconnected to function and chose a pragmatic way to ensure that. So instead of setting up a complicated way of keeping track of traffic and exchanging payments that might ultimately cancel out, they developed the system of peering instead.[2]

The largest backbones, known as Tier 1, were those that did not buy transit from any other backbone. Instead, they used peering to complete their connectivity, to enable their customers' traffic to reach anywhere. Thus, they did not pay to send traffic. Rather, they paid for the cables to carry the traffic. So long as their customers' traffic did not overload their cables, there was no extra cost for more traffic. Thus, the transit they sold their customers was sold by *bandwidth*—the amount of traffic it could carry—rather than the amount it carried.

As we will see, this trickled down to not needing to charge Wi-Fi users for their traffic. Although the Internet has undergone significant growth and changes since then, the underlying practicality has largely survived and governs Internet interconnection to this day.

Internet Access

The fundamental technology of the Internet has not changed over time, nor has the basis for interconnection and charging, be it for peering or transit, but the user price is dependent on the technology used to access the Internet, provided by users' ISPs. Going back in time, the original dial-up access was most closely associated with telephony and shared aspects of its pricing. That changed significantly when broadband was introduced and yet again when mobile broadband was introduced.

Dial-Up Access

Going back in time, it was not always the case that Internet access was priced to enable free Wi-Fi. In fact, the earliest examples go back before Wi-Fi was introduced in 1998, and even before the Internet itself was widespread. AOL was the largest online provider in the United States, and a press release from 1993, the year that AOL began to offer access to the Internet (as opposed to its own online services) spelled out this reasoning for its charges: "America Online expects that 90 percent of its customers will not use more than 5 hours per month so they'll just pay a fixed rate of $9.95. Heavy users will be able to purchase additional online time (beyond the initial 5 free hours) at the rate of $3.50 per hour."[3]

Set aside, for the moment, the charming notion that a "heavy user" is one with more than five hours per month of online access, and note that this was for dial-up access, which required the user to have a modem and use their computer to make a traditional phone call to reach AOL. The phone call was connected to an AOL modem using a circuit like any other phone call, over which the online traffic slowly flowed. Although the Internet is completely digital, between the user modem and the AOL modem the traffic was analog, like the voice calls that normally occupied those circuits. Those of us of the right age can still easily conjure up the beeping and screeching of the modems connecting, after which the modem (modulator-demodulator) translated the digital data into audio signals for delivery, and vice versa at the other end.

Capacity was limited by the number of modems AOL had in their network, and in fact, when AOL went to unlimited usage in 1996, at a cost of $19.95, usage skyrocketed. People stayed online for hours at a time, so many users had trouble connecting due to busy signals. The only reason to log off would have been for a call because dial-up prevented other calls being made or received. It was so bad that the CEO, Steve Case, had to send a note to subscribers asking them to treat the service like a pay phone and log off so others could access the limited number of AOL modems.

Dial-up access also used up circuits for the phone company, changing the calculations quite a bit in terms of network capacity. Five hours of monthly AOL usage may not have been a lot in terms of Internet access, but at the time the total average call time per line was around fifty minutes per day. The calculation significantly changed with unlimited services, and the phone companies had to adjust their own capacity.

In addition to not being able to make a phone call, because dial-up used the same network capacity as phone calls, the bandwidth of a dial-up connection was limited to fifty-six kilobits (kb) per second (Kbps). Kilobits per second measures the amount of data that can be sent over a connection, also known as the bandwidth. In this case, 56 Kbps is fifty-six thousand bits. A *bit* is the smallest unit of data, like an on-off switch representing a zero or one. Eight bits equal a *byte*, which represents a single character such as a letter or number. So 56 Kbps equals seven thousand bytes, or characters, per second. That is about five pages of this text per second: not so bad, perhaps, when most Internet content was text, but not feasible for multimedia content.

By way of perspective, to download a movie using a dial-up modem would have taken at least sixty hours at top speed—nothing like the high-definition, real-time streaming that we are used to today. Of course, at the time, the restrictions of dial-up matched the usage. Most of the Internet was text-based—emails and files—and therefore did not take great capacity. And the services were mostly asynchronous—not in real time. No one watched an email being pieced together the way you would listen to streaming audio, so delays were not noticed, nor did the sender expect an immediate response.

The early dial-up rates were thus usage-based in the same way as phone calls were—based on the time spent online rather than the amount of activity because of limits on the number of modems, similar to the telephone circuits. Eventually, however, as seen with AOL, the costs shifted to a flat monthly cost. This shift resulted from the market structure, as well as the underlying cost structure of the Internet.

The ISP market at the time was very competitive, for the simple reason that there were almost no entry barriers to setting up an ISP. A dial-up ISP did not have to invest in its own network. Instead, the ISP bought some modems to receive the calls, equipment to route the traffic onto the Internet, and transit connectivity to the rest of the Internet. As the number of customers increased, they could keep adding incremental capacity. By the year 2000, there were over seven thousand ISPs in North America.[4] Some of them were hyperlocal, others regional or national, but all faced many competitors, keeping prices low.

In the United States, at least, the development of the competitive ISP market was free from regulation, and that was the result of a series of regulatory decisions. The US FCC explicitly made decisions that enabled the growth of ISPs and adoption by consumers. In particular, the FCC decided that ISPs and other data services could access the regulated telephone network to offer service, but not be regulated themselves.[5]

In addition, another FCC decision exempted ISPs and similar data service providers from having to pay their telecom operator per-minute charges for incoming calls from customers, which would have precluded flat-rate pricing. Also, local calls were unmetered, keeping the costs down for users. By contrast, the per-minute charges for local calls common in Europe at the time clearly limited adoption and usage of the Internet during the dial-up phase.

Finally, the development of dial-up modems came from the earlier decision of the FCC to allow any equipment to connect to the network as long as it met certain standards. Before that, only equipment provided by the Bell System could be connected, resulting in no competition and few choices for telephones at the time. The decision was not made with modems in mind—it predated that—but it enabled companies to compete in developing modems and customers to choose their own and plug them in.

Given the strong level of competition in the United States, ISP pricing reflected cost. Although the dial-up part of Internet access required one modem per call to connect users with their ISPs, which constrained usage, the ISP then sent the traffic to and from the global Internet—and as we saw, the Internet has a fundamental cost difference with the phone network that enabled flat-rate pricing. By removing the reliance on dial-up modems and phone circuits, broadband service removed the last restraint to flat-rate pricing.

Broadband

The introduction of broadband in place of dial-up access had many benefits that we still enjoy today, including faster speeds and always-on Internet access. Telephone companies installed a new technology—digital subscriber line (DSL)—which eliminated the need for the dial-up modems and the need for using the telephone switch. Instead, DSL uses its own modem and routes traffic around the telephone switch directly to the global Internet.

By routing DSL traffic around the telephone switch, no telephone circuits are used. DSL also uses higher frequencies on the line than phone calls. The capacity on the telephone line allows for a spectrum of frequencies of the signals, just like the airwave spectrums are divided into AM and FM radio, broadcast television, Wi-Fi, wireless telephony, and myriad other uses. Just as with wireless, each use must occupy a different frequency so that they do not interfere with one another. As a result, phone calls can be made at the same time as DSL is used, and the DSL connection can always be on. Using different frequencies than the phone calls also removes the capacity limits facing dial-up modems, so broadband speeds are much faster, although there are limits on the speed of DSL as well.

At the same time, cable television companies were using their own networks to offer high-speed Internet access using a different technology called Data over Cable Service Interface Specification (DOCSIS). This technology reserved part of the cable capacity for Internet access and again resulted in faster speeds and always-on technology.

Broadband profoundly changed the way we used the Internet. Audio and video could be introduced because of the increased bandwidth, and services could be in real time because the networks were faster and had greater capacity. This made video streaming services such as YouTube and Netflix possible, as well as two-way real-time services such as gaming and video calling.

The introduction of broadband service did not just dramatically improve our use of the Internet, which we continue to enjoy through today, but also changed the underlying basis for pricing—with respect to both the market structure and the cost basis.

In terms of market structure, the introduction of broadband drastically reduced the number of ISPs by raising the barriers to entry. No longer could anyone set up an ISP with a few modems and a server connected to the Internet; broadband equipment had to be installed in the telephone or cable network. This reduction in the overall number of competitors did not necessarily eliminate competitive pricing, nor did it automatically lead to regulation as a means to control price. Essentially, four outcomes arose.

In the United States, where there was significant geographic overlap between cable TV companies and telephone networks, the FCC eventually paved the way for what was known as *facilities-based competition* among those companies, meaning that the cable company and the telephone company competed against each other using their own networks. In some areas, this competition was fortified through satellite, fixed wireless, or so-called over-builders that deployed their own new networks—such as Google Fiber, which rolled out a residential fiber network in a number of US cities, in competition with existing telephone and cable operators. The competition and coverage is not complete, however, but for the bulk of households, facilities-based competition was the approach taken.

In the European Union, many countries did not have cable networks, however, and so-called service-based competition was developed through regulation. Competitors were enabled to buy access to key parts of the incumbents' phone networks at regulated wholesale rates, allowing them to offer DSL service and compete in the retail market without deploying their own network.

In countries where these types of competition in fixed broadband were not feasible, the retail price of broadband was regulated, adopting the approach taken to telephony before it. For instance, in Bermuda, prior to opening the market, the incumbent had to subject all proposed broadband tariffs to regulatory review.[6] Finally, where there was very little fixed network to begin with, prospects for widespread broadband did not look encouraging until the emergence of mobile broadband, discussed ahead.

This description glosses over many technical characteristics and regulatory challenges, but the outcome was that in most countries, there was competition in broadband, albeit less than with dial-up access, and prices were below the monopoly level. However, broadband also shifted the cost basis for Internet access toward flat-rate pricing.

First, the time spent online with broadband does not incur any cost per se and in any case could not be the basis for pricing. With the Internet connection always on, time-based pricing would have resulted in continual charges. More to the point, however, no resources are used in keeping the connection on; they are only used when traffic is received or sent. For delivering this traffic to the rest of the Internet, the ISP pays a backbone provider.

As noted earlier, the transit that ISPs purchase from backbones is based on the bandwidth purchased rather than the traffic sent. Bandwidth is the maximum amount of data that can be exchanged over any given link. For instance, purchasing one gigabit per second (Gbps) of traffic allows the ISP to send up to that amount of traffic across the Internet per second. One

Gbps is equivalent to one thousand megabits per second (Mbps), or one million kilobits per second (Kbps). A typical home broadband connection may allow a maximum bandwidth of 25 Mbps (nearly four hundred fifty times faster than the fastest dial-up modem).

As a rule of thumb, an ISP then typically uses a *contention ratio* to decide how much Internet capacity to buy from a backbone in relation to how much it sells to its users. A typical contention ratio for home users might be 50:1. These are typically commercially sensitive numbers and may be falling as the price of capacity falls. However, for a 50:1 ratio, this means for every fifty subscribers who buy a 25 Mbps broadband connection, the ISP buys 25 Mbps worth of transit. This assumes (correctly) that not all users will be filling their connections at all times, which, after all, was the basis for packet switching in the first place.

At one level, this is similar to the decision a telephone company makes in terms of the number of subscribers it would have per number of circuits it can create. However, there is a crucial difference, as we have seen. When too many phone calls are made, the system blocks additional calls; when too much traffic is sent, the Internet connections slow down, but they will not stop. In any case, often transit arrangements accommodate increased bursts of traffic, and depending on the length of the bursts, there may not even be extra charges.

It is worth noting that transit represents a cost for the ISP, but in most developed countries the cost of transit is very low. For instance, in New York, transit might cost the equivalent of thirty cents per megabits per second per month, if bought in bulk. The transit cost per user could be as low as fifteen cents per user, depending on the bandwidth of their broadband connection and the ratio of users to transit capacity purchased. Thus, each user might be paying thirty or forty dollars per month for broadband to access that fifteen cents of transit.

There is thus an aggregate cost of increased usage, but it does not directly increase every time a customer uses the Internet. If you download a video at 3:00 a.m., for instance, when no one else is using their connections, it would not add to the cost for the ISP because it fits within their transit capacity. As everyone begins to stream movies during prime time, however, that action is likely to increase the amount of capacity used, and this peak time usage is what drives the ISP's cost by raising the monthly payments to the backbone.

Thus, there are increased costs with overall usage, and some ISPs have reflected it in their price, in two ways. Some ISPs offer plans with data caps, which indicate how much traffic the subscriber can use per month. The data cap is typically in measured in gigabytes (GB). According to the UK comparison site Broadband Genie, with a 10 GB monthly cap, a user can view thousands of web pages, make fifty-five hours of Skype calls, or watch about ninety minutes of a high-definition streaming video. Many data caps, where they exist, are for more than 10 GB, and unlimited plans are increasingly common.

Up to the data cap, there is a fixed price. If consumers go over, then an additional amount of data would need to be purchased. And there may be multiple plans available, with different data caps, so that users can choose the one closest to their needs. This is not very common today in many developed countries for fixed broadband, given competitive markets and that additional usage does not automatically add to the ISPs costs. As noted ahead, it is more common for mobile broadband, although unlimited—or effectively unlimited—plans for mobile broadband are also increasingly available in many countries.

A more common differentiator of broadband packages is the speed of the connection, which reflects how it buys capacity. *Speed* is a bit of a misnomer; in fact, it refers to the bandwidth of the connection. Nevertheless, the bandwidth impacts speed. You could think of the broadband connection as a funnel, through which the traffic can pass. The more megabits per second the connection can carry, the wider the funnel, and the faster the information can pass through to the user.

ISPs commonly offer packages with different speeds, with users paying more for greater bandwidth. The greater bandwidth will be useful for subscribers who expect to do a lot of interactive computing, such as gaming, or watch movies that require high bandwidth. As increases in bandwidth for users translate into higher costs of bandwidth for the ISP, they are reflected in higher monthly prices. However, once the plan is purchased, usage is typically free within the plan. Using Skype to call a Skype user in China does not have a cost to the user and results in no worries about the length of the call.

However, Skype provides a good illustration of the ongoing difference between telephony charging and Internet. Although it is true that Skype calls within Skype are free, regardless of the location of the caller or Skype user called, that is not true for all Skype calls. Skype offers a service called

Skype to Phone, via which someone using Skype can call someone on their traditional fixed or mobile phone, dialing their phone number. These calls are not free and do depend on the country called. While often the cost is in the pennies per minute, a Skype call to a mobile phone in the United Kingdom costs over twelve cents per minute, and to call some countries in Africa costs over fifty cents per minute. This is because the call must exit the Internet and enter the phone system to be completed, or terminated, by the phone company of the receiver. The phone companies still charge a rate for terminating those calls, regardless of where they originate, and those charges are passed on to the Skype caller.

I have the Skype app on my smartphone. What this means is that if someone calls me using Skype, the call is free for both of us—we can even add video. If they call me using Skype to Phone, however, I receive the call on the same phone, but it costs the person who called me and we cannot use video. Same device, same network, video calls are possible, and it is free. That highlights a difference between telephony and Internet these days.

One could argue that data caps or broadband speeds are a form of price discrimination, charging more for users who value their connections more, but there is an underlying cost rationale. Other forms of price discrimination are not done, however. Some of the challenge is technical; some of it is more behavioral.

We already noted that time-based charging does not make sense for broadband, which is always on but only uses resources when traffic is sent or received. The destination of the call is also used for telephony, but not for Internet traffic. It is not because the destination is unknowable: the ISP must route the traffic based on the underlying IP address, which can provide geographic information; that is why sometimes videos will not play because they are not available in a particular country. But users would not react well to destination-based pricing. Unlike with a phone number, users are typically not able to determine where a website is based or where a Skype call is going and would not welcome the surprise of paying more than they expected.

Although the trend is clearly toward unlimited usage, there are exceptions that prove the rule. In particular, mobile Internet often has different pricing than fixed.

Mobile Internet

Mobile technology changed everything for communications. Mobile voice cut the cord connecting our phones to our walls and then, with the Internet, liberated our work from our desks. Mobile broadband use now is greater than fixed use in most, if not all, countries.

First, let's step back and marvel at what is packed into a modern smartphone, just in terms of functionality and the number of devices it can replace in addition to a basic mobile phone. It also can take the place of a music player, a video player, a GPS, a camera, a video recorder, a flashlight, a watch, a wallet, a game console, and a small laptop computer with hard drive. There have already been serious impacts on sales in other markets such as cameras. This is a remarkable array of functionality, in a small, convenient device.

Mobile Internet as we know it today can basically be traced back to the introduction of the iPhone in 2007. At the time that AT&T rolled out the first iPhone in the United States, data plans were unlimited, and for good reason—there was not that much to do on a mobile phone before then, other than email and basic services. Apps were new, video was scarce, and pre-iPhone handsets did not have the screens or keyboards to do much online in any case.

That soon changed as apps increased in numbers, online video grew, and for many the mobile Internet became the main, if not only, way that people connected to the Internet. As mobile data usage increased, unlimited plans began to be phased out. The reason, however, was not necessarily the amount of data used because the underlying Internet cost structure is the same as for fixed. It is also not because of market structure because mobile technology fosters more competition in comparison to fixed broadband. Rather, mobile access introduces a new constraint that has a significant cost.

With respect to market structure, think about the difference in network deployment. Fixed telephony required deploying copper lines door to door, each connected individually all the way to an exchange. The copper has a cost, as does the digging or stringing of the wire, and then there is the cost of maintenance. The same is true today for deploying a fiber broadband network to homes.

In comparison, mobile signals are delivered from a tower with an antenna and a station at the base that delivers the signals to and from the network to the antenna. Once the tower is installed and the transmitter is turned on, everyone in the neighborhood receives the signal, even if they are just passing through. Anyone with a mobile phone can make or receive a call— and not just in their home or office, but also, as we well know, while they are walking, in a car, or on a train.

As a result, while fixed telephony was largely a natural monopoly, because of the high cost of deployment, mobile telephony was not, and in many countries three or even four operators soon were able to compete. As a result, competition replaced regulation as a means to keep prices down. The same is now true for broadband.

In advanced markets, it is common to sign mobile contracts for at least a year of service, so competition encompasses not only price, but also what is included in the contract. It can cover the number of phone calls that can be made in a month, the number of texts, and the amount of data that can be accessed. It can include new services such as access to music stream- ing. And it can include a subsidy for a new smartphone. Competition also involves rolling out better coverage, with newer, faster technologies, and it extended to AT&T securing an exclusive deal with Apple to roll out the iPhone in the first place.

On the other hand, there is one significant difference with fixed tech- nology. Mobile phones connect using wireless spectrum, and spectrum has some specific properties. First, to prevent interference, exclusive licenses are assigned to each mobile operator for their own slice of spectrum, often through an auction at significant cost. In one auction alone in 2015, con- ducted by the US FCC, operators bid a total of almost USD 45 billion. The spectrum won at auctions is used by all customers of the mobile operator, for both voice calls and Internet access.

At any point in time, the amount of spectrum is fixed to the amount held by the mobile operators, and over time the amount available in the most desirable bands is scarce, driving up the auction prices. As traffic increases, this leads to congestion, particularly in dense urban areas at peak times, and congestion makes it hard to make calls and use the mobile Inter- net. Until the next assignment of spectrum, there are only four things an operator can do to meet demand, which vary in affordability and feasibility.

First, the operator can subdivide its network into smaller cells. Mobile signals come from towers, and each tower serves a cell around it (hence the name *cellular service*), and each cell can serve a certain number of users and traffic. By dividing cells, with more transmitters, the number of cells increases, so that more people can be served. While the transmitters can shrink in size and cost, this approach takes time and money, and there is a limit to how small the cells can be.

Second, the operator can off-load traffic to Wi-Fi networks. Wi-Fi is not only on a different frequency than mobile networks; the frequency is also unlicensed, which is why any and all of us can install our own Wi-Fi networks in our homes without anyone's permission. As we walk into our house or connect to a public hotspot, our mobile devices can switch to the Wi-Fi network, allowing all Internet traffic, and even traditional phone calls, to go through the Wi-Fi and free up the valuable mobile spectrum. Mobile operators may also have their own network of public Wi-Fi spots, or strike deals with them, as a way of off-loading more traffic. This is promising and accounts for a significant amount of traffic but can only be used where there are Wi-Fi networks.

Third, there are successive generations of new mobile technologies. The first true mobile broadband technology was the third generation of mobile (3G); now, most traffic in many countries is 4G; and 5G is starting to be announced or deployed. Each generation is more efficient than the previous, allowing for greater bandwidth and more users. However, each new generation is introduced about every ten years, and once the upgrades have been made, at significant cost, then the operators must use the other approaches when they reach capacity.

Finally, operators can ration demand. This is not necessarily the preferred way to address congestion, but it may be the quickest and cheapest. This can be done with limited data plans, as introduced in the United States a number of years ago, which either keep users within the limits they have paid for or require payments for use above the limit. Even when unlimited plans were reintroduced in the United States several years ago, they included provisions that allow the operators to throttle a user's speed after they use a certain amount of data in a month and when they are in congested areas.

As a result, charging for data on mobile Internet is not because the service is the Internet, but because the service is mobile. Spectrum—the radio frequency used for mobile services—is scarce, and its usage has an opportunity cost for others, so demand can be rationed through pricing, with a bundle of data and charges for going over the quota. This situation has an even greater impact in developing markets, where users are even more reliant on mobile services.

Developing Countries

Users in developing countries also face usage prices, and also based on costs. Partly, this is because much of Internet access is mobile in developing countries because their fixed networks were never fully built out. Thus, the mobile usage has the same cost constraints as mobile anywhere, for the reasons we have just discussed. And partly it has to do with the nature of consumer arrangements with mobile operators.

In developing countries, most mobile Internet users do not have long-term contracts. Instead of the contracts that many of us sign on to for one or two years, which often include unlimited or nearly unlimited usage, most developing country users have prepaid plans, where they must buy their credits before using them, rather than paying at the end of the month. This is a result of a lack of financial accounts, unsteady sources of disposable income, and little possibility for credit. With prepaid plans, almost by definition, payment is made by usage.

Of course, the prepaid plans could provide access to large amounts of traffic at low cost, but for the most part they do not, and that has to do in part with differences in the underlying costs of the Internet. Increasingly, popular content uses a lot of bandwidth, whether it is video, games, or other multimedia content or services. And for reasons we will discuss in chapter 8, in some countries, a significant amount of it is hosted abroad.[7] As the cost of the international transit to reach that content is quite high still, it must be reflected in corresponding usage charges.

The developing countries are thus in a bit of a vicious cycle. Without a big base of users, there is little reason to host content and services in data centers in those countries or regions. But without local data centers, the cost of accessing Internet data remains high. The result is high usage prices, which inhibit uptake and usage, in the regions that may benefit the most from increased Internet access owing to the relative lack of traditional services.

Conclusion

Where there is scarcity, prices are a way to match demand to supply. What stops car lovers from all driving BMWs, wine lovers from drinking only old Bordeaux, gold lovers from more jewelry, and gadget lovers from buying the latest smartphone every time it is released? In a free market, increased demand will raise prices, and the prices in turn make buyers prioritize where to spend their disposable income.

What happens when the price is nothing? What is the result of not having usage charges on the Internet, not just at a coffee shop or other hotspot, but also at home, in the office, and for the most part on the road? Coupled with free content and services (discussed in the next chapter), this is one of the cornerstones of the success of the Internet.

It can take some getting used to. A number of years ago, I was speaking to a taxi driver in Paris, who was complaining about the cost of using the Internet with his mobile phone when high data charges were the norm in France. I could relate, because of the heavy roaming charges I was paying for data in France at the time. But when I told him I had an unlimited mobile data plan in the United States, he was a bit perplexed. He asked what would stop me from using it as a baby monitor, leaving one phone on by the baby and taking another with me. I had to admit, nothing would stop me, but I also doubted that anyone had ever tried.

Of course, now it is common to enjoy the free cost of always on services. We keep the Internet on all day (and night); using it for entertainment, as an encyclopedia, for work, and to keep up with our family and friends. We can even ask our ever-vigilant digital assistant a question out loud. We don't pause to consider the cost of what we are doing, and so it becomes a part of our lives.

Indeed, while AOL formerly noted that 90 percent of its users would not use more than five hours of service per month, recent surveys show that users now spend more than five hours *per day* online. And that is just using their mobile devices! Of course, websites and app developers, in turn, can design services that benefit from unlimited data, with games, video, social media, all available for unlimited use. And we can now use apps on our phones to access devices that continually secure our houses, track our fitness, and, yes, monitor our babies.

The flip side, however, is that operators must recover the cost of their networks and raise money for the upgrades to technology and capacity on which we now rely. For this, they have four potential sources: increasing the price for users, charging content providers, selling advertising, and government subsidies.

We can already see efforts to charge users to pay for the network, such as charging more for higher bandwidth, but there is likely a limit to what users will pay per month, and ultimately this rations demand and blunts some of the benefits of the Internet. Governments have also subsidized networks to help realize their own goals for a connected society, but in many countries, money is short, and deployment is largely left in the hands of the private sector.

This leaves charging content providers and/or selling advertising. Both of these are contentious. Content providers could be charged for better quality access to customers—in effect creating a fast lane for time-sensitive content, such as gaming services. However, this may be opposed by key stakeholders, including smaller providers who may not be able to afford the charges and users who want a large variety of content. Selling advertising requires detailed information about users and their preferences to be successful. This opens up significant debates about data protection and privacy and is covered in chapter 5.

As things stand, we benefit every day from the cost structure of the Internet: we do not have to think about cost every time we stream a movie or go online at Starbucks—a liberation very welcome to those of us who had to be very price conscious when making long-distance or international calls twenty years ago. Of course, on the flip side, this same cost structure benefits those with less benign uses for the Internet: spammers sending us unlimited unwanted emails, Russians spending their day sowing confusion through social media, and hackers diligently working their way into the systems upon which we increasingly trust our personal data.

How to promote the good, and prevent the bad, is an ongoing challenge gaining increased attention in the current techlash.

4   Something for Nothing

Half the money I spend on advertising is wasted; the trouble is I don't know which half.

—John Wanamaker

John Wanamaker owned sixteen department stores in the United States and Europe at the turn of the twentieth century. His quote laments the difficulty of assessing the value of advertising at the time. At best, one could try to place ads in the right context; ads in the sports section of a newspaper could be different than those in the business section. But beyond that, there was no way to know if the ad worked.

The Internet solved John Wanamaker's problem with advertising in spectacular fashion. It brings to mind the popular saying, "If you are not paying for the product, you are the product." Although it now applies to the Internet, the quote predates the Internet. Much of the Internet is free for us because it delivers our attention to paying advertisers, but the same has long been true about television, radio, free newspapers, and other media. The difference—and likely reason for the heightened popularity of the quote—is that we are effectively paying for the free online services with data.

It is here that the ethos of free takes on its own psychology. Many users don't know about the free standards underlying much of what they do online. Many also take free Starbucks Wi-Fi for granted, likely viewing it, correctly, as a marketing tool, but not considering why their home usage is typically not metered as well. But free online content and services almost became a birthright during the dot-com boom of the late 1990s. Not all of it was legal content, and not all of the services were sustainable, but the expectation of *free to the user* was baked into the Internet going mainstream.

Successful companies were then able to turn this ethos into profitable business models that answer the Wanamaker challenge.

Early Online Business Models

Many ads in John Wanamaker's day were for brand advertising, to establish identity and awareness among a target audience. More targeted retail ads, for stores, try to convert that awareness into sales. Broadly speaking, there are two challenges with these types of advertising: deciding where to place an ad and then determining whether it worked. Knowing the latter helps with the former. Over time, Internet technology helped solved both of these challenges, to put it mildly.

The earliest online ads were no more sophisticated than earlier media ads. ARPANET and NSFNET, both government networks, had an acceptable use policy that did not allow for-profit activities, including advertising. Despite the policy, the earliest commercial email on ARPANET was recorded in 1978, and despite strongly negative reactions its use grew to be known as unsolicited bulk email—or, more popularly, spam. Depending on definitions, the level of spam is more than 50 percent of email and may have been as high as 90 percent at one point. But as we will see in chapter 7, most of this is now blocked.

The term *spam* only comes indirectly from the canned lunch meat by that name. It directly comes from a Monty Python skit, in which a waitress reads out a menu of items that increasingly include spam, and a group of Vikings begins to chant "spam" until told to be quiet. It was then adopted in community chat groups (known as multiuser dungeons, or MUDs) in the 1980s, when chats were flooded with meaningless text like the mindless Viking chants in the skit. From there, the term made its way to unwanted emails flooding in-boxes.[1]

Even these early examples of spam address part of the Wanamaker challenge, however. It is possible to measure the response rate, and even keep track of sales, when people respond to the email or click on a link. But this shows that—not surprisingly—far more than half of spam emails are wasted. A good response rate for spam is, in one case that was measured, twenty-six sales out of 350 million emails sent![2] Why keep doing it? Because the cost of sending spam is almost free; the biggest challenge seems to be how to misspell words like Viagra (vaigra, V1AGRA, vi*agra) to get by the spam filters.

Later came banner ads. These are ads that appear at the top of a website or on the sides. These ads, like earlier media ads, are largely brand ads, and their placement was largely based on context—the content of the website and corresponding demographics of browsers of that website. These ads predate the commercial web, finding their first outlet on online portals such as AOL. The first web banner ads were shown in 1994, on the Hot-Wired website, including a futuristic one from AT&T asking, "Have you ever clicked your mouse right here? YOU WILL." In the first few weeks, given the novelty, upward of 80 percent of users did so.[3]

Although these ads were largely for branding, similar to TV ads, there are several critical differences. First, it was possible to count exactly how many people were served the ad, also known as an impression. Indeed, that was the common way that ads were paid at the time, by impression. Second, it was possible for the viewer to click on the ad and be taken to the advertiser's chosen website, which could also be measured. But still, in the beginning, everyone on the website saw the same ad, and not everyone was interested, so this type of advertising was not yet lucrative.

The first banner ads coincided with the start of the dot-com bubble, which lasted roughly from 1995 to 2000. It was still difficult to earn revenue on the Internet at this point. While advertising was not yet fully developed, users quickly grew an expectation of free content and services online for a variety of reasons. Partly, free content flowed from the original, noncommercial uses of NSFNET that was only decommissioned in 1995, and some of it was from individuals sharing their interests, as they continue to do through today. This included moderated discussion groups such as Usenet, which turned into Internet forums, and later the weblogs or blogs containing diaries, opinions, and other forms of individual expression. The earliest commercial content online was also free, but much, if not all, infringed on copyrights.

Napster, for instance, enabled people to share music files using peer-to-peer file-transfer technology, via which Napster connected a user who wanted a specific song with a user who had it, allowing the former to download the song from the latter's computer. This technology completely bypassed the copyright holders, meaning that musicians and record labels did not get paid, and it further entrenched the expectation among consumers that *digital* meant *free*. Although Napster was eventually sued and put out of business, that mindset still continued. Copyright holders—the music labels—were thus reluctant to sell their content online for fear of piracy.

During the bubble, other websites sprang up to offer legitimate—and costly—services, also for free. For instance, Kozmo.com was a delivery service that promised to bring items to buyers—at no charge—within one hour. It raised $250 million in venture capital funding and at its peak covered more than ten cities. It burned through money, though, unsurprisingly; the demand for free and quick delivery was healthy, and there seemed no way to start charging. Like many dot-coms at the time, Kozmo.com did not survive the bursting of the dot-com bubble; free did not pay in this case.

Such business models bring to mind a satirical ad on *Saturday Night Live*, a US sketch comedy show. The ad is for the company First CitiWide Change Bank, whose slogan is "We just make change." The manager boasts: "We will work with the customer to give that customer the change that he or she needs. If you come to us with a twenty-dollar bill, we can give you two tens, we can give you four fives—we can give you a ten and two fives. … We will give you the change equal to the amount of money that you want change for!" After some glowing customer testimonials, the manager tells the secret: "All the time, our customers ask us, 'How do you make money doing this?' The answer is simple: Volume."[4]

Just as making change earns nothing, no matter how many customers, the same was true for many free services at the time. During the boom, however, few were hampered by questions of revenues, much less profits. The related metrics of traffic, growth, and the number of customers were critical; the rest would work itself out. It was a free-for-all, and the stock market was in a frenzy, fueled by one initial public offering (IPO) after another, triggered in large part by the success of the Netscape IPO. Investor optimism—or perhaps *myopia* is a better word—was epitomized for me by the case of PalmPilot.

PalmPilot was the original popular personal digital assistant (PDA). The first versions were basically what was left over from an iPhone if you stripped away most features. In fact, it is easier to describe it as an electronic Filofax, as it was mainly used to store contacts, reminders, and a calendar. At least in the beginning, it had no connectivity, no keyboard (it used a form of stylized handwriting recognition), and no array of apps. Nonetheless, at the time it was very popular, particularly with early adopters; I have my own saved in my personal gadget graveyard somewhere.

PalmPilot was purchased by 3Com (mostly known for Ethernet), and in the height of the bubble, 3Com decided to sell 6 percent of PalmPilot in an

IPO. Based on its share price at the end of the first day of trading, PalmPilot was worth $53.3 billion. The parent company 3Com, on the same day, had a market capitalization of about half that, at $28 billion. How could 3Com be worth less? It still owned 94 percent of the more valuable PalmPilot.[5] That was a strong signal that the market was overvalued.

As it turns out, the NASDAQ stock index, home of many of the dot-com companies, peaked a few days after the PalmPilot IPO, in March 2000. Kozmo.com, PalmPilot, and many other stocks had been propelled by a perfect storm of hype and greed triggered by the popularization of the Internet and fueled by venture capitalists, stock analysts, and newly minted day traders. Like other speculative bubbles, the dot-com one was bound to burst—and when it did, investors lost real and paper fortunes.

The aftermath of the crash was like that of a forest fire: it left widespread devastation, but the cleared-out deadwood let sunshine in to allow a new generation to grow. The bubble laid the foundation for the subsequent growth of the digital economy. Telecom companies had invested significant amounts of money in backbone networks and providing broadband, enabling Internet access and growth. Data centers were built, which then housed the content and services that survived the crash. Engineers had taken jobs with the dot-coms and gained experience to help grow profitable businesses. And the dot-coms had invested into and upgraded office space, furniture, and equipment that could be used by the next generation. A number of the companies that survived, including Amazon, Apple, and Google, are now among the most valuable companies in the world.

Part of the reason these companies survived was their revenue models. Amazon and Apple, of course, always had a sales model for revenue generation, from e-commerce and computers, respectively. But the model for monetizing online content still looked grim. There were really two possible approaches: First, to successfully transpose offline models into online ones; that is, to sell content—newspapers, books, music—online through subscriptions or download fees. Second, to take advantage of the low online distribution costs and large market to distribute content for free, but paid through advertising.

At the time of the crash, neither approach still looked promising. Consumers were used to enjoying free online content, an ethos that began online before the dot-com bubble and was fueled by it, and it was hard to shake. Everyone likes free doughnuts, and no one wanted to risk the drubbing the American Red Cross took when it started to charge. Even if consumers were willing to pay, they did not want to pay each time and for everything. But the advertising model did not look promising, either. The ads at the time were not very effective, and the rates were low.

There was, however, one Internet subscription model that was earning revenue, and that was ISPs providing Internet access. Indeed, some at the time argued that without content, there would be no demand for access, so ISPs should compensate content providers. Clearly, however, the ISPs were not willing to go along with this, and it did not happen. If the argument sounds vaguely familiar, however, it may be because as content revenues took off, some ISPs flipped the argument roughly ten short years later, arguing that content providers should compensate *them*.[6] How did the flow of revenues reverse so quickly?

Growth of the Online Economy

Content owners clearly recognized the value of the Internet in terms of low-cost distribution, vividly demonstrated by the widespread impact of Napster, but that experience hardly encouraged an online sales model. The same economics that made it easy to share content over Napster would allow their content to be shared. Over time, this issue was solved quite well, starting with Apple convincing record companies to allow them to sell music through iTunes in 2003.

The selling point Steve Jobs used to get music rights was that the music would be protected from copying with digital rights management (DRM) tools and that it would only be made available to the relatively narrow base of Apple computer users. Those two restrictions were soon jettisoned, with the store being made available to Windows users soon after launch, and then Steve Jobs pushing back against DRM in an open letter. Within ten years, twenty-five billion songs had been purchased, and other vendors began selling and streaming music. Video also became available on iTunes for download in 2005, and soon after Netflix led the way with its subscription streaming service.

So eventually, audio and video content that was sold offline in physical format—CDs and DVDs—was made available online, along with newspapers, books, and other media. The economics of online sales was very attractive. Take music as an example. When you bought a CD, you had to go to the shop or order from Amazon and wait for it to be delivered. It could be out of stock; it could be out of circulation. With iTunes or Spotify, it can be played immediately, at home, in the car, in the city. And those services can also support a long tail of obscure content.[7] Likewise, Netflix first disrupted the video rental market by sending DVDs straight to the house, but then disrupted its own DVD model with its online streaming model. These markets lend themselves well to the digital economy. But what about the companies that continued to offer free online services? What options did they have for making money on the Internet?

Search Ads

Post-crash, with venture capital companies reluctant to support companies without a promise of revenues and then profits, a new business model was needed for online content. Display ads were not very effective, with some of the same characteristics and, for the advertisers, frustrations of traditional ads. The turnaround for online advertising came with search advertising, and its leader, although not pioneer, was Google. Search ads are those that appear next to the results of a search. Their success is built on a simple insight, perfectly executed.

If you go to a sports website, for instance, a display ad for a new car may introduce you to a new model, and there may be some chance that you were thinking of buying a new car anyway, and an even smaller chance that you were interested in that brand. Display ads—like traditional media ads—create brand awareness. But if you go into a search engine and search for "car dealer," there is a much higher chance that you are actually interested in a car and might click on an ad. This turns out to be a stunningly effective model for creating engagement, rather than just awareness.

A company called GoTo.com pioneered search ads two years before Google tried, but Google was (much) more effective, starting with search ads in 2000, around the time the bubble burst. As with any success, there are many reasons for this. One reason is that GoTo.com and other search providers before Google included paid search results among all the search results, while Google labeled them and put them on the side separate from the "organic" search results.[8] Thus, the search results were seen as neutral, being separate from the paid ads. The bigger picture, however, is also fairly straightforward: Google simply delivered much better search results than anyone else. That is a subjective statement, of course, but proved by

Google's quick and sustained success. This laid a solid base for generating ad revenue.

The simplicity of this model of advertising is that relevant ads can be delivered without any knowledge about the person doing the search—just based on the term searched. Rather than display ads, which were paid per view, or impression, search ads were paid only if someone clicked on the ad. The ads are meant to create engagement, rather than general brand awareness, and engagement was measured if the subscriber clicked on the ad—which in turn could lead to a sale. Google was only paid if the ad was clicked and thus collected search data to better refine the results and worked with advertisers to help increase engagement.

Advertisers now bid in an auction for popular keywords, against which their ads will be shown, and help determine the order. Today, some of the rates can be quite shocking. In 2017, the keyword *lawyer* was worth, on average, $54.86 per click.[9] And that was an average. The cost of *construction accident lawyer*—hard to be more specific about your needs than that!—was an average of $524.20 per click! In 2018, Google made $116 billion from advertising, the majority from search.

Of course, the keywords searched for are not the only information available or relevant. Context matters as well. For instance, a lawyer in California might not want to pay $524.20 for a click from someone in Maine; they can not only choose relevant search terms but also set parameters, such as the location to show the ad. According to Google, ads are then ranked, and displayed, based not just on the auction bid, but also on the quality of the ad and the context—including location, type of device, time of search, and "other user signals and attributes."[10]

Of course, any discussion about targeted ads eventually leads to privacy. One might think that search alone—and the terms that are gathered—are of relatively little consequence in terms of privacy. A search history might reveal something about tastes, politics, health, or family life, but probably not anything that is personally identifiable, that points to the person searching.

With enough search history, this has proven to not be true, however. In 2006, AOL publicly released twenty million searches, as a way to assist academic researchers to test and refine search methods. This involved 657,000 users, and to provide anonymity each searcher was given a number as an identifier to be able to compile searches from the same person without identifying them. Within a few days, however, the *New York Times* used the now public records to identify User 4417749 as Thelma Arnold, based on her searches. She agreed to be interviewed and was shocked when her search terms were read back to her by the reporter, responding, "I had no idea somebody was looking over my shoulder."[11]

The episode delivered a number of revelations. First, we learned that searches contain a lot of personally identifiable information, enabling some users to be identified. For some, it was easy, such as when people searched for themselves—a practice sometimes called *egosurfing*. We also learned that the searches can contain many disturbing, inspiring, bizarre terms. The AOL searches of User 927, also since identified, were so notable—and graphic— that they even inspired an off-Broadway play titled, eponymously, *User 927*. The searches make for gruesome reading, relating to a variety of sex acts that need not be specified here.

We also learned that search results alone have to be taken with a grain of salt: the user contacted by the *New York Times* seemed to be extraordinarily unhealthy based on her searches, but in fact she told the reporters that she liked to help her neighbors by searching on their medical symptoms (it was unclear whether the neighbors appreciated her help). Finally, and not surprisingly, violations of privacy can be dynamite. The identified user cancelled her AOL subscription after hearing about the release, and several AOL executives were fired or resigned.

Of course, not all companies can run search ads—in fact, very few. As any brief view of web pages will indicate, display ads are still used, so the next step was to find better ways to monetize them. In this effort, there have been significant changes in technology and accompanying business models that have impacted online advertising, effectively developing new ways to gather and deploy data.

Cookies

One change is the widespread use of cookies. If you have ever been shopping on an e-commerce site and come back to the site a few days later to find everything still in your basket, that is the result of cookies. Or do you notice after you shop on one site that the things you were shopping for show up in display ads on other sites? That is also the result of cookies. Basically, cookies are pieces of data sent from the website and stored on your computer, with information about you and your use of the website. They keep track of whether you were logged in and what you are looking at.

Like display ads, cookies were developed in the early days of the web; in fact, cookies were introduced by Netscape. One of their early uses was for e-commerce, to enable the shopping cart to be stored with the shopper instead of the store. These are known as *first-party cookies*, which are set by the website you are visiting. *Third-party cookies* soon followed, however; these enable, as the name implies, another party to set cookies on the website you are visiting. They can track users across websites and help ad companies to gather information and place ads.

The Internet Engineering Task Force (IETF) began working on specifications for cookies soon after they were introduced, and the resulting specifications recommended against third-party cookies. We spent a whole chapter talking about the benefits of open Internet standards, but the downside of voluntarily adopted standards and recommendations is that they can be ignored—and in this case, they clearly were.

While researching this book, I looked in my browser at all the websites that had left cookies on our family computer. I started counting the alphabetical list, and when I hit two hundred, I was still in the *a*'s—at alinghi .com, a website for the Swiss sailboat that won the America's Cup in 2003 and 2007 and lost in 2010. That's an old website visit, still stored in my computer. This is not a self-help book, and apparently I am not one to talk, but browsers do provide options to remove old cookies and limit new ones. There are also regulations and policies about cookies: in Europe, since 2011, websites are required to inform visitors about their cookies and seek consent to use them.

Cookies can be used to serve ads to consumers, based on the preferences revealed by their browsing history. Over times, cookies were supplemented by other means of gathering information. At the same time, the business model of advertising has also been changing.

Accounts

Think about the number of passwords you have. How you set a password is a security issue covered in chapter 6. For now, each password signifies an online account, and each of these accounts contains personal information. Why else would you need a password? Again, the use of accounts is a practice that dates back to the earliest online portals of the dot-com era and like other early practices has gained in use and impact. An account can help gather personalized information in a number of ways.

First, personal information may be given up front when setting up the account. An account for a fitness tracker, for instance, might ask gender, age, height, and weight, all reasonable to determine your fitness and progress. Second, the account may gather information over time based on your activities. And finally, the account may be used to log into, or link with, other accounts, to gather further information about your diet, weight, and more.

The results can be revealing. We can, of course, in the first instance begin to receive advertising related to our health or activities. Some may find that useful—there is a reason companies pay for advertising, after all—while others find it very off-putting. Insurance companies are beginning to provide discounts for users who share their fitness data, which may lead to premium increases for those who don't. Some insurance companies even share the data with employers as part of the management of employer-provided health insurance in the United States.[12] This can lead to new problems, as the data could possibly reveal an illness that could have serious personal or professional repercussions if leaked.

There is also the law of unintended consequences. Strava is a website where runners or cyclists can track their best times and share them. At one point, the site decided to provide a "heatmap" of all of its users' shared activities. It made for impressive viewing, but quickly it was determined that those patterns could reveal the location—and even layout—of sensitive US military installations in countries such as Afghanistan, where the soldiers' runs were clearly the only activity in the region and tracked the contours of the compounds.[13]

Of course, that example is just for health trackers. Accounts are prevalent online, for Google, Facebook, Amazon, and many other websites. Here again there are always two sides to the coin. The provision of personal information into an account may be intrinsic to the website. Facebook is a social media site for connecting to our friends. We need an account to organize our postings and pictures, and the account needs to know who we are to connect us with our family, friends, and colleagues.

But, as ever, there are some issues. A key problem online is that we have so many websites that it is hard to keep track of all the passwords—but using the same password everywhere can be dangerous. One solution is that we can use our account from one site to log into other sites. This can simplify our lives—we don't have to setup new accounts everywhere—but it also increases the concentration of data about us.

Programmatic Ads

At the same time, the business model of advertising has also been changing over time as ad networks have emerged. Instead of a website selling ads directly to advertisers interested in displaying ads next to their site, an ad network can act in the middle. Websites with ad space (also known as inventory) can make that space available to the ad network, while advertisers can go to the ad network to place their ads. The ad network then matches the ads to the websites based on the context of the site and preferences of the advertisers and manages the flow of money and information between the websites and the advertisers. This can make the market much more efficient, ensuring more revenue for the websites and better placement for advertisers.

Ad networks do not just have to serve contextual display ads based on the website. Given the amount of data available, it is possible to target people rather than websites. The technology allows different banner ads to be shown to different users. On a contextual basis, an ad network might place a beer ad on a sports website for all viewers to see. But figuring out that a particular user is a beer drinker and placing beer ads on other websites that they visit may be much more effective than earlier display ads. This is called *programmatic advertising*, which is efficient, but has some downsides.

The issue is that by following users, and their perceived tastes, the context of the website might not be considered. Beer ads may show up on a wine website—that might be a bit embarrassing but could still be effective. The beer ad might also show up next to a news story about drunk driving—and this has happened—which sends a terrible signal. The news story is completely undermined, the beer company is (hopefully) mortified, and they will both blame the ad network.

And, like many other areas of life, politics has intervened. Ads showing up in controversial websites have led to boycotts of the advertiser. One organization, Sleeping Giants, emerged after the 2016 US presidential election to put pressure on companies whose ads showed up on a particular (right-wing) website, mainly by tweeting, or retweeting, screenshots of the ads on the website. As a result, thousands of companies stopped the ads. Many of the companies expressed surprise that their ads showed up there.

The issue is that, with programmatic advertising, a company's ads can show up in upward of four hundred thousand websites, depending on the targeting parameters. No one could keep track of all those sites, even if they wanted to—and until they were at the receiving end of a boycott, no one really wanted to. The solution is to blacklist websites where ads should never show up or, perhaps even safer, provide a whitelist of websites where ads should show up. Either way, advertisers may feel the need to play a part in choosing where their advertising is placed, as in pre-Internet days.

Mobile Advertising

Mobile phones change the advertising game significantly. The use of smartphones now spans the spectrum of ages and backgrounds, when they are available and affordable, and for many of us, they are indispensable. And they are a significant source of advertising revenue. Much of what we discussed previously holds for a mobile phone: we can use it to access subscription content—music, video, and more—and we can use it to search and browse, supported by ad revenues. But there are three features of mobile phones that set them apart and in some ways make them possibly more valuable for ads.

First, of course, the main feature of mobile phones is that they are mobile. Not only can they go with you, but they always know where you are. They also know where you have been, where you parked your car and where you are going when you get back in, what shops you are in, what cities you visit. It can know how much you exercise and what appointments you have.

While that is obvious today every time we use a map or look for the closest restaurant, or where we parked our car, location awareness has always been a feature of mobile phones. Even before smartphones, the first mobile networks had to know where we were, at all times, to be able to deliver calls and text messages to us. How else would the network know you were in a different neighborhood, or even a different country? Indeed, the first mobile ads were text messages, and if they could access your location from your mobile operator, they could point you to a nearby store or sale.

For a vivid illustration of the data gathered today, on an iPhone there is a feature called Significant Locations, showing where you have been. For instance, I can see how many times I went to the local market in the past year or two and exactly how long I spent there. When the feature was first introduced, once an iPhone was unlocked, the significant locations could be accessed by anyone knowing what to look for. This led Professor Noel Sharkey, a computing expert, to warn: "This is shocking. Every place you go, where you shop, where you have a drink—it is all recorded. This is a divorce lawyer's dream." Indeed.

That is no longer possible, because the user passcode has to be entered again before the significant locations are shown. The significant location feature itself can also be turned off. There is also a disclaimer that the data are encrypted and cannot be read by Apple. So though Significant Locations has locked down the data, it still provides a vivid illustration of what our phones know. And, of course, our location information is nevertheless shared with third parties, even without the use of the Significant Locations feature. First, there are multiple ways that our location can be determined: our mobile companies still know where we are, and we can also be located from apps that use our GPS location and from Wi-Fi signals. This can be used to provide targeted ads.

The second difference with mobile phones is the use of apps. There are millions of apps available, and an increasing amount of time spent online is through apps, as opposed to a mobile or fixed browser. And in emerging countries where computers and home connections are rarer, the percentage is likely even higher.

Although Apple was not the first to produce a smartphone with apps, it produced the one that defined them. It took a year after the launch of the iPhone for Steve Jobs to decide to open the App Store to third-party apps, which soon took off, to put it mildly. As with websites, most apps are free—around 96 percent. Some of these are supported by ads, some are subsidized, and some are ads themselves—for a car, for instance. The others are paid, and Apple—along with other app store operators—keeps 30 percent of the revenues.

In between free and paid apps are so-called freemium apps, which are free to download and use, but additional features can be purchased. A particularly successful example of a freemium app is the game *Candy Crush Saga*, first released in 2012. It can be played for free, but users can purchase special actions to help clear the board. A small number of players spent a lot of money, and just four years after the release, the developer, King, was purchased for $5.9 billion. To put that in perspective, the year *Candy Crush* was first released, Lucasfilm, the developer of *Star Wars*, was sold to Disney for $4 billion in cash and stock. The *Star Wars* franchise of more than thirty years was worth significantly less than the freemium franchise of four years.

The final difference with mobile phones is that they tend to be personal, rather than shared by a family (at home) or for work (in the office). They are also linked to an Apple or Google account. This eliminates the noise that comes from having multiple users of a shared family computer. Thus, advertising directed at a mobile phone can be very targeted.

Of course, a mobile phone also has challenges. The screen is small, it is hard to type, and not everyone wants to engage. Nonetheless, mobile ad revenues are in the hundreds of billions and growing fast, as there are now over three billion smartphones.

Ad Blockers

The reaction to advertising has been strong for some people. As discussed in the next chapter, much of the reaction has been to the personal data used to deliver the ads, but there are also attempts not to get ads in the first place. There are a variety of tools available to do that, and a variety of justifications to do so.

Essentially, from the user perspective, advertising can have several impacts. It increases the amount of data that is being downloaded, which can cost money for those paying for their data. In addition, the ads can slow down the delivery of the web page. In one study, 39 percent less data was used when ads were blocked, and the pages loaded 44 percent faster—not to mention the autoplay ads that can startle with sound and alert people around you that your attention may be elsewhere.

From the website perspective, however, an ad blocker has a financial impact, removing the basis for providing free content. If banner ads are not served, there are no payments for impressions, and if ads are not clicked, there are no payments for clicks. Taking the revenue out of the equation removes the support for the free content, and without the free content, the usage of the Internet would change in significant ways.

As with almost everything Internet, technology gives and technology takes away. Websites can turn around and use software that blocks their content from reaching users who are using ad-blocking software. Both sides lose out in that case: the website does not get the ad revenue, and the user does not get the content.

Another solution is an appeal to our better angels. Websites such as that for the *Guardian* newspaper ask for contributions to be able to continue to fund their content; the *Guardian* also has a subscription model enabling users to pay to receive an ad-free version of its content. The remaining solution is to simply charge a subscription to all, which many newspapers do, while sometimes offering access to several free articles per month.

Supporting free content is not a new question, nor just a question about use of technology. It is like copying a CD or reading a magazine at the bookstore. Yes, the ad ecosystem should make ads less burdensome; that is a valid market response. But if everyone free rides, there is no more ride. Of course, blocking ads is also a symptom of an underlying concern with the data that drives them, which is addressed in the next chapter.

Offline Is Moving Online

Every Super Bowl, one number that never fails to be mentioned is the cost of running an ad. In 2020, the number was at least USD 5 million for thirty seconds. And for that money, these ads are dissected, rated, rewatched online, and discussed, for days afterward. Yet at the end of the day, they are little different than the ads that prompted John Wanamaker to lament the wasted 50 percent of his spend. That might all be about to change, as Internet technology continues to extend in depth and breadth. In particular, the barrier between online and offline is retracting, if not dissolving.

In the continuing quest to target the right ads and determine if they are successful, technology and new business models are being brought to bear. Take three traditional offline examples: television advertising, store purchases, and your refrigerator. Online, it is very easy to serve targeted ads to someone watching a video, but with TV everyone gets the same ad. Online, it is very easy to see if someone who clicks on an ad then purchases the product, but not possible to see if they buy it in a store. Finally, it is easy to see what someone fills their fridge with if they shop online, but not possible to see how it is consumed. This is all changing, however.

Internet television—that is, pay TV delivered using Internet technology—is more similar to watching streaming television on an iPad than it is different. The provider can gather data about the person watching and insert digital ads, just like on a website. That is true even for broadcast TV ads, if someone is using a smart TV (i.e., one that is Internet-enabled). In fact, smart TVs are priced low because of the value of the data that is gathered—and sold—about the users.[14] Will targeted ads take over the Super

Bowl? Maybe not, because jointly watching the ads has become part of the experience. But for the game before the Super Bowl—why not?

Likewise, offline behavior has been linked online. The holy grail is to follow a user from ad view to purchase. Again, that is not difficult online, if you click on an ad and purchase the product. Offline, it has been moving in steps. First, it was possible to use location technology to see who is entering a store and whether they viewed an ad beforehand. But it wasn't clear that they had purchased. Now, by combining credit card data with online behavior, it is possible, and it is being done. This linking has boosted the spend on ads significantly.[15] By all accounts, personally identifiable data is not shared between companies when the link is made, but it still increases the amount of online data.

And in another merger of online and offline, the Internet of Things (IoT) embeds Internet connections into an array of devices inside and outside our homes, with a variety of uses, which can include helping complete the loop between ads and ordering. Smart refrigerators, for instance, can already be used to order groceries from a touchscreen, and some also have cameras to keep track of what goes in and out. It is a short step to the refrigerators suggesting new foods, providing coupons, and even directly ordering certain favorite foods when they are about to run out.

Conclusion

To distill the debate regarding online services, an incredible array of services is available to us at no charge, in return for data about us that can be used to sell advertising to pay for the services. We can get free music and videos, online storage, email and message services, social media—the list goes on and on. And these services have brought us great benefits. Email has changed the way that we communicate, search has changed the way we access information, and social media the way we interact with our family, friends, colleagues, customers, and even strangers.

The rise of this advertising-funded content has led to a remarkable turnaround in the fortunes of ISPs versus content providers. Where less than twenty years ago there was no clear revenue model for content providers, who looked to ISPs as a possible source of revenues, today the revenue—and market capitalization—of the content providers has overtaken the ISPs. Now some ISPs are responding by seeking a share of revenues from the content providers and by trying to become content providers themselves and offer advertising.

It has also generated an enormous—almost unimaginable—amount of data about us, our surroundings, and our interactions. In addition to the services that we enjoy, this data is being used for machine learning and artificial intelligence, to drive the next generation of services. On the flip side, the data is generating many of the concerns that are arising with the Internet: it helps fuel the growth of the largest online companies, there are concerns about our privacy and data protection, and cybersecurity is an ever-present threat. These topics are all covered in the next part.

II   The Downside of Free

5   Did We Give Away Our Privacy?

All human beings have three lives: public, private, and secret.
—Gabriel García Márquez

Walking down the street in any city is a public act. Our friends might recognize us, someone famous may be photographed, the police can issue a ticket if we do something wrong, and a family member could keep an eye on us if they are worried. But the goal of our walk may be private: a job interview, a meeting at the bank, an appointment at a medical clinic, or a rendezvous at a hotel. Those meetings may also be secret. Our current employer may not know we are searching, the bank may be about to foreclose on our house, the medical clinic was for plastic surgery, or the rendezvous was an affair.

In an analog world, the privacy risks of this walk were generally well understood. Will the person we meet tell someone else? Has someone seen us enter a building? Will any paperwork from our meetings leak? We have a personal or professional expectation of privacy, bolstered by laws or reputation. If someone we met with violated our privacy, we probably would know who it was and might have some sort of recourse. We weren't carrying a digital lookout in our pocket, with free services that have changed the economics of privacy.

The right to privacy was enshrined in the UN Universal Declaration of Human Rights in 1948, in article 12: "No one shall be subjected to arbitrary interference with his privacy, family, home or correspondence, nor to attacks upon his honor and reputation. Everyone has the right to the protection of the law against such interference or attacks."[1] The main worry at the time was physical privacy, and the main offender was likely to be government.

That was a decidedly analog time, and with the onset of the digital age, the focus shifted to virtual privacy and the concerns broadened with the technological possibilities. I think it is safe to say that no teenager in history ever took a camera, went to the store and bought some film, loaded it up at home, undressed, took pictures, dropped off the film for developing, picked up the pictures, chose a favorite, put it in an envelope, put on a stamp, and mailed it to someone they liked.

And even if that did happen, there were limits on the downside. The recipient could keep it in a safe place or destroy it. And even if things went bad, the damage would be embarrassing, but limited in place and time. The cost of printing more copies and willingness of a store to do that would limit the ability to pass it out. The school yearbook would never print it. No editor would dream of taking the responsibility of publishing such a picture. In the physical world, everything takes time, and money, and there are gatekeepers, all of which provided some guardrails.

Not so, clearly, in the virtual world. The smartphone—loaded with free apps—not only makes it easier to do, the consequences can be far worse. The recipient cannot credibly destroy the picture or find a fully safe place to store it. If things go bad, the picture can be copied almost infinitely at the press of a finger. It can be uploaded on a platform that does not have an editor and may only take the picture down upon request. And even if it is deleted from the platform, someone else may have copied it.

Of course, this a very specific example, although one that has caused and will cause true harm for people. In general, though, the ethos of free seems to have removed, or at least widened, our guardrails. Using free services, we share our public lives, some private details, and possibly some secrets. We know what we are sharing, but we do not necessarily know how it is combined with the digital detritus left by our browsing, online interactions, real-world interactions, and location. And we do not always know what is then done with the data.

In 2013, the UN General Assembly affirmed that offline rights apply equally online and that this applies in particular to the right to privacy in the digital age. It adopted a resolution affirming that "the same rights that people have offline must also be protected online, including the right to privacy."[2] At the same time, countries also began clarifying laws reflecting the new realities of privacy.

So though the right to privacy remains, the practice of privacy has shifted significantly. Starting with the basics, the Internet Society, noting that there is no one definition, provided a common understanding of *online privacy* as "the right to determine when, how, and to what extent personal data can be shared with others."[3] A common definition of personal data, in turn, is "any information relating to an identified or identifiable individual."[4] Clearly, this is a simple rendition of a complicated legal and regulatory issue, but a good starting point for discussion.

Here we will focus on the economics of privacy issues, using these commonsense definitions and examples rather than applying any legal standards. Two important points to consider in this discussion are consent and context. My credit card details are clearly personal data, over which I should have control. To buy something online, I must provide it to the online retailer, which in turn has to convey it to the card company for approval. I may choose to have it stored in my computer or with the retailer to simplify future purchases.

The question is whether I have consented for other uses without understanding the terms and conditions, or whether the data is used in another context without my consent. For instance, as described in the previous chapter, our credit card purchases may be matched with our ads we have seen online. Is that happening to me? Is it anonymous? Did I consent to it? Could I stop it if I wanted to?

The deeper question is, who owns my personal data? It sounds axiomatic that *personal data* belongs to me, but most online actions have at least one other party. Whatever I buy online was sold by someone: Is that information just mine? What about the retailer? If I send an email to someone, is that just mine? What about the recipient? The same holds true for streaming a movie, arranging a date, getting a ride. The property rights are not defined, and as with the clean air example in the first chapter, government is increasingly called upon to establish rules and regulations.

And we all have cause to pause and wonder about unknowns. A few years ago, before lunch, I asked my colleagues for the name of a nearby restaurant we had recently tried so I could call for a reservation. They reminded me of the name; it was a popular brasserie. I began typing it into search on my phone browser to look up the number. I typed *b, r, a* ... At this point it could have pointed me to a lingerie shop, but it did not at all. The right brasserie appeared as one of the first choices under the autocomplete suggestions, none of which related to undergarments. Was my phone listening?

So many have wondered the same thing that some academics actually conducted a rigorous study, concluding that, in fact, your phone is not listening to you.[5] That may be surprising, but in one sense, why would it need to? I had been to that restaurant before quite recently with my phone, it was just before lunch, and I have never had any online interest in lingerie.

On the other hand, you might want to watch what you are saying in front of your television. Samsung's Smart TV policy at one point noted, "Please be aware that if your spoken words include personal or other sensitive information, that information will be among the data captured and transmitted to a third party through your use of Voice Recognition." In other words, be careful: your TV is listening.[6]

There is thus a general worry about the loss of privacy from new digital technologies and Internet services, expressed in aphorisms such as "privacy is dead." And there is specific concern about our data resulting from a number of recent events. First, Edward Snowden leaked documents taken from the US National Security Agency (NSA) that reveal the extent of government surveillance of online services and telecommunications records. Second, the personal data that Cambridge Analytica harvested from Facebook demonstrated just how much personal information could be reaped from a seemingly innocent online quiz. And third, a steady stream of news about data breaches, from the US government, retailers, credit agencies, and others, has put our private data in play. Yet people still use online services. This is sometimes known as the *privacy paradox*.

The Privacy Paradox

The privacy paradox refers to the observation that users worry about privacy but do not translate their worry into behavior. That is to say, in surveys, people will state that they are worried about data privacy in general or have low trust for online entities in particular. Yet usage for websites about which concerns are voiced, such as social media sites or e-commerce, continues to rise.[7]

There are clearly questions about the evidence. People may overstate their worries to survey takers if they think that is the "right" thing to say. And it is hard to link the concerns to behavior—that is, to determine whether those who say they are concerned about privacy are still using those sites. It is also hard, though, not to puzzle over the increasing concern with data privacy set against the continued growth of online services.

Starting with the basics, people clearly put personal information on the Internet, which might relate to relationships, sexual orientation, health, politics, faith, job, or other aspects of their personal life. And, broadly speaking, there may be several attitudes toward keeping this information private.

First, some people are what one researcher called *privacy fundamentalists*; that is, the idea that any entity has personal information about them simply does not sit well.[8] They may abstain from using online services as much as possible, and they may use a wide variety of tools to anonymize or protect their online engagement. This could be as simple as using a fake name online, but it also includes technology such as using a virtual private network (VPN) to protect their transmissions, encryption on their devices, or using the dark web to hide their traces. Included in this group may be some with a secret to hide. It could be their sexuality, a medical condition, their faith or lack thereof, or their politics. But that is not necessary to become a privacy fundamentalist, nor is it even sufficient.

I would stress here quite strongly that people with "nothing to hide" can—and do—worry deeply about privacy. The notion that we should not be worried about privacy so long as we have nothing to hide is simplistic and, strictly speaking, runs against our human right to privacy. And the idea that someone might have to follow every statement of concern about privacy with the disclaimer "not that I have anything to hide" minimizes the plight of those who cannot add that disclaimer honestly.

This issue was encapsulated in a statement from then Google CEO Eric Schmidt, who said with regard to sharing information with Google that "if you have something that you don't want anyone to know, maybe you shouldn't be doing it in the first place." He himself though once blacklisted a publication that published personal information about him, including earnings and political donations—but it was all information found through Google.[9]

But more broadly, this notion of not having anything to hide conflates the context of what is public, private, and secret. Having a child is public information and that the child was conceived is not a secret, but the details are definitely private.

There is also a group that does exhibit a privacy paradox. While not a uniform group, these people—and I include myself here, by the way—do use social media, e-commerce, online banking, electronic voting, location services, fitness trackers, and a wide variety of other services that include personally identifiable information. Most, if not all, of this group have at least an awareness of the risks, if only based on the stream of stories about abuses of personal data, and it may alter their behavior, but not stop it. Economics can help explain this paradox.

Economics of Privacy

Let's start first with what we know about our privacy and what we are getting in return. The data we know we are giving, we are not giving for free, we are giving for services. We use a fitness tracker to track our fitness, and the data is the baseline for that. We use an online map to go from A to B, and it needs to know where we started and where we are going. We use YouTube to watch videos, and it has to know what videos we want to watch to show them to us. And we use Facebook to communicate with family, friends, colleagues, and other communities, and it has to know who we are and who we know.

In return, consumers generally recognize that they receive value. According to one recent study, Facebook is worth at least $1,000 per year to users; that was what was needed on average to pay someone to leave Facebook. In economic terms, this is known as the *consumer surplus*—the difference between what we would be willing to pay for something and what we actually pay. Because Facebook is free for users, the consumer surplus is maximized. The authors of the study also noted that Facebook is worth more to us than we are to Facebook: at the time of the study, given the total market value of the company and the number of users, the value per user from an investor viewpoint was $250.[10]

Another study looked at what people would accept to give up various digital goods. It showed people requiring $3,600 per year on average to stop using online maps, $8,400 to give up using email, and $17,500 to live without online search.[11] These are clearly big numbers, showing that people derive a lot of value from these services, particularly as they are free to use. Overall, however, technology has long been shown to deliver significant value beyond its direct revenues. Another study shows that between 1948 and 2001, companies retained less than 4 percent of the total value of their technologies, the rest of the social returns going to consumers.[12]

So it is not surprising that an awareness, and even alarm, about data privacy does not always translate into a life of online abstinence. There are clear benefits that may outweigh the risks. However, people may not fully account for the risks, which highlights two important, and relatively new, strands of economics: information economics and behavioral economics. Both strands help explain how people make choices, which may lead to suboptimal or inefficient outcomes.

We already saw how people shift their preferences when a Hershey's Kiss becomes free, compared to a Lindt truffle. This is an example of behavioral economics, which shows not only that people do not always act rationally, but also that often they act irrationally in a predictable way. It is a short leap from the chocolate experiment to taking a free service over a paid service with better privacy controls.

In the chocolate case, it was pretty clear which was the better chocolate. That might not be so clear, of course, with respect to online services and their privacy controls. This brings us to information economics, which studies how information impacts economic decisions—in particular, when not all information is known or available. In general, we may often operate under imperfect or incomplete information.

The related questions are therefore, first, whether users have all the information needed to make a rational decision with regard to privacy and, second, whether they would make rational decisions even with that information.[13]

Information Economics

For starters, most websites and online services have terms and conditions providing the privacy policy and information. Many are not read, but even if read, there can still be incomplete information about privacy.

A consumer advocacy group in Australia looked at the user agreements for the Amazon Kindle Voyage e-reader. They noted that there were at least eight documents, with over seventy-three thousand words in total. That is roughly the length of this book. To highlight the challenge, they videotaped an actor reading the documents, and it took nine hours in total.[14] It was, I hope, less interesting than this book.

Even after reading those policies, we still do not know for sure what is done with our data. When the policies say that data can be shared with third parties, for instance, it may not be clear exactly which third parties and what data are shared. Even if a law requires more disclosure about the third parties, we do not know specifically with what entities the data are shared. We also cannot confirm the conditions under which they are shared and what those companies are doing with the data.[15]

Using the elements of information economics, let's take the example of location data. There is clearly incomplete information for the average user about how location data can be used in general. For instance, the *New York Times* did a study of mobile location data with eye-opening results.[16] They found that at least one thousand apps contain code to share location data with third-party companies, and one person's location, accurate to a few yards, may be updated up to fourteen thousand times per day! The *Times* tested twenty apps thought to be sharing data and found seventeen of them sharing locations with seventy companies, including one weather app alone sharing with forty companies.

The data can then be used for targeted advertising; one advertising company tracks people going to the emergency room and can send them ads for personal injury lawyers. The maps identified the phones of those standing around President Trump during the presidential inauguration and could presumably track where they went next. While the data are anonymized, the *Times* was able to identify specific users and show them the paths of their travels: which doctor they went to, where they spent the night, and other personal information. Users agree that an app can use their location, but it is not always clear that it is used for advertising—and even if it is mentioned, it would not say, for instance, how often the location is shared, with which companies, and what it is used for.

This highlights that data has a unique feature for something of value. It's not like putting gold in a safe; the gold is either there or gone, but either way there is certainty. It is not like your car, which can only be in one place at a time, or a house owned by one family at a time. It is not even like less intrinsic stores of value such as a bank account, where your money can be loaned out to others, but is always available if you want to take it back, and is guaranteed in case of a crash. Data can be in more than one place at once, and additional uses do not necessarily detract from its value; they could even add to it. And what can happen to that data? We do not have full information about that, either.

At one end of the spectrum, nothing happens to the data. The data are either not kept, deleted after a certain period, or kept safely internal to the company. At the other end of the spectrum, the company is breached, and the data are used for identity theft, financial theft, blackmail, or other public purposes (more on cybersecurity in the next chapter). Along the spectrum, there are a variety of possibilities. First, the data can be used internally in the company as per the privacy policy to provide services—notably, advertising. This can include combining it with other data gathered by the company or by a third party for analysis or use. At the extreme, it can be used by the company or shared in ways that fall outside of the privacy policy but fall short of an outside data breach.

Slightly separate from this, how likely are you to find out how the data were used or abused? Here, there is significant uncertainty. You may never be sure that your data are used according to the privacy policy because it is hard to prove a positive, in a sense. And if your identity is stolen, you may never be able to tie it to a particular data breach or abuse. In between, however, there may be some signals of how the data are used.

We often see the result of cookies on our computers—when we go back to a website and our shopping choices are still in the cart or when our shopping choices keep appearing in other websites as ads. And, frustratingly, they do not seem to disappear even if we buy what we were looking for. On the other hand, companies are conscious of, and most work to avoid, what is sometimes referred to as the *creep factor*. That is when we viscerally come face to face with what the data reveal about us. It is a jolt for us, and counterproductive for the company, but people's thresholds vary as to when they might experience this.

My first memory of the creep factor dates back a few years. My wife gave me the first version of the iPod Touch for my birthday—this is the one that looked like an iPhone, but without mobile phone functionality. Before turning off the light, I was trying out the installed apps. I opened the map application and clicked on My Locations. How could it know my location? Not only did this iPod not have built-in GPS to determine location, it also did not have cellular capability, which would have allowed it to determine my location from cell phone towers.

I was skeptical, but I was wrong: the location dot appeared on the map over our house. It felt almost like crosshairs. How could it know where we were? Surfing the web through the iPod, which was connected to my home Wi-Fi, I learned that my Wi-Fi was in fact the culprit. It turns out companies were driving down every street, registering the location of every Wi-Fi signal, so that location could be determined by matching the Wi-Fi signal picked up by the iPod with the database. I also learned that the reaction to this feature varies significantly; when I told my wife how my new iPod knew our exact location, she was non-plussed.

But every now and then, we are all confronted by the creep factor, perhaps no more so than recently with the case of Cambridge Analytica. In this case, a researcher created a quiz, taken by several hundreds of thousands of users, which accessed the data of their Facebook friends, a total of eighty-seven million users. The privacy policy at the time allowed for the access, but not the subsequent uses, and Facebook asked Cambridge Analytica to delete the data. As we now know, it did not, and used it to target ads in the 2016 US presidential election.

With no intent to downplay the chain of events that had significant repercussions for all involved—impacts on Facebook, the closing of Cambridge Analytica, and the election itself—there are several takeaways here. First, privacy policies may have loopholes or unforeseen outcomes. Second, it is an illustration yet again of how hard it is to control intangible data: you can ask someone to delete something, but you never know if it is truly gone. And finally, but for the subsequent disclosure, no one receiving those ads would have fully understood that they were being targeted or why.

Behavioral Economics

Even armed with the knowledge of what data we are providing, knowing how it might be used, and understanding that there is risk, people will still use smartphones, apps, and online services. In assessing the risks, we have some general biases, which behavioral economists have uncovered.

First, we must recognize that data privacy is not the only area where awareness of a risk does not translate into action. Look no further than those huddling in the cold outside a building—even a hospital—smoking a cigarette. And for those who argue that privacy policies are simply too long and complicated to understand, what could be more succinct and to the point than the four words on the side of a cigarette packet in the United States: Smoking Can Kill You. Actually, the United Kingdom version gets right to the point: Smoking Kills. And, yet, every day, millions of cigarettes are taken out of those packs.

And there is no need to focus on smoking. Many sports have dangers that fail to dissuade, or even help attract, participants. And even more mundane, consider driving or riding a motorcycle from point A to point B. Many still resist seat belts, helmets, and other safety features. Some do it in lieu of flying, which is statistically safer. So a clear understanding of risk does not always change everyone's behavior.

Why? There are many aspects of behavioral economics that cover the decision to share our data, and no full agreement as to which ones are correct.[17] We may overestimate our own understanding of what data may be available about us and how it can be used, as well as our ability to prevent harm. In addition, at whatever level of risk we understand, we discount the future and prefer the immediate benefits of the online service to a longer-run possible harm from the data.

Solutions

So, what can we do about privacy? And yes, we have—everyone has—a role to play. Some companies can clearly act as better stewards of our data. Governments can help correct market failures with appropriate regulations. And nonprofits such as the Internet Society (with which I work) and the World Wide Web Foundation provide critical advocacy. But we as users also play a role, just as we play a role in other public campaigns for the environment, smoking prevention, and car safety.

Payment Models

By coincidence, the day I began writing this section started with an announcement from Mark Zuckerberg about how Facebook was changing its business model to build in more privacy, describing his "vision and principles around building a privacy-focused messaging and social networking platform."[18] That announcement was followed by commentary, as one would expect—some cynical, some encouraging, some hopeful. The change itself is likely to take a number of years, but in the meantime, what is clear is that companies are aware of the need to generate (or restore lost) trust and aware of the challenges they face.

As noted earlier, awareness of privacy issues is ever increasing based on recent revelations and scandals. The companies themselves are beginning to address the issues, alongside the development of new technologies and business models. Many of the concerns result from websites that provide free services paid for with advertising revenue, targeted using our personal data. Would it make a difference to change the payment model? Two somewhat diametrically opposed models have been proposed and attempted. One model consists of paying for an ad-free version of the online service. The other model consists of being paid in return for our data.

There are already examples of services that we can pay to have ad-free, such as the *Guardian* newspaper or the Spotify music service. But many of these companies do not necessarily gather much data, and even if the ads are targeted, they are largely contextual. We are mainly paying to reduce the clutter of ads, to improve the viewing experience, to support good journalism, and to use less broadband data for ads. Similar companies that charge for their services, such as Netflix, still keep track of data to recommend programming that we would like.

On the other hand, there have been proposals that more data-intensive platforms such as Facebook could or should charge for ad-free services. By one calculation, Facebook makes eighty-two dollars per user per year, and thus would only have to charge seven dollars per month in the United States to replace ad revenue. Facebook would still keep track of our Facebook friends and what we say to them—that is the service—but the analysis of data would not be needed anymore to deliver ads. But, of course, not everyone might want to pay for service, depriving us of their network effects, and not everyone might be able to afford to pay, depriving them of the benefits.[19]

The other model, then, is for websites to pay us for our data. The idea is that these companies aggregate data, typically anonymized, and then sell it to advertisers and others, sharing the money with the users. The users can take ownership over, and make money from, their personal data, and the companies can aggregate and learn from or profit from the data.

There are several problems with this idea. First, at least at this point, the earnings received by users who try this are low. One BBC reporter tried a few services offered by small companies. He received thirteen cents for answering ten online questions, one cent per month for selling his location data, and a ten-dollar Visa card for selling his Google profile data, his location, and other information.[20] It was relatively little money, and the companies did not even offer any useful services in return; for instance, they did not offer mapping, but just offered to buy the location data from an existing service. It is not clear that they could afford to pay the user and generate useful services.

One reason that our individual data is worth relatively little is because the data only has real value when aggregated with that of other users—when it becomes *big data*. Knowing the movies that I like, for instance, might help Netflix make some obvious recommendations—based on actors, directors, or genre—but the real value is when my likes and dislikes can be compared with a large dataset of other users to identify movies that others with my tastes liked. The data is critical, but so is the algorithm; a Netflix Prize of USD 1 million was awarded to a team that was able to improve Netflix's predictions for ratings by 10 percent, based on a database of one hundred million customer ratings.

Serving ads benefits similarly from aggregating data and improving algorithms. Retail store loyalty is hard fought over, and it turns out that there a few points at which it can be modified or established. Having a baby is one of them, so the Target chain of department stores in the United States decided to make an effort to market to pregnant women, to turn them into regular customers when their babies were born.[21] The challenge, of course, was determining whether a woman was pregnant in order to win her loyalty.

If you looked at any one woman's shopping at Target over time, it would likely be impossible to pinpoint when she became pregnant based on her purchases. It turns out that if a smart data scientist looks at all women shopping at Target over time, it is possible. Target was able to identify purchases, including unscented lotion, nutritional supplements, cotton balls, and hand sanitizers, that together enabled them to not only predict pregnancy, but also estimate the due date with some degree of certainty.

So Target started sending out coupons for baby items to women they identified as being pregnant. Soon, the father of a teenage girl came to his local Target, furious that they had assumed his daughter, who received the coupons, was pregnant. A few days later, he sheepishly came back and admitted that Target knew she was pregnant before he did.

This is the power of big data in action—and a reminder that with power comes responsibility, or at least caution. As a result, Target began to sprinkle baby ads into regular advertising booklets a few at a time, and this proved more successful. Clearly, in this case, any single woman's shopping list would be worth little, while all women's shopping lists are worth their weight in gold.

The second issue with paying users for data is the possibility of what I call the *day care paradox*. If you have ever had children in day care, you know the pressure of having to pick them up by a certain time and the reaction of the staff if you are late. And you probably don't have to have worked at one to know how you would feel if parents were continually late. It's not like shutting down the McDonalds at closing time and depriving a late customer of their Big Mac: you have to stay open until the last child is picked up.

In this context, a group of researchers in Israel went to ten private day care centers and counted late arrivals for four weeks. In the fifth week, at the behest of the researchers, six of the day care centers instituted a fine for those parents who were more than ten minutes late (without telling anyone it was an experiment). Economics should work its magic and encourage parents to come on time and avoid the fine. However, psychology was stronger, and the number of late-coming parents *increased* for a few weeks before it stabilized at a higher rate.[22]

The authors' theory was that there was an incomplete contract before the fine: it was not fully specified what would happen if parents were late once or more, and thus parents—likely desperate to keep their child's spot at the center—ensured that they were not late as much as possible. The fine completed the contract, and parents could be comfortable in the knowledge of what would happen if they were late: they would simply have to pay a fine. There was no threat of further repercussions. I would go a bit further and argue that the social stigma and guilt of keeping the hard-working staff late was removed by paying them to stay late.

Coming back to the privacy paradox, being paid for your data not only does not necessarily reduce the amount of data available about you but may shift the social contract. Having paid for the data, the provider may feel a level of ownership and control over that data, more than they would have if they did not pay for it. It is worth noting in this context that people were paid to take the quiz at the origins of the Cambridge Analytica scandal.

Privacy by Design

Humans have proven bad at adapting themselves to some aspects of new technology, so it is better if the technology adapts itself to human characteristics. Take the vexing problem of passwords. We try to make them as simple as possible, we write them down in convenient places, and we reuse them and reuse them.

This was demonstrated in somewhat comical fashion when Kanye West made a televised visit to President Donald Trump in the Oval Office and unlocked his phone to show a picture. He did so with the camera rolling on him, which revealed that the code to unlock his phone was *000000*. Likewise, Mark Zuckerberg had his Twitter account taken over after LinkedIn was breached because he used the same (simple) password, *dadada*, on both. We will cover fully the folly of this when we discuss cybersecurity in the next chapter, but it also provides a good example of why we need technologies that provide privacy by design: we cannot rely on all users to configure privacy.

These examples may be extreme, but many of us were guilty of using easy passwords until we were forced to use capitals, numbers, and even symbols. This alone may not help if we write them down, so other technologies are being introduced to help us. Starting with our devices, there are increasing measures to keep them private. First, increasing authentication technologies, moving from passwords to fingerprints to facial recognition. Other techniques include two-factor authentication, in which a code is sent by email or SMS, which should only be received by the owner of the phone. And if all else fails, the information in the phone might be encrypted automatically to prevent being able to extract information.

These defaults borrow heavily from some of the findings of behavioral economics. If humans act irrationally in a predictable way, such as not implementing the simplest security precautions, then they can be *nudged* into using more safe precautions.[23] The theory of nudging is also called *libertarian paternalism* by its developers. Paternalism changes the default to help us help ourselves, but the libertarian aspect allows us to turn it off. A stricter form would not make the default choice optional.

Likewise, we can set our privacy on our phones and in our browsers. On an iPhone, you can turn off location services completely or turn it on by setting the permissions for each app that asks for your location. Through a browser, one can control websites' access to location data, the microphone, camera, and other features. However, the default for many features is typically still toward sharing; for instance, many people are surprised by the tracking of significant locations on an iPhone because they did not know about the feature when it was introduced and were not asked. The nudge would be to have the feature turned off by default.

Privacy-friendly business models have also been attempted. This is a broad definition of privacy by design, but these companies build privacy directly into their business models. There are a number of such services, covering a variety of services. For instance, DuckDuckGo is a search engine geared to protect privacy. It notes in its privacy policy that it "does not collect or share personal information."[24] It has raised funding and monetizes search the old-fashioned way, by simply serving up ads related to the term being searched. It had average usage of about thirty-six million searches per day in early 2019.[25] Impressive, but Google gets the same number of searches in about eight minutes.[26]

Although an initiative like this is, of course, noteworthy, and choice is good, it is unlikely to be disruptive. This is probably of interest only to privacy fundamentalists and will not likely shift privacy protection for the rest of us. The largest companies in search—notably Google, but also Baidu in China and Microsoft with its Bing search engine—have a significant head start. They have a significant head start in developing their search algorithms, they have a significant head start in terms of computing power, and they have a significant head start in terms of infrastructure to deliver the search results.

Not only that, this head start is self-perpetuating. The more users and the more searches, the more the companies can learn and refine their search algorithms. After all, a search company gets pretty instantaneous feedback. If the user chooses the first link on the list of search results, something went right; if they scroll through a few pages and then keep refining their search, there is something to learn. And, of course, the accompanying ad revenues help finance further research and investment.

We will discuss the growth and implications of the large Internet platforms in chapter 7, but for now, the privacy policies of the large companies—with the most users—will make the biggest difference. And there have been changes in recent years; if you know where to look, there is more transparency, and more control also is possible. Facebook, for instance, has a page for their users called Your Ad Preferences, which shows how the user is categorized for ad purposes and allows them to make changes.

The Pew Research Center released a study of Facebook users in the United States in early 2019.[27] Seventy-four percent of users knew that this feature existed. Of those, 59 percent said that the categories represented them somewhat or very accurately. In one category, only 51 percent of users had been given a political label in their ad preferences, and of those 73 percent said it accurately described their views. Speaking for a sample of one, my Facebook ad preferences reflected the activity of my daughters on our family computer more than my own, and my (strong) political beliefs were not picked up at all.

Governments

The main question, in economic terms, is whether the issue of privacy represents a market failure—which, by definition, the market cannot correct by itself. Will the pressure of increased scrutiny and campaigns from users lead to better outcomes alone, or is government action needed?

The need for government privacy regulations certainly did not start with the Internet. Health records, banking, government documents, and others have always required privacy. The Internet just made things more complicated. It is one thing, for instance, when health records were kept on paper in the doctor's office, in the hospital, or with the insurance company, where their presence could be established, monitored, or shredded. It's another when they are put in the cloud for processing, sometimes outside the country, and can be copied and shared without cost.

We need more information about our privacy and assurance that the information is correct and being followed. This can be done through self-regulation but requires monitoring or enforcement through a third party or with government involvement. Even when government is involved, however, it does not need to get involved with every step.

Take the example of food labeling. The government can set standards for food labeling but allow companies to provide the information. Testing for compliance could be done by a third party or the government, while enforcement would ultimately be done by the government. Something similar could be done for company privacy policies—listing what information must be in the policies for users and how to ensure compliance.

Of course, there may be food ingredients that are not acceptable and are banned outright, or those that companies will remove voluntarily and highlight that in their marketing pitched at consumers. For livestock, a label is not sufficient. Noting that a steak is 100 percent beef does not convey more than a bare minimum of information for consumers; instead, there are standards and inspections for how the cows are treated and processed as consumers cannot, and probably would not want to, gather that information firsthand.

With respect to data, many countries have privacy laws with a wide variety of specifications that can differ depending on the type of information. The recent EU General Data Protection Regulation (GDPR) of 2018 provides strong privacy protections for personal data, particularly for sensitive personal data including genetic data, sexual orientation, and political preferences.[28] The law is a landmark act that provides individuals with rights and control over their data and puts increased obligations on companies to account for the data, as well as sets fines for noncompliance.

In general, regulations can include transparency about what is being done with the data, along with monitoring and enforcement if a violation occurs. In addition, it could be important to include more specific regulations about what should be done and what should not be done with our data. For instance, the GDPR has provisions stating that if data held by a company is encrypted, then if it is taken it may not be considered a data breach or incur any fines from a data breach.[29]

It is also important to address internal use of personal data as insiders have a unique ability to access their companies' data. For instance, Uber used a God View feature enabling employees to track specific customers in cars, including celebrities, journalists, and ex-boyfriends or ex-girlfriends. This feature was actually shown off at company events but unraveled when a guest at an Uber party tipped off a friend in an Uber everyone was following via God View. The US Federal Trade Commission (FTC) came to a settlement with the company whereby its privacy practices would be monitored by a third-party company for twenty years.

Third parties can play a broader role in privacy as well—for instance, through certifications. TrustArc (formerly TRUSTe) provides privacy certifications, such as ones showing that a website complies with US online privacy regulations for children. However, TrustArc itself has been fined for not conducting adequate assessments of the websites it certified.[30] In any case, the privacy certifications themselves need to be recognized and trusted to help generate trust in the websites using them.

Another aspect that typically needs to be regulated is cross-border data transfers, where data goes outside the jurisdiction of the country. It is important to guarantee that the conditions of cross-border transfers are understood and that the destination country ensures the same levels of privacy and security expected in the originating country. Europe has imposed such regulations for many years—for instance, requiring US companies to conform to European data privacy regulations to store data from European companies.

In this respect, countries with strong data-protection policies and their companies that have developed strong reputations can gain a competitive advantage. Switzerland, for instance, has leveraged its reputation as a stable and neutral country with a long history of banking confidentiality to become an attractive location for data centers to protect data. In addition, a number of Swiss companies have focused on offering enhanced privacy services, such as ProtonMail, which provides secure email services.

As for addressing behavioral issues, part of the issue is increased understanding of the risks and alternatives of online services. In this regard, a number of the steps with regard to incomplete information will also help impact behavior. Transparency will provide information about companies' use of data, and regulations requiring users to opt-in to certain practices can nudge users toward more informed privacy choices.

In addition, there is education. Take the practice of sexting, raised at the beginning of this chapter, which is easy with a smartphone and a data plan. Governments clearly cannot regulate the actions of a teenage libido—or an adult one, for that matter. However, my children in primary school had a morning with the police learning bicycle safety. A crossing guard helps them navigate the street in front of the school. I learned how to drive in a graded class in high school. Why not teach online safety to all children in the schools? That would begin to provide education about the risks.

Finally, there may be areas where it is not possible to change behavior because of the benefits of online usage: better protection is the ultimate solution. In this, users will play a critical role in pushing for these better privacy protections, from companies and from governments, and in using those protections in their best interests.

Users

The role of users is paramount. It is, at the end of the day, our personal data and our privacy in the mix. Users can act on an individual basis, and advocacy groups help provide a voice. For starters, we can translate our concerns into actions—taking available steps to protect our data, such as understanding privacy policies, deleting cookies from browsers, keeping track of privacy settings on browsers and mobile phones, and other actions to protect online security, including installing software security upgrades and setting adequate passwords.

However, at the end of the day, personal information cannot always be separated from functionality. I cannot completely turn off the location service on my phone because it is necessary for the mobile phone to connect to a cell, and the telephone company thus knows my location and uses it to route calls and data. Of course, I might not want a flashlight app to share my location with advertisers, so I would like to block that use. But if I want to use a map app for directions, the phone has to know my location as well. If I want to use Uber, it has to know where I am. So limiting the availability of data may not be possible or may severely limit benefits.

The same is true for social media apps, the purpose of which is to enable us to share personal information. For instance, LinkedIn is a professional social media platform that can be used to find a new job or to find clients. To do so, we have to provide relevant information about our work experience and make it searchable in some way so that potential employers can find us. At the same time, we might not want our current employer to realize that we are looking for a new job. In other words, putting personal information on the site can be very beneficial, but we need control over how it is used.

Thus, changes would be beneficial to help users to realize the benefits of the Internet services, those requiring personal information, but without the privacy costs. Here, users can use the tools of the Internet to advocate—to push companies to do the right thing and push governments when that is not enough. There are already cases in which users have signaled their concerns about privacy.

As early as 1990, individuals successfully protested a plan by Lotus and Experian to release a direct marketing CD set with information on 120 million Americans. In Europe, Max Schrems successfully challenged the EU Safe Harbor privacy arrangement with the United States based on details on surveillance released by Edward Snowden. In essence, EU data-protection laws only allowed data transfers to non-EU countries if the country provides adequate protection. Schrems argued that the Snowden revelations about Facebook revealed that the data transferred by Facebook was not adequately protected; the Court of Justice of the European Union agreed and ruled the Safe Harbor agreement was invalid. More recently, Alastair Mactaggart, a real estate developer, spearheaded a citizen initiative to pass a new privacy law in California, which led the legislature to pass the California Computer Privacy Act of 2018, which is comparable to the European GDPR.

And end users have allies. The Internet Society, World Wide Web Foundation, Electronic Frontier Foundation, Privacy International, and others have all helped educate users and governments and push for better privacy regulations and company policies.

When individuals and organizations succeed at promoting better privacy practices and business models change, new technology becomes available, and regulations are passed, users still have a role to play. Users must educate themselves, make informed choices, and play their part in protecting their privacy. If there were no benefits from Internet access, we could easily protect our privacy. But there are benefits, and we all have to monitor our privacy settings, push for better solutions from companies and governments, adopt new technologies where possible, and be vigilant to the impact of our actions, on ourselves and others.

Data Brokers

There is one significant exception to the business models discussed here. Our vision of the privacy trade-off is that we trade our personal information for services that we use. We find a service that we like, we sign up, provide any needed information, and then use the service. If we do not actually read the terms and conditions, we are at least given the opportunity. We might be able to control our privacy preferences, see what the service has collected, and unregister if we are not comfortable with the trade-off.

The big exception to this rule is *data brokers*. These are companies that develop large databases about individuals and sell them to help target advertising or calculate people's credit scores. We never sign up with them, we receive no service in return from them, and it is not clear if we can unregister. One observer calls these companies *privacy deathstars* based on the growth of online data, with the result that "everyone now is invisibly attached to a living, breathing database that tracks their every move."[31]

A number of these companies developed early in the computer age, leveraging the ability to develop and process large databases, but grew in breadth and depth with the Internet. Today one of the largest, Acxiom, collects more than ten thousand indicators on 2.5 billion consumers in sixty-two countries. If you live in the United States and have ever wondered why you are asked for your home zip code when you pay by credit card in a store, it is because that is almost always enough to personally identify you and add to the data collected about your purchase activity.[32]

These companies are understandably secretive. It is difficult to find out what data are gathered, how they are gathered, and how they are used. For instance, Acxiom allows users in the United States to see what data they have, but the process is quite cumbersome. To do so, you make the request on their website, if you can find the page. It costs five dollars for processing, and that must be sent in the form of a check: though the company is happy to take our data online, it will not accept an online payment to see that data. Then, you wait two weeks to get access to your information. It is not clear what, if anything, you can do if the information is wrong.

Investigations have shown that these brokers classify us by race, religion, marital status, income, and other personal metrics, and put us into buckets with names such as Urban Melting Pot or Salt of Society, which are used for marketing purposes. And the resulting data may be easy to acquire. A researcher was able to buy the online dating profiles of one million people for EUR 136 from a company dealing in dating profiles, with pictures and all the intimate details one might expect people to give to a dating site.[33] It is unlikely that many users know that their profiles may be bought and sold in this fashion.

And there have been harms. Cambridge Analytica was essentially a data broker, with a focus on politics, and its data extended beyond what it took from Facebook. A small data analytics company in Ecuador accidentally exposed a database on a server that contained personal information on more than twenty million Ecuadorian citizens (more than the number of living citizens), including children and over seven million financial records with salaries, account numbers, and balances. It appears the company gathered the data from government sources and left them on a database without a password until it was discovered.

Again, these are companies that have no customer relationship with the subjects in their database, no terms and conditions we can review or agree to, no services we receive in return. And they are essentially unregulated, at least in the United States under current laws; recent European privacy laws may provide some limits that are beginning to be explored. Other governments are more reactive, as Ecuador began to quickly push through a data protection law after the mass data exposure.

Ultimately, though, these companies are beginning to make changes in their business models toward privacy, based on their own market assessments or as a result of government policy. For instance, some data brokers are under investigation for potential violations of the European Union's new data protections and are making changes in their business practices. Users and governments can play a significant role in helping push for these changes.

Conclusion

Free services are based on an exchange of value between users, who provide data to companies in return for services. These services provide us with previously unimaginable benefits. They enable us to tweet our thoughts to the world, share our experiences with our friends, stay in touch with our children, find routes with the least traffic, and more. They have also provided companies with information about our private lives.

Data privacy is a complicated issue to address. There are differences in the sensitivity of the data, differences in consumers' attitudes toward their data, and differences in how the data may be used, or abused. On top of that, there is imperfect information about what is happening with the data, which every now and then is pierced in dramatic fashion with a revelation that forces us to confront the situation.

And the impact is complicated. We are not presented with a situation of quick cause and effect—that if you put that information into a website and press Enter, it will be combined with certain other data, resulting in a definite and predictable outcome. You can search for a new job and not be fired by your boss in the next five minutes, arrange an affair online without being divorced the next day, or pay your taxes electronically without having your identity immediately stolen.

On the other hand, with the accumulation of information and experience, the privacy paradox is slowly undone. We learn more about how our data is used and change our behavior in beneficial ways, while companies begin to protect their own brand reputations and governments bridge the gaps. This process has been accelerated in recent years by the increase in cybersecurity concerns, covered in the next chapter.

6 Is Our Data Secure?

There are only two kinds of companies—those that have been hacked, and those that will be.

—Robert Mueller, FBI director, 2012

For a museum display, Ford fused the left-hand side of a 1965 Ford Mustang with the right-hand side of a 2015 Ford Mustang.[1] The display demonstrates how much changed in cars over the fifty year span. In purely functional terms, the cars are basically the same: both can carry four passengers at the speed limit. In terms of comfort, electronics, and features, however, the cars are light-years apart. But though cup holders, GPS, Bluetooth, and stereo make the journey nicer, the life-changing difference—literally—is with regard to safety.

The 1965 Ford Mustang only had lap seat belts standard in the front, no head rests, and lap belts in the back were optional. The 2015 Ford Mustang has shoulder seat belts all around, eight airbags, and it automatically makes an emergency 911 call if one of the airbags deploys. Whereas the 1965 model debuted a light in the glove box, the 2015 one has an airbag in the glove box door to protect the passenger's knees. The 2015 version does not just protect passengers in case of a crash, it also helps prevent them with electronic traction and stability control and a four-wheel antilock brake system. Crash avoidance, blind spot detection, and lane-departure systems are available as options.

Getting into any car in the 1960s was a leap of faith. There were no safety standards or tests. Ralph Nader's seminal book *Unsafe at any Speed* was published in 1965, and it demonstrated the resistance to safety measures on the part of automobile manufacturers at the time.[2] The book is credited with starting the long process of making cars safer, starting with the passage of seat belt laws and the creation of the US Department of Transportation.

But it was not just a matter of building safer cars—it was also a change in culture. I can remember as a boy riding in the back of a pickup truck or station wagon, with no constraints or second thoughts—which is now not just illegal, but also unimaginable. The resulting increase in safety is striking: controlling for millions of vehicle miles traveled, there were almost five times as many fatalities in 1965 as in 2015.

Today, putting our personal information into a website is also a bit of a leap of faith. The Internet was not originally designed with security in mind. It was designed as a distributed system, connecting multiple networks, with no central core in which to place security. Instead, the key was seen to be trusting those using it, which was easy in the early days when it was used to share resources among academics and researchers who knew one another. According to one of the early pioneers, David D. Clark, an MIT scientist, "It's not that we didn't think about security. We knew that there were untrustworthy people out there, and we thought we could exclude them."[3]

At the same time, early applications, such as file-sharing and email, were very basic to promote collaboration. There was no thought at the time of online banking or health services. Indeed, as noted above, the US National Science Foundation Network (NSFNET), which served the research and education community until 1995, began with an acceptable use policy against commercial use of the Internet.

As discussed in chapter 2, the Internet is based on open standards and uses open-source software, built on collaboration and for free access and use. That is one of its enduring strengths, but without security built in, it has proved a challenge to increase security. And many of the free services available over the Internet—and the paid ones—have not prioritized security at the behest of speed to market and cost saving.

When asked why he robbed banks, Willie Sutton is said to have responded, "Because that's where the money is." While he made off with his share of cash, he was also caught a few times, so imagine his reaction to learning that online thieves—from the comfort of some unknown location—stole $101 million from the central bank of Bangladesh, and might have taken $1 billion but for a typo that led to suspicions. And there was no need for a gun or a mask or a getaway car. Today the Internet is where the money is, along with health data, campaign strategies, business plans, personal pictures, and so on.

Take, for example, Ashley Madison, a website with the express purpose of enabling married men and women to cheat with one another. Its tagline is, "Life is short. Have an affair." To be clear, I was never a client—which I can easily prove, as it turns out, because the website was hacked in 2015 and all of the thirty-seven million users' names were put online, where they can be searched.[4] I use this example because it illustrates many of the problems with today's security levels and the corresponding risks.

The website recognized that married people would want to keep their affairs quiet, marketing the ability to have discreet relationships. In the end, it did not really deliver on either part of its marketing slogan. The data revealed that there may not have been that many relationships started through Ashley Madison (many of the women's profiles were apparently fake, there to attract men to the site); the fact that all the data was breached revealed that the company could not keep anything discreet, either. Of course, the company cannot guarantee a relationship, but it at least should have paid more attention to security.

The aftermath of the breach revealed a number of shoddy and fraudulent practices at the company, in addition to the use of female bots to attract male customers. The company advertised its security with a number of security seals and awards displayed on its website, but all of them were made up. Users were offered the option to pay nineteen dollars to delete their information, to be able to fully hide their tracks—but Ashley Madison did not actually delete the data, which was released in the hack. Indeed, this deceit may have actually motivated the hackers to release the data out of an odd sense of moral outrage.

The aftermath also inflicted untold costs on those involved. First and foremost, the users with a desire for, if not practice of, discreet relationships were outed. Some were blackmailed, some divorced, and some tragically committed suicide. The CEO, who was forced out, had his own extramarital affair revealed through the release of stolen emails. The company, predictably, was sued in a class-action suit for $578 million and faced government sanctions. But, as we will explore ahead, unlike many of the relationships harmed in its wake, the company is still in business and in fact claims an increase in business.

There is, of course, a morality tale to be told in dividing the blame among the users and their usage of the site, the site itself, and, of course, the hackers. For our purposes, the interesting point is that a company with the main selling point of discretion was not able to protect its data, and users could not protect themselves from the breach. And the released information indicated a number of mistakes by the company that led to the breach, some of which they knew about and ignored.

Stepping back, a recent study showed that 95 percent of such data breaches could have been prevented.[5] There are two main causes of breaches that can be averted.

First, many breaches attack known vulnerabilities in online systems. We are all used to updating the operating system on our computer or phone. One of the reasons is to patch a defect that could allow a breach. But not all of us update each patch all of the time, and that leaves us exposed. Organizations operating hundreds or thousands of devices with different systems connecting them may not devote enough resources to security or may be worried about testing the compatibility of upgrades, and this leaves them exposed to hackers searching for systems that have not been updated.

Second is the phenomenon known as *social engineering* in which an employee is tricked into providing their password. We have all received so-called phishing emails asking us to log into a familiar site to address an urgent matter. Doing so allows the hacker to capture the user's email address or user name and the associated password. The hacker then may use that information directly to enter the real version of the website or may find out where else the user may go and hope they use the same login details—which, human nature being what it is, is quite common.

These phishing attacks highlight the asymmetric advantage held by the hackers. They can send out millions of emails and just need one person to click on the wrong link to start their attack. A company I work with decided to teach employees about cyberattacks by sending out fake phishing emails. I spotted the first three fairly easily, but the fourth came on my phone as I was headed to a meeting in a taxicab in Cairo, which can be a full-on sensory experience. The email seemed urgent, I was preoccupied, and I clicked on the link. That could have been enough for the hackers, but luckily it just said, "oops—you fell for our fake phishing email" and gave some pointers.

Several years ago, Target stores had a major breach that resulted from such vulnerabilities.[6] The hackers were able to install software through a phishing email sent to an employee of a third-party vendor providing work on refrigeration, heating, and air conditioning. With a little sleuthing, they apparently determined that the third-party vendor worked with Target and installed some software that captured the password to get into the Target system. From there, they were able to work their way through the system to install software that captured shoppers' credit card details when they swiped their cards in the store.

This took place during the busy holiday season, and they were able to capture forty million credit card details before the breach was detected. Many were sold for up to forty-five dollars apiece before the credit card companies were able to cancel the cards, for a total take likely over $50 million. The total costs of the breach were much greater than that, however. The credit card companies had to replace the cards for a cost of at least $240 million. While the shoppers were not responsible for fraudulent expenditures, they were more vulnerable to identity theft and received credit protection. A few executives were fired. And Target was sued.

There were a number of points where this story could have ended differently. The employee could have avoided the phishing email. The third-party vendor was using free consumer virus protection that did not detect the password-capture software. Target did not realize that its connected contractor was not well protected, but Target itself had not changed a few of its own passwords from the default. And there were a number of other vulnerabilities in the Target system that allowed the hackers to gather the credit card information, store it on Target's own servers, and retrieve it. As is often the case, the customers themselves were faultless. In particular, they were not even shopping online—they were in the store—but the systems were still connected and vulnerable.

The hackers put a significant amount of effort into this breach, knowing the value to them of the credit card details they could steal. While in this case the breach was likely preventable at a number of key turning points, that is not always the case. If 95 percent of breaches are preventable, that means 5 percent are not. For instance, though many breaches result from known vulnerabilities in systems, a vulnerability is by definition unknown before it is discovered. Such a vulnerability, known as a *zero-day* vulnerability, is valuable because it cannot be defended against, and they are often hoarded or sold, sometimes back to the company responsible so they can create a patch.[7]

In a zero-day attack, although a breach cannot be prevented, the impact can be mitigated (as is the case for any breach, regardless of the cause). The easiest way, of course, is to not store data of which a breach could be costly. For instance, the Ashley Madison breach was made worse by the release of the details of users who had paid to be deleted. But ultimately, data is essential to the operation of an online service, and some must be stored. It does not have to be easy to use, however. Encryption of data—that is, applying a code to scramble the data—is virtually irreversible if done correctly. Yet in one analysis of breaches, only 1 percent of organizations breached reported that their data had been encrypted, rendering it of no use to the hackers.[8]

This, then, is the economic paradox at the heart of cybersecurity. The victims are not abstract or distant: they are the companies' own customers. The economic costs of a breach can include harmed corporate reputation, lost customers and sales, lower stock price, lost jobs for executives, significant costs to repair the damage, and lawsuits. Yet the number of preventable breaches keeps increasing, along with the amount of data breached, and executives and their boards have not all been fully shaken out of their complacency yet. What can explain this?

Typically, when there is an economic paradox such as this, when one cannot understand the marketplace outcomes, one looks for a market failure. As we have discussed, a market failure cannot sort itself out. A third party is required to intervene. This brings us to the economics of cybersecurity, in which there are three potential market failures, and third-party solutions are needed.[9]

Public Goods

The very strength of the Internet model masks an underlying weakness. As discussed in chapter 2, Internet protocols are open standards and often rely on open-source software, which anyone can use without payment: both companies for their own use in hardware and software and end users. This has all the features of an economic *public good*.

Take the example of public broadcast television as a public good. Once the signal is transmitted, anyone with a television can watch the channels; in economic terms, it is *nonexcludable*. Further, my watching does not take away the ability of anyone else to watch; again, in economic terms, it is *nonrival*. In other words, it is free to watch the channel, and there is no impact on anyone else by doing so. This is much different than most goods, such as the television used to view the public broadcasts. I can be stopped from buying one if I am not willing to pay the price, and if I do buy one, that television is no longer available for anyone else to buy.

Public goods have many great qualities, with many social benefits. However, they are not just public because anyone can use them; in a sense, they are also public because they are typically facilitated or financed by government, even if provided by private companies. This is because of the inherent market failure of public goods.

Think about what would happen if a for-profit company decided to offer a public broadcast channel, with educational and cultural broadcasting and no advertising. They start broadcasting and ask people to pay. People would realize quickly that they would be able to receive the channel even if they did not pay, so long as others paid, and a free-rider problem would emerge. As a result, public broadcasters in many countries, such as the BBC in Britain, charge an obligatory license fee to every household with a TV to finance the cost of the broadcasts.

I am happy to say that Switzerland, where almost anything can be put to a referendum, voted in 2018 on whether or not to keep the $450 annual public broadcast fee mandatory. A no would have allowed free riding on the programming paid for by those who continued to contribute, but I am happy to report that over 70 percent of those who voted chose to keep the fee mandatory.

In our case, the standards at the heart of the Internet have all the characteristics of a public good, including open-source standards. They are clearly nonrival: anyone can use the technology without taking the ability away from anyone else to use it. They are also nonexcludable: even if a license fee is charged, no one is denied access. However, as discussed earlier, the Internet standards developed by the IETF and W3C have a long history and stated purpose of providing freely available standards.

The development of open-source software is also a public good. Once it is done by someone, it is available to all, and this can lead to free riding. This is not to say that the development of open source is not an incredible achievement of researchers, engineers, and companies volunteering together to build software for all, and in many cases there are less defects than in proprietary software. However, it is possible for pieces to slip through the cracks.

A particular downside is a lack of resources to invest in improving the software, including for security purposes.[10] For example, OpenSSL is an open-source software library for securing online transactions and is used by many large websites, including Google, and companies making servers, including Cisco. In 2014, the Heartbleed bug was revealed; it had made users vulnerable to hackers for the previous two years. The bug was viewed as potentially catastrophic, estimated to impact up to 20 percent of secure web servers—making them not secure—and the cost of identifying the risks and addressing them was estimated at $500 million.

In the aftermath, it was quickly determined that the initiative developing OpenSSL had been receiving $2,000 a year in donations, with only one full-time employee and a few volunteers. The Core Infrastructure Initiative was quickly set up with funding from many of the major software companies to fund OpenSSL and other similar critical open-source initiatives. Although the wake-up call could have been much worse if the bug was more widely exploited, it shows the mismatch between the importance of the software and the available resources. It also highlights many of the positive aspects of open source, which should not be dismissed: the willingness of volunteers to work on the software, the responsibility of the community that found and reported the bug, and the quick reaction once the underlying lack of resources was identified.

Information Asymmetry

The OpenSSL story highlights another market failure in cybersecurity: as consumers, we have very little way of knowing how securely our software, devices, and systems are created. This is known generally in economics as *asymmetric information*, a market failure that comes up often in our lives. It comes up whenever one side of a potential transaction has more information about the transaction than the other side.

When you buy a used car, the seller knows more about the condition of their car than the buyer ever could; when buying car insurance, the driver knows more about their driving habits than the insurer does; and entering a restaurant, the chef knows more about the quality of the food and kitchen hygiene than the diner. When the truth is revealed, it might be too late.

This market failure impacts the willingness to buy or sell a good or service. Think about the price of car insurance in a competitive market.

Companies have to set the yearly premium and the deductible that the owner pays in case of an accident. What happens if a company has one plan, with a premium and deductible aimed at the average driver? Bad drivers will happily take that plan because it is a good deal given their driving history. Good drivers, on the other hand, will find it to be too much and go elsewhere. So the insurance company will be serving more bad drivers than good and will have to continually raise the premium and/or the deductible until they are stuck with the riskiest drivers. This type of situation is sometimes known as a *death spiral*.

That insurance company would prefer to elicit a credible signal to separate the good drivers from the bad. A signal is credible if only the party wanting to share positive information—the good driver—could afford to make it. For instance, a car insurance company can offer two plans—one with a high premium and low deductibles, and another with a low premium with high deductibles. Someone who knows they are a bad driver is unlikely to want to pay high deductibles every accident, but a good driver could afford to do that. They will save money by taking the low annual premium and only pay the high deductible in the rare case they cause an accident.

But sometimes there is no way to make a signal credible. Your toothpaste may say it has fluoride in it to help fight cavities, but how do you know for sure? How do you know if your airbag is going to work in a crash? You can test drive a car, but you can't test the airbags. Will your new hair dryer really shut down if it falls in your bathtub? And restaurant reviewers cannot know how hygienic the kitchen is when they are sitting in the dining room.

In some cases, private organizations will do the testing on behalf of consumers: think of Consumer Reports for many products, the European New Car Assessment Program for car safety, or UL (formerly Underwriters Laboratories) for electrical appliances. But often, the solution in these cases of market failure is government. The government can set standards; it can provide consumer protection for false claims; it can test products itself; and it can impose liability in case of failure (as discussed further ahead).

This brings us to cybersecurity. The OpenSSL case in one way is not about asymmetric information per se; it was an honest mistake that even the hard-working volunteer developers did not know about. On the other hand, until it was investigated, few realized how much trust they were putting into software supported with so few resources. The Ashley Madison case was willful: users in general relied on false claims of security and in particular could not know that the records they had paid to have deleted were not, in fact, deleted. The company knew it, but the users did not.

The bigger issue is that even companies that have put significant resources into cybersecurity have trouble providing a credible signal that they have done so. As a user, about to choose a critical service such as an online bank, how can we determine which really have put resources into protection and which ones are simply stating that they have done so? Prior to the announcement that all three billion Yahoo! user accounts were hacked, how could the average user have known that they were at greater risk using Yahoo! than Gmail?

One source of cybersecurity ratings relates to insurance. Cybersecurity insurance is potentially a significant market, given the exposure of companies to hacks.[11] However, insurers have difficulty providing cyber-risk policies, given the lack of information about attacks, exposure, and risk. Companies are emerging to help the insurance industry by rating the exposure of organizations seeking insurance from cyberattacks. For instance, one initiative by the insurance industry helps its customers identify products and services that lower cybersecurity risks. Such a joint insurance initiative is relatively rare, but interestingly similar to one that the industry undertook in the 1950s to increase road safety.[12]

At the end of the day, if organizations cannot make credible claims—certified by third parties—of their cybersecurity levels, and know that none of their competitors can either, why should a company fully invest in cybersecurity? Users will not be able to test which services have the best security in any case, so why bother? That is the ultimate market failure with asymmetric information in this situation: there is no guaranteed upside of investing more in cybersecurity, so the investment will not be sufficient.

It is made worse by the fact there is not enough downside from underinvesting, as we see next.

Negative Externalities

An externality is another example of market failure. It comes up when an economic activity has an impact on others—negative or positive—that is not reflected in the cost. The result is inefficient because too much, or too little, of a good or service is produced by not considering the full social impacts.

If you are trying to sell your house, the state of your neighbor's property can have an impact. Your neighbor mowing the lawn, trimming the hedges, painting the house, throwing away junk from the backyard can all make your house more attractive. On any given day though, your neighbor will not factor your house value into his or her decision to clear up. That is the impact of an externality. They also arise more generally with pollution. Dumping waste into a river only impacts those downstream.

Typically, if moral suasion does not work—either with your neighbor or a chemical plant—third-party action is required. For neighbors, that could be a homeowners' association that can set and enforce standards. Often, though, government action is needed to remedy externalities. The government can set minimal standards on pollution or in certain cases, such as for leaded gasoline, where any amount is too much, it can ban something outright.

In economic terms, it can also impose a tax at least equal to the cost imposed by the activity—for instance, taxing a fuel that creates pollution or taxing the pollution itself. This forces the producer to internalize the externality by accounting for the social cost and the economic cost and producing less of what is causing the externality.

Data breaches can cause significant negative externalities because typically the organization that was breached does not bear the full cost of the breach. Go back to the case of Target. To my knowledge, the third-party vendor that was the launching pad for the attack on Target did not bear any of the resulting cost, other than probably losing the account with Target.

Much of the cost was borne by the credit card companies to replace the stolen cards, although they were able to recover some costs in lawsuits against Target. The consumers successfully sued to recover $10 million, but after legal fees that was very little for forty million customers. The CEO was forced out, but with a large severance package. The stock price fell 10 percent, but quickly bounced back. And customers continued to shop at Target.

Of course, Target did bear a significant cost for the breach—likely over $200 million after insurance payouts. But much of the cost was after the fact, as a result of legal settlements; the default is that the banks and consumers basically bear their own costs. Ashley Madison likewise faced a massive class-action lawsuit, but in the end, it was settled for just $11.2 million (before legal fees), with each exposed user eligible for up to just $3,500, based on submitting valid claims. For instance, those who had paid nineteen dollars to have their accounts deleted will just be refunded the nineteen dollars because they were not deleted, but they receive nothing more for the impact on their personal lives. Perhaps it is not so amazing that the website is still in business in this light.

Of course, if you do not expect to bear all the costs of a breach, then you may not make all efforts to prevent it, leading to a market failure of preventable data breaches with significant costs borne by innocent parties. Users in particular are usually left out of the picture. For instance, even if there is no immediate cost, sometimes the data breach can lead to identity theft in the long run, with no or little compensation. Even if users are able to recover money, the default is that they have to sue and show specific harm, and it is hard to link identity theft to a particular data breach.

Much of this situation arises from the fact that software vendors are not liable for damages caused by bugs or vulnerabilities. Take the example of a *password manager*, a program that creates unique and complicated passwords for a user for each site and then automatically fills it in when using that site. This is a good way for users to reduce risks because password reuse is common and a way for hackers who have stolen one password to enter multiple sites. By using a password manager, however, users are putting all their eggs in one basket: if the password manager is breached successfully, then the hacker can potentially get a user's master password that enables access to all the rest of his or her passwords.

The cost to the user could be enormous, exposing them to theft, blackmail, and more. The cost of a breach to the password manager? Potentially not much at all. A review of the terms and conditions of a number of these warn users—in all capital letters—that they may only receive a refund of the cost of the software.

One password manager, LastPass, is known to have been breached, but with no evidence that consumers' master passwords were compromised, although they were prompted to change them to be sure. And the terms and conditions may not protect the company in that situation from lawsuits, lost customers, reputational risk, and even bankruptcy. But it does not send a good signal to the user of the value of their passwords.

The impact of a data breach must be internalized to reduce the externalities of a breach, and government action is the best, if not only, way to achieve that. Laws that shift protection to users and third parties harmed by a breach would help, particularly in the case of fraud or negligence. This is clearly what happened in the auto industry with safety.

One might argue that this will raise the cost of providing services, particularly free online services, but there has to be a balance. A password manager, health website, financial account, all house important, sensitive data that deserve to be protected. And though that protection will cost money, the cost will not just protect the company and its users from a breach, but also deliver broader social benefits by increasing online trust—a nice positive externality. This is particularly important in cases in which the users cannot assess the cyber-risks themselves.

Conclusion

The car industry has come a long way in the past fifty years with respect to safety. While a number of features such as airbags had to be mandated due to industry resistance, today there is competition over safety features. Now cars feature not just front airbags, but side airbags, overhead airbags, airbags to protect passengers' knees, and even an outside airbag to protect pedestrians from hitting the windscreen. In addition to protecting passengers if a crash occurs, there are features to help avoid crashes in the first place.

To help us find out more about safety, there are not just mandates, but tests. We can learn the ratings of cars we are about to buy, and car manufacturers unhappy about their safety ratings can improve them. There is also liability. In the wake of defects that resulted in a number of deaths, one airbag manufacturer recently went bankrupt after paying for recalls and settlements to victims' families. This provides an incentive, even after the tests, to ensure that quality is maintained and defects are promptly reported and repaired.

This is the shift that must take place for cybersecurity. As an example of the difference in approaches in different sectors, several years ago a Jeep Wrangler was hacked and taken over remotely. Jeep had installed an Internet-enabled entertainment system, and several researchers found vulnerabilities that enabled them to take over the car using its wireless connection.

Luckily, they were responsible security researchers, and they invited a *Wired* reporter to test-drive a hacked Jeep to demonstrate the bug.[13] They took over the transmission, and the terrified reporter ended up in a ditch, unhurt but shaken. Jeep issued a patch, but argued that the hack was vandalism, and not a product defect. In other words, the hack was essentially covered as software, without liability, and not by the stricter rules of automobile safety. The problem is not likely to get better—a Ford F-150 pickup truck from 2016 has 150 million lines of code, well more than Windows 7, an F-35 fighter, and a Boeing 787 combined, and all ripe for hacking with an Internet connection.[14]

As more and more devices and vehicles are software-driven and Internet-enabled, not to mention self-driving, the idea of software liability may need to be revisited, to impose the same level of liability on the Internet-enabled component of a product as on the rest of the product. That should be accompanied with a more encompassing safety environment. This can include changes at a number of levels.

First, many of the tools to increase privacy discussed earlier can also increase security. Companies providing technology can adapt security features to human behavior, rather than hoping that humans adapt themselves to security features. That can include prompting better passwords, nudging users to update their software or making it automatic, and automatically encrypting data in devices and in transit. Much of this is already starting to occur; it should be encouraged and continue.

Many of these features will come with commercial software; at the same time, developers of the open standards at the heart of the Internet will have to continue addressing security issues, and support for critical open-source efforts will need to continue to be supplemented as needed. This will help address the public goods aspect of these standards and software.

Third parties can play a significant role in developing standards, conducting tests, and providing safety ratings to guide us in choosing the services and devices that we use online. We see this starting with ratings to help insurance companies assess risk, which needs to extend to providing ratings to assist users. This will help make information about security less asymmetric.

And finally, there is a role for governments, which can pass laws on data protection, provide mandates, ensure that data breaches are responsibly disclosed, and, where needed, explore when and how to impose liability on critical software so that organizations internalize the costs of security breaches to a greater extent.

These efforts will clearly cost time and money to implement and do not absolve all of us from learning—and implementing—safe online practices. However, the costs of not doing this are high as well—not just on the organizations and users directly impacted by a breach, but more broadly on digital trust, which is critical as more of our lives migrate online.

7   Platform Power

At the heart of capitalism is creative destruction.
—Joseph Schumpeter

Waiting for a cab on a snowy evening in Paris in 2008, the founders of Uber had the same frustration that many of us have with taxis. There weren't enough of them and no sign of where to find an empty one. One of the founders, inspired by a scene from a James Bond movie, had already had the idea of using smartphones with maps to match drivers with passengers.[1] His plan was to buy a fleet of luxury cars and share the cost among the users. That would have saved the frustration of waiting in the cold for a cab, but given the cost of the limos, it may not have reduced the wait time very much on a busy evening.

The other founder, fatefully, talked him out of buying limousines—convincing him to find professional drivers with their own black luxury cars and use the app as a platform to match passengers with drivers.[2] Later, of course, the service was opened to any qualified driver with any qualifying car, and the first industry was fully "Uberized." Now other ridesharing platforms have emerged, taxi drivers have felt the impact, and there are concerns about local regulations and work conditions for the drivers—but no question about the power of such platforms to engender revolutionary changes.

Over the past twenty years, Internet companies have become among the most valuable in the world, including Alphabet (parent company of Google), Amazon, and Facebook. At the same time, newer companies such as Uber and Airbnb grew fast to significant valuations. Each company occupies its own niche in search, e-commerce, social media, ridesharing, and accommodations, and they are moving into other spaces as well. They are all innovative, invest significantly, and continue to expand globally.

It is easy to explain how these companies were able to enter markets and grow, based on open standards and permissionless innovation. The basic Internet standards are available to anyone to develop services without having to reinvent the wheel, and the services themselves can be offered, and used, without the permission of any entity. In addition, a host of companies provide the building blocks of growth for creating, hosting, and expanding a web and/or mobile app service. Many of the new companies are platforms, connecting providers with users and thus avoiding the need to invest heavily in the services provided, and many of these rely on advertising models to be able to provide free services.

Based on these characteristics, they have all disrupted older companies or even industries, engaging in the creative destruction that has characterized modern economies. *Creative destruction* is the process—identified by economist Joseph Schumpeter—whereby a company innovates a new product that pushes out incumbent companies and may gain some degree of market power, but then falls victim to new rivals with further innovations seeking their own taste of market power.

In the Internet space, think about the size and reach of Amazon, for instance, having emerged as the largest online retailer in the United States and pretty much any other country where it competes. Yet there are now significant questions about the size and market power of Amazon and other online companies. Are these companies themselves susceptible to disruption, or did they effectively raise economic drawbridges in their wake that block the next generation of disruptors? And do they have a preferential bridge to the next generation of services?

First, we will review the characteristics of market power, illustrating the role of barriers to entry in determining the competitiveness of markets and the role of prices in measuring the impact of the resulting competitiveness. Then we demonstrate how these characteristics apply to online services and the challenges for applying competition policy. Price plays an important role in competition policy—market power traditionally leads to price increases—and thus free services that remain free are more difficult to assess using existing tools, so new approaches are being explored.

Introduction to Market Power

In general, market power is the ability to set prices, rather than take the market price. A key feature of market power is barriers to entry that make it difficult for competitors to enter a market, allowing one or more sellers in the market to profitably raise price above cost, which is where it would otherwise be if there was perfect competition. These barriers can be natural—for instance, in markets with high capital costs that lead to economies of scale—or they could be artificial—for instance, if a company buys up the supplies of a key input to keep them from rivals. The result could be a market failure or a natural evolution of markets.

Let us unpack the issues step by step.

A monopoly is an extreme case of market power in which barriers to entry result in only one seller of a product or service. Generally speaking, monopolies are common in our daily lives. Sometimes they are inevitable; in other cases, they are viewed as desirable. In either case, they are typically the result of government policy, rather than a failure of policy.

Electricity, water, and gas are all typically provided by utilities, which are considered to be natural monopolies because of the cost of the networks required to connect every household. Once one network has connected the houses or apartments on your street, a second one would be uneconomical to build, and it would be difficult to win enough customers to make it sustainable. The threat of a natural monopoly is that with no risk of competitors entering the market, the monopolist can raise prices. To address this concern, the natural monopoly utilities are often state-owned, but even if they are private companies, the rates charged are regulated so that the utilities can cover their costs but not reap monopoly profits. We saw in chapter 3 how this applied to telephone networks, and the impact on broadband services.

However, high prices are not the only potential costs of monopoly. A British economist, John Hicks, famously noted that "the best of all monopoly profits is a quiet life."[3] More descriptively, US Judge Learned Hand wrote in a famous antitrust case that "possession of unchallenged economic power deadens initiative, discourages thrift, and depresses energy; that immunity from competition is a narcotic, and rivalry is a stimulant, to industrial progress; that the spur of constant stress is necessary to counteract an inevitable disposition to let well enough alone."[4]

In other words, price is not the only concern with monopolies: customer service, quality, and innovation also may suffer without any competitive pressures. As a result, there has been a movement in many countries to try to introduce competition for natural monopolists where feasible. Of most relevance here, in telecommunications, in a number of countries regulators have established ways for competing companies to offer service using key elements of the network of the incumbent provider. This is particularly noticeable, and relevant, with regard to broadband service, where companies can compete quite vigorously using the incumbent's network on price, speeds, or amount of traffic, as is often the case in Europe.

A second form of common, and sanctioned, monopoly comes from patents. In the case of pharmaceuticals, for instance, the impact of the patent is noticeable: for a given period, such as twenty years, the patent holder is able to charge high prices. The high prices charged are, in fact, the whole point of the patent. They provide the incentive to take risks and innovate to create the new drugs. When the patent expires, generic companies can enter the market, and prices will fall. In other cases, such as mobile phone technologies, the patent holders will typically broadly license their patents so that there is competition in the resulting phones, but as we have seen, the cost of the patent licenses can be a relatively significant amount of the phone's selling cost.

These monopolies result from entry barriers that cannot be surmounted because of costs or legal constraints, leaving the provider with 100 percent of the market. Much more common is a company with market power, not monopoly, which has a market share that falls short of 100 percent of the market. But market share is not the only indicator of market power; the key is how the market share is won and what the company does with it.

One way to get high market share is to offer a better service than anyone else, at a lower price. It may be through a more efficient process, through better technology, or as a result of an innovative business plan. Customers find the product or service attractive, and the company builds market share as a result. Other companies will have an incentive to compete with new innovations. If they succeed, creative destruction ensues, and a new company may emerge with a high market share. Such competition promotes innovation and choice and provides benefits for consumers. This is why we say that we "Google" something online: Google was so much better at search that it is hard to remember the earlier search engines.

A company may also have high market share because there are barriers to entry that fall short of a natural monopoly. For instance, the cost of developing and building a large commercial airliner is in the billions. Hence, there are essentially only two companies left—Airbus and Boeing—and even they rely on at least indirect government support. This market structure is intrinsic to the cost of building a large commercial airliner, and so long as the companies compete with one another on price, new models, and delivery, there is no competition issue.

In general terms, it is permissible to have market power, but it is not permissible to monopolize a market. Achieving a monopoly position by outlasting rivals as a result of "superior skill, foresight, and industry" is acceptable, according to US Judge Learned Hand, who notes that "the successful competitor, having been urged to compete, must not be turned upon when he wins."[5] However, other ways to build or leverage market power cause harms.

For instance, if a company is able to buy all of a key input to a product, or otherwise keep it out of the hands of competitors at any reasonable price, then the company will build up market share and be able to charge higher prices. That would be an abuse of market power. This was the way of the trusts in the United States in the late 1800s, which led to the passage of the groundbreaking antitrust laws to contain such results.

Further, leveraging market power legitimately won in one market into other markets is not permissible. For instance, IBM preceded its success in computers with success in the market for tabulating machines, electromechanical devices used to summarize results printed on punch cards—for example, for processing census data. IBM leased the machines to clients and required them to buy their punch cards at a price above cost. It was a good way to price discriminate—to earn more from users who used the tabulating machines more based on their purchase of cards. However, punch cards can intrinsically be a competitive product because it is relatively easy to make them, and in 1936 the US Supreme Court ruled that IBM could not require its customers to buy its punch cards.

Thus, though market share is an indicator of market power, a test of the impact of market power is measured by higher prices. Neither indicator alone is sufficient to establish market power. Note that anyone can raise prices—from the smallest fruit seller to the largest auto company. The question is whether it is profitable to do so. If a vendor of punch cards raises prices and there are competitors, then it would quickly lose market share, and the decision would be antiproductive but not anticompetitive. IBM, on the other hand, was able to tie punch cards to the lease of the machine, raise the price of punch cards, and increase profits.

Turning back to supply and demand, a key concept in assessing market outcomes is economic, or social, welfare, which measures the total benefits of a market outcome for consumers and producers together. Overall, the lower the price, the better for consumers: they pay less and can afford more (along the demand curve). At the market price where supply equals demand, social welfare is maximized. The last unit is sold at a price where the consumer's willingness to pay equals the producer's costs. This is said to be an *efficient outcome*. Any more units sold would be below the producers' costs, and would not be efficient.

If a company with market power raises prices, two things happen. First, whatever is purchased costs more than the perfectly competitive price; consumers pay more for what they buy, which is transferred into the pocket of the company with market power. Second, less is sold because some cannot pay the higher price, even if they would be willing to pay the cost of producing the product. This loss in social welfare is known as *deadweight loss*. That can be the result of market failure. Here, subsequent to a competition review, government action could be taken to avoid these impacts on social welfare and move toward a more efficient market.

Any competition review of monopolization and its impacts is after the fact. There is, however, one opportunity to prevent market power, and that is at the stage of merger or acquisition, to determine whether it could result in an anticompetitive outcome. This could be done for what is called a *horizontal merger*—when two companies compete in the same market, thereby eliminating competition between them—and it could be done in a *vertical merger*—when a company buys a supplier of an input, for instance, which may impact the ability of rival companies to compete.

In our focus on market power, we have so far focused on *power*. However, it is also important to define the relevant *market*, which is critical because that is the battleground over which any action is reviewed. Say Pepsi and Coca-Cola are about to merge. If the relevant market is carbonated cola drinks, then the two companies would have a high market share, with a likely chance that prices could be raised, and the merger would surely be rejected. If, however, the relevant market is all drinks—including water!—then the two companies would be relatively inconsequential in that market and the merger of little concern.

Of course, the correct market definition is somewhere in between. Effectively the question is, what would constrain the price charged by the merged company? If there is evidence that people would switch from cola to other carbonated drinks if the merged company raised the price of cola, then those drinks would be included in the market definition. If the price of carbonated drinks went up and people would switch to other soft drinks, then those would also be included. When there is nothing left that would constrain a price rise, the market is defined, and the potential impact of the merger would be analyzed with respect to the impact on that market.

So, in summary, market power exists when a company with a high market share is able to profitably charge a high price. A high market share can come from having a great product at a low price, so that is not market power. A high price can be charged by anyone, but usually it is not profitable as market share would fall. So the ability to charge a high price, while still maintaining a high market share, is the key to market power. That can result from entry barriers that prevent competitors from entering or effectively competing, or it can come from using a strong market position won in one market to get market power in a related market.

Historically, it was hard to imagine that market power could be acquired by Internet companies. Anyone could easily enter the online market, and once in the market prices were typically free. There was significant competition online in many areas, and in others there were plenty of offline competitors. When Google entered, there were other search engines; Facebook faced other social media; and Amazon competed online and with traditional retailers. The story turned out to be not so simple, but let's start at the beginning.

Online Barriers to Entry

One of the iconic symbols of computer entrepreneurship is the garage. Hewlett-Packard, Microsoft, and Apple were all started in the garages of their young founders. In the online space, Amazon and Google also started their growth in garages. The next wave of Internet companies did not even really need a specific place to start. Facebook was started in a dorm room,

Airbnb in the first apartment that was rented out. All this is to say that the cost to enter most online markets is intrinsically low. It is quick and easy to put together a website or mobile app, and no garage is needed for early manufacturing, for inventory, or to host servers.

And in some ways the barriers to entry are actually falling. As we have seen, the relevant Internet and web standards are open and freely available. There are many free tools that can help people put together a commercial website, and initial hosting costs are low. To enable growth, cloud services are available to provide the underlying computer power to avoid having to spend a lot on equipment and the teams to run the sites, and content-delivery networks can distribute the content globally. To tap into smartphones, online app stores can take over distribution and manage any payments. And, last but not least, online ad networks can help services monetize their content.

The result has been a remarkable amount of creative destruction, in several waves. An early wave, which was perhaps the most predictable, came from digital media. Online media began to quickly take on traditional media, and advertising revenue for traditional media began to fall. For instance, where it is available, Craigslist basically made classified ads obsolete. As professional media began to be available online, traditional physical media—namely, books, CDs, and then DVDs—and their retailers began to decline, and now it is harder to find a bookstore and probably impossible to find a store devoted to CDs or DVDs.

Traditional communications also began to be impacted. Free voice-over-IP services such as Skype began to eat into traditional telephony, particularly for otherwise expensive international calls, and also began to offer new business services, including conference calls and video calls. SMS texts—formerly a solid revenue earner for mobile operators in many countries—began to be challenged by messaging services, including WhatsApp, which uses traditional telephone numbers but sends the messages over the Internet. Radio was challenged by streaming music services such as Spotify, and television—broadcast and pay TV—is challenged by video downloads and streaming services such as Netflix.

This is not that surprising because all of these services lend themselves well to digitalization: media can easily be converted or created online and then shared. Traditional providers, once their concerns regarding copyright violations were assuaged, contributed to the trend. Music, TV, magazines, newspapers, and movies are licensed to online retailers, including Apple and Netflix, and to mobile stores such as Google Play. Traditional media may or may not like the new digital world, but they are now firmly part of it.

While television studios have created Hulu for streaming video and Disney has created Disney+ for streaming, the more significant form of competition may now be taking place in the other direction. Netflix began producing its own content several years ago, including television and movies, which now compete significantly with traditional media companies— not just for sales but also during award season. They have been joined more recently by Apple TV and Amazon Prime, both investing heavily in their own content.

Uberization

Some traditional sectors that clearly thought they were safe proved to be anything but. Soon after an auction of two hundred of the medallions needed to operate a yellow taxicab in New York City, the *New York Times* published an article entitled "$1 Million Medallions Stifling the Dreams of Cabdrivers." It noted that a pair of medallions to operate a "minifleet" sold for more than $2.5 million. The article stated that "city and industry officials have cast [rising medallion prices] as a sign of confidence in the future of yellow cabs."[6] That article was written in November of 2013, two years *after* Uber started operating in the city.

Just a few years later, there were sixty-five thousand Uber drivers, compared with 13,500 yellow cabs, and the dream of owning a medallion had turned into a financial nightmare. It has since come out, though, that the rise in medallion values was fueled by aggressive lending practices, based on the premise of ever-rising medallion values, a bubble that burst at least in part as a result of ride-hailing services.[7]

Uber made no investments in cars and hired no drivers; it simply matches customers and drivers who own cars. The same is true with Airbnb matching hosts and renters. They have increased supply and variety, lowered prices, and added convenience for customers, and that had a significant impact. Other companies in this category of platforms include TaskRabbit and Amazon Mechanical Turk, which have created an online market for labor, a key part of what is now known as the *gig economy*.

One reason that many did not see this wave of disruption coming was that they had created sectors built around trust. Getting in a car or falling asleep in a lodging are among our most vulnerable moments, and taxi companies and hotel chains invest in developing trust among their customers to overcome natural reluctance. Each uses branded cars or buildings and is subject to local laws and a local regulator that can help provide consumer protection. It seemed impossible that a global business could be built around people who would pay to get into a stranger's car or take a room with a stranger or, for that matter, that drivers would pick up strangers or owners allow strangers into their homes. But they do.

It still seems remarkable, but the way trust developed was to create a culture of sharing and to have each side rate the other. So, for instance, every rider rates the driver, and vice versa, so that bad drivers are dropped and bad passengers cannot get rides. Of course, homes were treated badly, and in some cases the worst happened to drivers or passengers. The companies had to respond and develop procedures to prevent this and insurance to mitigate it if it happened, but by and large they were able to do so, to the great benefit of Uber, Airbnb, and the other platforms.

The creative destruction of these regulated sectors has led to significant amounts of pushback.[8] Broadly speaking, there are two reasons that sectors might be regulated—economic and social—and opposition to the new platforms is coming for both reasons.

In economic terms, for instance, New York issued a limited number of taxi medallions in the 1930s to prevent the excess competition that arose during the Great Depression as too many cabs chased too few riders. Of course, the system took on a life of its own: as the medallions rose in value, there was resistance to increasing the number of medallions as doing so would depress the value of the medallions. This, of course, created excess demand over time and left room for competing services, culminating in the ride-hailing services.

In social terms, regulations can stem from a number of rationales. Some protect workers from bad working conditions, such as taxi drivers spending too much time at the wheel. Of course, these and other regulations protect consumers from dangerous drivers and protect other drivers and pedestrians. Other social regulations ensure accessibility of taxicabs, for instance, to make them usable for all who need them.

Not surprisingly, objections to Uber and other ride-hailing platforms fall along economic and social grounds. Economically, taxi drivers in many cities have protested cheaper competition from ride-hailing services, resulting in the services being banned intermittently in cities such as London. On social grounds, objections also arise because they lead to more congestion in cities as the drivers circle for new fares. The cars may also not meet taxicab requirements, such as for accessibility. And finally, the drivers are not considered employees, and thus must bear all costs on their own, with no guaranteed minimum earnings, insurance, pension, or other social protections.

Airbnb has also received many social objections. Neighbors complain sometimes about the constant turnover of guests, who do not have the same investment in the neighborhood as longer-term tenants or owners. And some are investing in properties solely to rent them out on Airbnb, reducing the stock and affordability of the remaining properties for residents. As a result, cities have imposed regulations and taxes in an attempt to even the balance.

These disputes clearly did not stop the growth of these new platforms, given in particular the benefit of not having to invest directly in the services provided through their platforms. However, the disputes have not yet played out as new forms of competition emerge, worker protections need to be addressed, and cities address long-term social issues including congestion of roads and affordability of housing.

Content Platforms

Traditional media are not just addressing online availability of their content, but also are now competing with a whole new source of content—everyone. We can send out our opinions through blogs, tweets, and posts, stream our music or podcasts, and upload videos onto YouTube. Stars have been discovered online and careers can be made. News is being delivered, policy is discussed, and sometimes horrific events are livestreamed. Companies that host the content do not have to create it; instead they act as intermediaries between the users who generate the content and those who consume it. These platforms compete with traditional media in many ways—particularly for users' attention and advertiser revenues.

These online platforms generate significant revenue from content, without actually creating any content. On social media, the posts and messages created by users is the content that is shared. On other sites, such as YouTube, users generate the content that is uploaded for other users to discover. Such platforms have generated a number of policy issues, in part because of their favorable economics.

The success of this business model seems clear—letting others create popular content with all the costs that entails. However, it was not always evident. We have already covered the challenges of monetizing online content in the late 1990s, and that certainly impacted the prospects of such platforms, as with any other online property. However, at the same time, platforms faced perhaps a more significant constraint, and that was editorial responsibility and liability for the content.

In traditional media, editorial responsibility and liability go hand in hand. The publisher of a newspaper chooses every story, writes every headline, and authorizes every ad. If a story is false or defamatory, the editor has responsibility, whether it is legal or reputational. The same is true for television, where the broadcaster secures the rights to all content or develops and approves its own content. Even live television, which cannot be fully scripted and controlled, can lead to a fine, at least in the United States, resulting in some broadcasts being delayed by a few seconds to give the network time to block any offending content.

Traditionally, the only way to reach a mass audience before the advent of online platforms was through a publisher. I could write a letter to the editor, for instance, but the chance of it being printed is very low, and impossible if it is false, rude, or crazy. Not so online, where the same message can be tweeted and ricochet forever. Of course, platforms might not want to be associated with the content, or it might infringe on copyright.

In the late 1990s, as the platforms started, a fundamental challenge emerged. When platform owners chose to block content, for whatever reason, some courts ruled that blocking any content turned the platform legally into a publisher, with editorial responsibility over all content. As a result, this led to the somewhat perverse outcome that it was better not to edit any content than to take on the responsibility for all content.

To stimulate investment, laws were passed (notably in the US and Europe) that treated platforms as intermediaries with a safe harbor from liability—in the United States, famously, this is referred to in shorthand as Section 230 (of the US Communications Decency Act). Platforms could filter content that was uploaded without taking on responsibility for filtering all content. In return, however, they were responsible for taking down content upon lawful request. This was true for general content, which might invite scrutiny for political, religious, cultural, or other sensitivities, depending on the country, and it was also true for material that infringed on copyright.[9]

Along with the increased value of advertising, as discussed earlier, this safe harbor led to the initial growth of platforms from the late 1990s. And these companies grew quickly, given the economics of online platforms. However, as we will see ahead, the platforms led to a new set of challenges, including economic ones related to competition and market power and social ones related to the content that is available on the platforms and the impact of that content on society.

Winner Takes All

Given the economics, particularly for platforms, there are a number of large Internet companies growing with remarkable speed and strength. What is noteworthy is their growth not just in absolute terms, but also relative to their competitors. Google has 90 percent of search in some countries, Facebook has billions of users, and Amazon has a large share of the US online retail market. Of course, many of these companies have a Chinese doppelgänger—Alibaba, Tencent, Baidu—but in China, the same dynamic has emerged with those companies.

Why was it easy for the current wave of large Internet companies to enter and grow, but harder for their competitors to follow them? For the economics, we can look on the demand side and also the cost side. Further, even well-meaning regulation sometimes had unintended consequences of raising barriers to entry. To start, though, online companies generally benefit from playing in a winner-takes-all market.

In the physical world, there are always constraints on the growth of a company, and always room for at least one strong runner-up. The best restaurant in town will fill up; the classrooms of the best professor reach capacity; concerts have a limited number of seats; and vacation flights will sell out. Consider the recent travails of Tesla: it had more than five hundred thousand orders for its Model 3 family car but had significant challenges ramping up production capacity, with significant investments required and a number of quality challenges, leaving room for competitors to develop and market their own alternatives.

Compare that with online services. Online companies have to make little or no investment, at least in the short run, to grow capacity. The marginal cost of another customer, another download, is essentially zero. Take a mobile gaming app, for instance. Once uploaded, the distribution costs are covered by the app store, and once downloaded, the user runs it on their device, using their Internet access if needed, with no further input from the developer or app store—until the next update, which can be distributed easily through the app store again. There is thus no supply constraint on a popular game, which can quickly grow in popularity.

The first mobile game to pass $1 billion in revenue—*Puzzle & Dragons*—shot up quickly in sales after a TV ad in Japan in 2012, with very little increase in cost to meet the increased demand. Of course, what goes up can come down, and soon another game took its top spot. The developers had a good run, though. In the year the game peaked, it had only about forty developers, and most of the revenues went straight to profits. In total, the game made USD 7 billion, and when demand fell, there was no empty factory or stockpile of unused inventory dragging down the company. While these online games can grow quickly, there are no barriers to entry and thus no market power; they are popular for a period and then, with no cost, players move on to new games.

Online services such as search engines and social media have a few more forces at work, however. They clearly benefit from the winner-takes-all phenomenon that applies to games, but also from network effects. They also have a cost structure more demanding than a mobile gaming app to develop and operate the service, which leads to economies of scale. The leading services thus benefit from advantages on both the demand side and the cost side, advantages that have proven difficult for runners-up to overcome.

This is particularly true if the content or services are free. One way to enter a market typically is with a low price, as a way to have consumers try the product or service and hopefully switch allegiance. However, a new social media service cannot undercut Facebook on price, and a new search engine cannot undercut Google; they are already free. To understand the additional hurdles a challenger must face, it is important to understand the forces that led to the growth of the incumbent in the first place.

Network Effects

On the demand side, the economics of online services clearly favor growth and raise entry barriers because of network effects. Again, these arise when the benefits of a service increase with the number of users—and they are what make common Internet standards so valuable. With respect to online services, network effects are key to social media such as Facebook and Snapchat.

The more users on the platform, the greater the benefits to other users. No one wants to be the first user of a social media service because it would not be very social. On the other hand, no one would have minded being the first customer of Amazon—all that mattered to him was that he received his book. Although as a small bonus, Amazon named a corporate building after him.[10]

Although price is always an important factor in attracting customers, and particularly for new companies attracting new customers, an attractive price is particularly important when network effects are involved. The more initial users there are, the more alluring the service is for additional users. Free is the most attractive price, and here the role of free is clearly—once again—critical. The earliest users of services such as Snapchat did not need to pay, so there was no barrier to adopting, making it easy to try. The fact that the price remains free for new users keeps the ball rolling.

A variation on network effects is the two-sided market. For a service such as YouTube, users are interested in content. An increase in the number of users makes it more attractive for content, while more content makes it more attractive to users. Of course, the users of YouTube also create the content for others, in a positive feedback loop of growth. Again, this makes it difficult for a new competitor to enter this market: not only is it necessary to attract users, but one must also attract content that is attractive to users. Uber and Airbnb are also examples of two-sided markets.

Network effects lead to switching costs for consumers and, in a two-sided market, also for sellers. It is hard to switch from a social media site because the value is in your network of contacts, and it may be difficult to export information to a different site; with Uber, users build up a solid rating reputation that takes time to build up elsewhere (which is also true for the drivers); and Amazon and Netflix, in addition to their content, know our preferences and give recommendations.

These demand-side benefits may extend into adjacent markets also as the companies move into television streaming, car entertainment, smart speakers, smart watches, home security, and other areas no doubt in the planning stages. Is it possible, practical, or likely to mix and match these devices, or will an Android household stay Android or an Alexa one stay Alexa? Although you must pay for the devices, the apps used across the devices within the same family are generally free. The convenience is unquestioned, the benefits to the provider clear.

Economies of Scale

On the cost side, the entry barriers for online companies seem deceptively few, but they are large and growing. First, as noted, the entry costs are low to build a website and grow a business online, particularly if third parties are providing all the content or services. However, even if entry is easy, growth is harder than it seems, particularly in a market that already has a clear leader.

The first thing users notice with a new service is its website. Although it is true that almost anyone can build an online website using free tools, it is also true that almost anyone can tell how well it was built. In the physical world, bank buildings tend to be grand and imposing. Likewise for other institutions based on long-term trust: law offices, health clinics, accountants. The reason for investing in fancy offices is not just to create a nice place to work or to make an inviting environment for clients, but to send a credible signal that a company has no plans to take the money and run, that it will be there when you need it.

A good website sends a similar signal.[11] When a website does not work well, when it is very basic or poorly designed, we may be more reluctant to order something, to put in our credit card number, or to input personal information. For instance, if we are buying something like a pair of shoes, which may not fit, we want to be confident not only that the right shoes will arrive, but also that they will be accepted as a return if needed. A quality online retail website, signaling that the company can be trusted, can cost up to $500,000.[12] That can act as a barrier to entry for smaller companies seeking to invest, but without it there may not be enough users to grow.

Once the website or app is built, the economies of scale are almost overwhelming. The same website can fundamentally serve a million or a billion users. The cost of reproducing a video or streaming a song one more time is effectively zero, and the cost of the Internet access is carried by the users. But quality of service is critical, and a popular website hosted on a single server in a single location would quickly be overwhelmed.

Studies show, for instance, that slow response times—also known as high latency—cost companies valuable sales or views. Several years ago, Amazon calculated that if a page takes one second longer to load, that costs them $1.6 billion per year in sales; Google stated that a four-tenths of a second slowdown costs eight million searches per day.[13]

As a result, large online companies have invested a significant amount of money to speed the delivery of their web pages. The essential elements to do this are increased computing power to process the data, hosted in data centers closer to the users, with more capacity to distribute the data. Such resources are available through large cloud companies and content-delivery networks, which host the computing power and deliver the data around the world.

However, the largest online companies build their own data centers; some have invested in fiber-optic cables to connect their data centers and even designed and built their own servers, of which there may be millions. These investments are costly—according to one study, online companies invest $75 billion per year in infrastructure—and provide economies of scale which are hard to match.[14]

For an entrant, all investments in similar capacity must be deeply considered, particularly those that will be sunk costs. A *sunk cost* is a cost that has been incurred and cannot be recovered. Take, for instance, a ticket to a concert. If you paid for it, and it cannot be sold or refunded, then it is a sunk cost. If you fall ill on the day of the concert, you may feel pressure to go because of the cost of the ticket. That is the *sunk cost fallacy*. The time to consider the cost was before buying the ticket; afterward, it is a sunk cost that can be ignored. Not everyone is swayed by the fallacy, though: the entire fitness industry is propped up by people who sign up on January 2, show up twice, and treat the membership as a sunk cost for the rest of the year.

Before making investments, companies need to seriously consider sunk costs, their own and others. Sunk costs can have a significant impact on competition. With current Internet companies having sunk billions into algorithms, custom servers, bespoke data centers, and their brand names, new entrants will consider their entry carefully, knowing that incumbents will have every incentive to compete hard to protect their position. This is particularly the case in a winner-takes-all situation. Entrants have to manage to find a path to revenues, grow their network, and invest in providing high quality of service. And they also may have to get over inadvertent barriers raised by policymakers.

The Law of Unintended Consequences

The open and global nature of the Internet has led to its unprecedented growth in the number of users and the depth and breadth of their use. Not all users, and not all usage, is good, however, often taking advantage of the intermediary role of platforms, so there is significant effort toward protecting the experience of those online. These efforts, by policymakers and by companies and others in the Internet community, have often had the unintended consequence of increasing consolidation in the Internet.

For instance, immunity for intermediaries was meant to help promote the growth of the online platforms. And as we have seen, their growth has been spectacular, with implications few may have expected—in particular, that one platform might be able to reach billions of users and that platforms could be used to impact elections, radicalize terrorists, stir hatred, and spread disinformation. The same channels can also be used to circulate copyright-infringing material to a significant audience very quickly.

As a result, the intermediary safe harbor is—perhaps inevitably—under pressure. In the United States, an exception to immunity from liability has been enacted. A US bill passed in 2018 requires platforms to filter material related to sex trafficking, weakening the immunity from intermediary liability.[15] More recently, President Trump signed an executive order to remove the Section 230 immunity if a social network edits a post. This came in response to Twitter adding fact-checking labels to two of his tweets for the first time. Whether or not this move proves successful, it adds to the pressure on the safe harbor.

In Europe, on the other hand, a law was passed requiring platforms to better filter copyright material, rather than simply take it down upon notice.[16] There has also been understandable pressure to filter hate speech and terrorist content, which are driven by social concerns but may have economic consequences.

These changes may lead to further consolidation of online companies. As the markets grow, it becomes harder and harder to fully filter all content effectively and efficiently. YouTube, for instance, has five hundred hours of video uploaded every minute. Working eight-hour days, it would require ninety thousand people just to watch the new content coming in, much less make any difficult decisions about what to do with the content. Clearly, that is impossible. Instead, software programs are used to identify content that may infringe on copyright or other laws. For instance, Google has developed a tool for its YouTube platform called Content ID, to identify copyrighted material that was uploaded without permission, which cost more than USD 100 million to develop over ten years.[17] No entrant could invest that much time and money into such a program up front.

Other regulatory actions also have an impact on concentration. The GDPR that came into effect in 2018 has compliance costs for online companies that gather personal data. As discussed earlier, personal data can be used to target online ads. One study looked at the market share of ad networks in terms of their website reach in the month before and after the GDPR went into effect. The study showed that the impact of the GDPR corresponded to the size of the vendor: the smallest ones in the study lost over 30 percent of their reach of websites, whereas the largest—Google—gained just under 1 percent. The study attributes this to the resources available to the largest ad networks and to risk aversion leading websites to drop the smallest ones in case they were not compliant.[18]

Other efforts to improve the Internet have, at least indirectly, contributed to the consolidation on the Internet. Take spam, for instance. On the one hand, it forms an enormous part of email traffic—over 50 percent. But on the other hand, for many of us it has all but disappeared from our inboxes. Part of it is being stopped at the source; part of it is intercepted before it reaches us; and some of it may end up in our junk mailbox. All of these efforts cost money, however, and improvements in spam filters are generally proprietary. The result is that there are relatively few email services these days that can effectively filter spam, and all are provided by large Internet companies.

It is now difficult to enter the market because while a new email provider is on the learning curve of blocking spam, their users will feel bombarded with junk mail and may give up on the new provider. It takes a significant amount of email to train spam filters as to what to block and not block, and also a significant investment to develop the needed algorithms, and it is difficult for entrants to scale up over time without losing customers. There are open-source spam filters, but they suffer from the same constraints.

These increased costs may have particular resonance in developing countries attempting to bridge the digital divide (as discussed further in the next chapter). For instance, where a small email provider might have started in a local market and grown with the market, now users—even within governments—are more likely to turn to the large international providers, partly because they are free, and partly because they are relatively free from spam. Likewise, more generally actions to correct the market failures around cybersecurity also have significant costs. This is true for data centers and for hosting providers, which must help protect their clients.

The outcomes, while inadvertent, make it more difficult to compete and should be considered when new laws are passed or new developments are promoted.

Competition Policy

Of course, market power is not new or unique to the Internet, or even the digital age. However, it is proving challenging to address with traditional tools, in no small part because many services are offered to users free of charge.

Using the ability to raise price as a measure of market power in a review of market power is challenging for Internet platforms on which services are free. This clearly did not apply to most products and services over time, other than advertising sponsored traditional media such as broadcast television. But the challenge for addressing market power for Internet companies goes further than price. There is also the issue of the impact of market power on innovation and on service quality and the impact on any competitors who cannot enter a market, to the extent those can be determined and are taken into account.

Consider Google. Google was started by two Stanford University students, first on campus and then in a friend's garage. Its growth was clearly based on its innovative new search algorithm, which was simply better than others at the time. After twenty years, there is no evidence, to paraphrase the words of Hicks, of deadened initiative, discouraged thrift, and depressed energy. In fact, if anything, the opposite is true based on a stream of announcements about new services and features.

Google has famously noted that "competition is a click away," meaning that just as many were using earlier search engines and tried Google and did not go back, Google could suffer the same fate.[19] Of course, Google offers a lot more than search these days: it offers Gmail, Google Docs, Google Maps, Google Drive, Google Hangouts, and so on. And then of course there is Android on phones, and the Chrome operating system (OS) and the Chrome browser. In short, there are a lot more services, and they are all free, other than the devices on which they are installed.

But here is where it gets a bit tricky. When searching for an address, Google search results include a map of the results at the top of the page, using Google Maps. This is very convenient, and it is an excellent mapping service. But we used to use MapQuest, which lost significant market share after Google started showing Google Maps results. Here we come to the issue of moving from a market with a well-established position into another adjacent one, as we saw with IBM and punch cards. But here, Google Map results are also free, and there is evidence that they were better than MapQuest at the time.

We now come to a fork in the road. In the United States, the FTC examined the so-called search bias of Google displaying its own services in response to search queries but decided unanimously to close the case. Then FTC Chairman Jon Leibowitz noted that "the American antitrust laws protect competition, not competitors"; the latter had complained about the impact of this practice on their business because of a loss of visitors from related searches.[20] In other words, there was no harm to consumers.

On the other hand, in Europe, a review of this practice relating to the display of Google Shopping results led to a fine of EUR 2.42 billion, in a case brought by British shopping comparison site, Foundem. Competition Commissioner Margrethe Vestager said: "Google has given its own comparison shopping service an illegal advantage by abusing its dominance in general Internet search. It has promoted its own service, and demoted rival services. It has harmed competition and consumers. That's illegal under EU antitrust rules."[21]

The EU result is different than in the US result, based on similar complaints, which highlights a difference in approach. While both seek to protect competition, the United States applies a consumer welfare standard in which harm is primarily measured through higher prices. Nonprice impacts on quality, consumer choice, and innovation can be taken into consideration, but it is hard to determine how these are, or should be, weighed against free prices.[22] At the same time, the EU seeks to protect competition, but that includes protecting competitors from harm from a dominant company, which would ultimately impact incentives to innovate and compete with lower prices. So far, the EU approach has been more interventionist in online markets where prices are free.

The current argument against large online providers is proving difficult to analyze for an array of reasons. They benefit from characteristics of the Internet—namely, the winner-takes-all outcome—and characteristics of their services—namely, network effects and economies of scale. In their core areas—Google in search, Facebook in social media, Amazon in e-commerce—they succeeded with good products that are popular with users and are free or competitively priced.

And in any case, what market would they have power in? In 2018, Amazon had roughly 50 percent of online retail sales in the United States, representing 5 percent of total retail sales. So is Amazon a big fish in the small pond of online retailers, or a small fish in the big pond of all retailers? Is messaging a unique service, or does it compete with phone calls, text messages, email, and other forms of communications? Finally, the companies are adamantly not enjoying the quiet life: their free services are still free, their paid services are still reasonable. And they are restless, offering an endless array of new content and services.

I still see three areas where there remains concern.

First, there is the traditional area of monopolization or abuse of dominant position, including companies successfully moving into adjacent markets and potentially crowding out competitors. This is an area where traditional competition policy—notably in Europe—is active, can evolve, and offers an alternative to the approach in the United States. The EU and several countries, including the United Kingdom and Australia, have begun to study how to address digital challenges in competition policy.

There is also a more general concern about the impact of large companies on their societies. Some of this harkens back to the early days of US antitrust policies, captured by Louis Brandeis, who was concerned about the "curse of bigness" and the impact of large corporations on democracy.[23] We see that today in discussions about the impact that online companies have on content and more generally on privacy and data protection. Competition policy may alleviate the size of the companies, but the more general concerns about content and privacy are outside its remit.

Finally, what is truly new here is the role of data that is gathered by the companies. In particular, the quality and quantity of data that companies have regarding consumers may be the most significant barrier to entry. It has two potential impacts. First, the data is at the heart of privacy concerns and cybersecurity breaches, as we have already examined, and second, it may allow monopolization—not just into adjacent markets, but also into future markets. Options to address the latter concerns may well help alleviate the former concerns as well.

Data as the Difference

It is possible that a new metric is needed to measure market power, especially when services are offered for free. Where normally a profitable increase in price was a strong metric, the new metric may be the ability to profitably gather data—and monetize it through advertising—without losing market share. Where before prices led to profits, now data is the new coin of the realm. Where before a merger may have led to less competition and the ability to raise prices, now a merger may lead to increased data gathering, which can be monetized. Where before a company with market power in one product may have leveraged that into a complementary product to increase prices, now it may leverage one online service into another using data and to gain more data.

Competition policy is critical to economic welfare, by regulating natural monopolies, preventing the achievement of artificial monopoly through mergers, and preventing anticompetitive harms. However, over the long run, creative destruction may ultimately play a larger role in preventing sustained market power from emerging. And data may hinder this process for some companies going forward because of the data needed to develop new services, including notably artificial intelligence (AI).

In ICT, for instance, antitrust challenges in the US certainly impacted the market behavior of the Bell System, IBM, and then Microsoft, and they impacted the development of the Internet. As a result of a 1956 Consent Decree, the Bell System was required to license patents for the transistor for free, paving the way for Silicon Valley, and it later openly licensed Unix as well, which helped deliver TCP/IP and open-source software. Later challenges to the Bell System enabled third-party devices such as modems to be attached to the network. Eventually, challenges led to the breakup of the Bell System itself.

IBM and Microsoft both underwent their own large antitrust cases; the one against IBM was eventually dismissed, and the one against Microsoft ended in a limited settlement. During those times, IBM was ultimately supplanted by Microsoft and other PC companies, and then Microsoft itself saw the rise of Google and other online companies. Of course, IBM and Microsoft still exist, and thrive, but without the dominance they possessed at the peak of their powers. There is some debate about the role that the antitrust cases played in distracting the companies and modifying their behavior, but new technology and business models also played a significant role in the shift.

As we have seen, online companies benefit from significant advantages—low cost of inputs for platforms, network effects, winner-take-all outcomes, and others. But new companies can also benefit from the same effects and possibly even new benefits based on their business strategy or technology. Thus, existing search engines gave way to Google, and Myspace gave way to Facebook. However, going forward there may be one critical difference, and that is the role of data. Not only does it drive advertising revenues, but it can also help enter new markets.

One example is Amazon Marketplace, acting as a platform where third-party vendors can sell their products. This generates competition with Amazon's own sales. Amazon has also introduced its own house brand, AmazonBasics, which is starting to compete with the traditional brands Amazon and the Marketplace retailers sell. The result is that the data gathered by Amazon leads to two concerns: First, that Amazon can gather data about sales on the Marketplace to refine its own sales of the same items, working directly with manufacturers, at the expense of the independent vendors. And second, that it can use these data to refine its own AmazonBasics brand offerings.

On the other hand, even understanding this, many retailers are dependent on Amazon and find it difficult to leave the Marketplace. This is an expression of market power—the ability to profitably increase data gathering. At the same time, independent online retailers have a difficult time entering or competing without access to the same data.[24] The need for data acts as a barrier to entry.

Going forward, machine learning is being used to develop AI, and machine learning requires data. Take what is for us a simple task, differentiating a dog from a cat. It turns out to be difficult to program a computer to recognize the difference because dogs and cats share so many features—fur, tails, and so on. But if you had millions of pictures of cats and dogs, particularly if they were already labeled as such, you could feed them through the computer, which could develop its own algorithm for telling the difference—effectively the way we effortlessly did when we were children. This example is not a likely moneymaker, but it demonstrates the value of having good data in developing AI.

More to the point, the YouTube Content ID system described earlier also depends on machine learning. First, it develops the tools to fingerprint the content, then it uses machine learning—based on an enormous amount of uploaded audio and video—to refine the system over time. In particular, it learns to identify tricks used to get around the system. With the largest store of user-uploaded video, as well as investment in machine learning, Google can develop the most sophisticated Content ID system to detect copyright violations which, to be clear, is valuable for the copyright holders.

One solution to data disparities is to focus on a form of data sharing between companies. The idea is to provide access to existing datasets to lower barriers and enable new companies to develop their own business model to enter the market. It leverages two salient points about personal data. First, data is virtual, not physical; it can be shared so that more than one company has access to the same data at the same time. Second, the raw data is created by the actions of the users: which rides they took, which products they purchased.

However, any data-sharing approach should acknowledge that the existing companies are successful not just because of the data, but because of what their algorithms do with the data. In fact, it is probably on the basis of good algorithms that the companies grew and were able to gather more data, upon which to refine the algorithms further, and so on.

One can thus differentiate between *user data* and *processed data*. The former is an input that could be shared, while the latter is a proprietary outcome that should not be shared. The ability to share user data could increase competition and choice for consumers. The large platforms would be able to continue to provide service, while smaller firms have access to data that would enable them to innovate and grow. The devil is in the details, however. First, what are the conditions under which data must be shared? Second, what is the format for sharing the data? And third, how can we protect privacy without rendering the data useless?

The result of an antitrust review could thus be—instead of, or on top of, a fine—a requirement to share data with entrants. This would require a competition law finding against a company, along with a new approach to a remedy that would withstand challenge. In addition, it would require the consent of those whose data would be shared, built upon a guarantee of privacy and data protection.

One way to do this is individual data sharing. For example, our reputation is important to us on platforms such as Uber, and a barrier to a new rideshare program is that we might be reluctant to move and start over with a new rating. The same is true for a driver whose reputation is also valuable. This data is entered by drivers and passengers, and allowing it to be portable would increase competition. To the extent that the data is subsequently processed or analyzed by Uber, however, those results should be proprietary because they result from investment and create competitive advantage.[25]

Such data portability is already included in the European GDPR and would allow users to take their own data from one company to another. This was decided in the context of privacy, but it also impacts market power. It lowers the cost of switching services and thereby barriers to entry. However, it does not allow a continual flow of data from an existing service to a new one: it is a one-time transfer of historical data.

A modification of this approach would be to create personal data stores, which would intermediate between users and platforms, gathering raw data and then sharing it with any service that is chosen. This could provide a continual flow of data—chosen by the user—to the platform or platforms of their choice. An example is Solid, created by the inventor of the web, Sir Tim Berners-Lee, which provides users a Solid Pod to store their personal data and the ability to decide who can read or write data stored in the Pod.[26] A Pod is a personal storage place, which is online and can be accessed from anywhere, by anyone with permission.

Of course, there is a collective action problem that we have hinted at previously. The value of our individual data is only truly unlocked when it is aggregated. That is the essence of a data company, and it is the key to machine learning. If you only know which movies I like, it is hard to make recommendations, and if you only know where I went with Uber, it is harder to design a ridesharing platform. So, to be successful, an organization would need a significant amount of aggregate data, not just data on one user at a time.

With any form of data sharing, privacy and security are critical issues. Data ported or shared between companies would need to be secured while stored and in transit, and users would have to consent to each company's terms and conditions—or standard terms and conditions might be imposed regarding any moved data.

A final approach might be to keep the data within each service, but allow or require interoperability between services. This might be to access data on different services, or it might be to create cross-platform services. This is how the telephone network was opened to competition—by ensuring that competing networks can interconnect with the incumbent and make calls to each other's subscribers, using a shared numbering system and common standards. Following an antitrust review, similar approaches could be used for online messaging services, for instance, to overcome the advantages in network benefits that the larger services have by enabling smaller services to access them.

These approaches all entail a number of risks. Not just in terms of the security and privacy of any data that is transferred or shared, but also in adapting competition policy to the Internet space while adhering to its underlying goals and principles. Many services are free to consumers; others sell services at low prices. The services are popular, innovation is high, and quality continues to increase. Harms to competitors today, or in future services, can have a long-term impact on choice and innovation. However, they must be addressed in ways that enhance overall economic welfare, including for the companies that have succeeded so well in providing the online services— once unimaginable—that many of us could not do without.[27]

Conclusion

Concentration is common in the digital age, in no small part because of network effects on the demand side and economies of scale on the supply side. Nonetheless, successful companies have built their market position on the back of innovative services that meet, or even create, consumer demands. However, there is a question about the Internet companies and the durability of their market position. While there have already been competition reviews of some companies, there are significant questions regarding what comes next.

In the short run—that is, with a static outlook—the question relates to assessing and addressing market power. Europe has already taken a few actions against some large companies, while the United States has held back for the most part. In the longer run—that is, with a dynamic outlook—one wonders whether creative destruction is effectively altered as a result of the accumulation of data. In other words, is the data that is being gathered today going to be relevant for tomorrow's services? And if so, will it make it harder for new companies to enter the market tomorrow? Should that change the public policy approach today?

The ICT industry, from its inception, has been marked by innovative companies that have grown large but then have been subject to creative destruction. In many cases, the large companies have been subject to competition policy reviews, which directly or indirect constrained their actions, but ultimately new companies emerged, offering different products or services. Perhaps the key question for policy makers is whether this time is different—whether the data that companies have provides the bridge to the future that previous companies did not have.

Free services generate a virtuous circle for data gathering. Users try the services because they are free, often generating network effects and economies of scale for the companies, which increases the number of users. As the companies grow, they innovate or acquire their way into new free services, which generate further amounts of data. This data then helps with the machine learning needed to move into new future services. We will return to this question in chapter 9, looking at the future of the Internet.

8   The Digital Divide

Human potential is the only limitless resource we have in this world.
—Carly Fiorina

In the weeks leading up to the opening of the Apple App Store in July 2008, a young Kenyan by the name of Wilfred Mworia created an app to highlight events in Nairobi. The only hitch was that the iPhone didn't work in Nairobi then—and even if it had, he did not have one. No problem. He developed the app with a simulator, which is software that acts like an iPhone but runs on a computer; it is meant to be part of the development process, not the whole process. He noted that even without the iPhone, "I can still have a world market for my work."[1] Mworia identified an opportunity and took action, but he faced difficulties others did not have.

I have done a significant amount of policy work in Africa for governments, the World Bank, and companies. And this story always reminds me of the urgency of closing the digital divide to provide equal opportunity for all. While this chapter focuses for the most part on Africa, given the lag in many countries and my experience there, the lessons here resonate for other developing countries in Latin America and Asia.

Everyone likes free access, but it can be a game changer in developing countries. Open standards lower the cost of developing Internet-enabled networks and online services. Unmetered Internet provides access without needing to moderate usage based on affordability. And free online services can provide connections to friends and family, entertainment, education, and job opportunities.

The results can leapfrog many aspects of development. That is commonly said of mobile networks, which leapfrogged the development of fixed telephone networks in developing countries. But the concept applies to online services as well. Where banks are few and far between, mobile money can allow users to save and spend; where vocational training is a pipe dream, online courses can step in; where families are separated, they can communicate cheaply and send remittances; where government resources are stretched, services can be offered online.

Getting to free is not cheap, however. Networks have to be built and connected internationally to deliver the Internet traffic. The cost of providing Internet access has to be driven down to be affordable for public hot spots or private subscribers. Devices can entail a significant investment for many, and even the costs to charge the devices can be formidable where there is no electric grid. And then services have to be offered or developed, and content has to be provided, in the correct language, with local relevance, and with sufficient advertising or other monetary support.

The Mobile Difference

It is impossible to overstate the impact of mobile Internet access in developing countries. For users in developed countries such as Switzerland, a smartphone seems like the physical embodiment of the Internet age, a window to the online world. However, for much of the time on our phones we are using Wi-Fi attached to a fixed broadband network, whether at home, in the office, at the airport, or in a café.

Fixed networks have near universal coverage in most, if not all, developed countries, and the networks are all upgraded to offer broadband. As the Internet grows in popularity, increasingly fiber optics are being deployed in the network, up to the house, providing us with ever-higher speeds. A Wi-Fi connection to these fixed-line connections enables us to access the Internet anywhere in or around our residences conveniently, without cables, using a variety of devices. The same is true for our offices and many places in between.

The devices can include our computers, but also our smartphones, which will switch automatically from the mobile network to Wi-Fi when you get in range. Indeed, to save on mobile data usage and capacity, we can set our phones to perform certain functions, such as updates, only when on Wi-Fi. Even traditional phone calls can default to Wi-Fi calling instead of a mobile signal. This is called *offloading*, whereby the mobile networks put traffic through Wi-Fi; according to Cisco Systems, over 50 percent of mobile traffic is offloaded.

For many of us in developed markets, it is possible that relatively little of importance is done when out of range of Wi-Fi. It is hard to think of many places where one can sit and engage online that do not have access to Wi-Fi. Otherwise, standing, walking, riding, we are often using preloaded apps and content and do not need to be online. That is clearly not everywhere, and not always, of course. But if you have ever tried to save on data roaming costs by relying on Wi-Fi when in a foreign country, access can be fairly continual, from airport hotspots on arrival, to the hotel, restaurants and cafés, offices, and public hotspots.

On the other hand, most, if not all, developing countries did not have a significant fixed network when the Internet began to grow. Fixed telephony was a natural monopoly, provided by either the state or a regulated company, with many of the enjoyments of the quiet life of a monopolist discussed in the previous chapter. The cost of deploying a wire to an establishment was high, quality was not always good, and there was still significant unmet demand. In Tanzania, for instance, in the 1990s, more people were waiting for a fixed line than those who already had one.[2]

The challenge with the fixed lines is that each residence needs a separate copper line connecting it all the way to the telecom switch. Mobile technology did away with this dilemma. Putting up one tower with a mobile transmitter could serve an entire neighborhood. That tower did not even need to be served by any wires: a diesel generator could provide power, and the traffic could be sent to the tower with wireless technology. That is not ideal, but it works.

As a result, mobile telephony was not ever considered a natural monopoly: competition was often introduced from the start, with many countries having at least three providers. Mobile operators needed access to spectrum over which to send their signals, but there was so much demand from operators that governments soon discovered that they could auction spectrum licenses for significant revenues, which also avoided some of the inefficiencies when spectrum was assigned to companies based on administrative processes. And these operators can all share access to the towers and the corresponding operational costs to make it cheaper to deploy networks.

Of course, many other elements needed to be provided, but they could be upgraded as demand grew. As mobile traffic increased with broadband usage, fiber connectivity replaced wireless technology for backhaul from mobile towers to the rest of the Internet. International connections were first done with satellite, and then submarine cables began circling continents, bringing fast, cheaper connections. And the mobile technology itself keeps being upgraded, from the first and second generation (2G) for voice, to 3G, which was the first offering full Internet access, to 4G, with 5G emerging.

Updating from a voice network to the mobile Internet costs a fraction of the cost of deploying the network in the first place. In fact, the economics of supplying mobile Internet are so favorable compared with fixed that there was a complete flip between supply and demand. Where there was more demand than could be met in most countries using fixed lines ten or fifteen years ago, now with mobile, there is more supply than is being used. With fixed, you would only serve houses on the waiting list; with mobile, everyone in the neighborhood gets the signal, but not everyone will subscribe.

Demand-Side Switch

Given the increase in supply from mobile Internet, it is important to focus on demand for Internet to make sure that everyone who *can* go online *does* go online. Take, for instance, Rwanda, where President Paul Kagame led the fight to end the genocide over twenty years ago and forged a lasting peace. He has charted a path of using ICT to move the country from its agrarian base to a knowledge-based economy, with a series of five-year plans as part of the Vision 2020 initiative. To get there more rapidly, mobile Internet was the only solution. By the end of 2019, there were only 11,393 fixed telephone subscriptions in the country, out of a population of just over twelve million, and even less fixed broadband.

Mobile was the only alternative for real widespread connectivity, and the mobile network for voice was quickly built out to cover virtually the entire population, with about eighty mobile voice subscriptions per one hundred inhabitants today. In addition, virtually the entire country is covered by mobile Internet, with nearly 100 percent able to receive a 4G signal.

Yet in Rwanda, only just over 17 percent of the people are mobile broadband subscribers as of the end of 2018.[3] Note in addition that some people may have multiple subscriptions—for instance, for work and home—so the actual population penetration is likely to be below 17 percent. Note also that a further 43 percent of the population has a mobile Internet subscription that is prebroadband, using an older technology (EDGE and GPRS), but still able to access the Internet.

The same dynamic is true to different degrees in other countries, many of which have effectively 100 percent mobile broadband coverage. So what is holding people back? At one level, that is a difficult question to answer. There are not many surveys of non-Internet users, certainly compared with surveys of Internet users, for the simple reason that by definition nonusers cannot be easily reached over the Internet; they must be surveyed in person. From countries where such surveys do take place, a few trends emerge.[4]

First, as one might suspect, cost is an issue. The cost of not just monthly access but also the smart device can be a significant constraint. The ITU and UNESCO Broadband Commission for Sustainable Development advocates a target for entry-level broadband packages to cost less than 2 percent of average income in all countries by 2025; more than eighty countries still have not reached that level for mobile broadband.[5] In some countries, it is still a double-digit percent of average income, such as the Democratic Republic of Congo, where it is 33 percent of income.[6] But even 2 percent of income is a good amount of money, particularly for just 1 GB of data per month, which may not be enough to allow meaningful access to a broad range of content and services.

With 1 GB, you could send about ten thousand emails: not bad if that's all you do, but if you like music, 1 GB is equivalent to 160 songs from Spotify.[7] Average mobile usage in the United States is under 10 GB per month, but average residential fixed broadband usage is 268 GB! And that does not count usage at work. So cost is clearly a limiting factor in developing countries. But other factors play a large role, as noted in the following quote from Kofi Annan, then secretary general of the United Nations, under whose leadership the World Summit on the Information Society was convened in 2003: "The so-called digital divide is actually several gaps in one. There is a technological divide—great gaps in infrastructure. There is a content divide. A lot of web-based information is simply not relevant to the real needs of people. … There is a commercial divide. E-commerce is linking some countries and companies ever more closely together. But others run the risk of further marginalization."[8]

As hard as it may be to believe, lack of interest in the Internet is a significant issue driving the digital divide. How could everyone not find the

Internet indispensable? For many, who can hardly make it through a conversation, a meal, a class, or, unfortunately, even a drive without a quick peek at the screen, there is no lack of interesting content. In fact, there is so much content that it is our time and attention that are scarce. Dip a toe into YouTube and you can quickly submerge. But what any one of us finds interesting is not universally interesting.

This can come down to two overlapping issues—language and relevance. More than 50 percent of web pages are in English, and no other language even approaches 10 percent.[9] On the other hand, only about 20 percent of the world speaks English, and for most it is a second language. But even if someone speaks English, the content may not be relevant. For instance, most of the content I interact with on the Internet is very specific to my context—for news, political commentary, for researching this book, or for catching the local bus. And for looking at English Premier League football results, which to be fair is slightly more universal.

If you don't speak English, then there is a further divide between languages that use the same alphabet and those that do not. Until recently, domain names (www.example.com) and email addresses (michael@example.com) had to basically use the English alphabet—not even French with accents and other characters. Owing to some hard work by ICANN, and the Universal Acceptance Steering Group (UASG), internationalized domain names are beginning to catch on, and IETF is working on standards for using these in email addresses. That itself benefits a huge swath of Internet users, and potential users, in Asia, the Middle East, and elsewhere.

One large source of content that is locally relevant and in the right language is posts and messages in social media from friends, relatives, and colleagues. But of course, this requires that a critical mass is also using social media, which is not always the case. Network effects work both ways: if a lot of people you know are using something, it makes it irresistible; if no one is using it, it is very resistible. But it can be a strong magnet for going online and being able to communicate and keep in touch for free. It is such a magnet that some people who are using Facebook do not even realize that they are using the Internet.[10]

The final significant reason people do not go online is a lack of digital skills. It can seem daunting to go online and learn how to navigate the web, send emails, and use apps. That is particularly true for those with limited or no literacy. Other, less common reasons for not going online include worries about privacy and security, and avoiding dangerous content.[11]

These issues together are critical. A significant milestone of 50 percent of the world population online was passed recently. We should definitely celebrate that. However, that of course leaves the other 50 percent—and to make things worse, adoption rates have slowed down significantly. Today in Africa, which has the lowest regional Internet penetration levels, annual growth in the number of users is below 10 percent, and for areas with higher penetration rates, the growth rate is even lower.

The previous technology to experience fast and widespread growth levels was mobile voice. Mobile voice well exceeds Internet penetration, and growth rates for mobile phones slowed much later in the adoption cycle than for Internet adoption. This can be relatively easily explained by comparing the characteristics of mobile voice with the four factors that are getting in the way of Internet adoption.

First, availability of mobile voice is historically higher than mobile broadband because mobile voice networks are not always fully updated to mobile broadband until there is demand. Costs for having phone service are lower than for mobile Internet subscriptions; a basic phone for voice is much cheaper than a smartphone, while mobile data is an additional cost. Also, for a mobile phone, content is not an issue; they are used to call and text, so all content is communications. And they are also much easier to use than the Internet once one knows how to dial the phone.

Solutions

As the Internet began to emerge, mobile broadband did not exist, and public policy first focused on infrastructure, particularly in those countries where the fixed network was falling short. The gap was clearly on the supply side of the market. In addition to not having enough fixed network, there was little backbone in many countries and little international connectivity between countries.

Significant work went into addressing these challenges, not just by national governments, but also regional organizations and international governmental organizations such as the World Bank. These groups helped develop policies to reform the telecom sector by introducing competition and then helped develop infrastructure. Most recently, Internet companies, including Facebook and Google, have been investing in infrastructure in developing countries, including submarine cables to bring traffic there and partnerships with operators to assist with developing networks within countries.

Now that the focus has shifted to the demand side as a result of mobile broadband availability, the solutions are significantly different. As we consider these solutions, it helps divide people into three broad groups: First, those who could not go online, even if they wanted to, because of a lack of Internet-enabled networks where they live or work. Second, those who do have access to the Internet, if they wanted it, but have not yet chosen to go online, for the reasons given earlier. And finally, those who already are online. We will not focus significantly on the last group, other than to note that the solutions for the previous groups will also be of benefit to the latter group: Who wouldn't want more affordable services, more relevant content, and easier-to-use devices?

Availability

One of the many remarkable facts about the Internet is that it predominantly runs over privately funded infrastructure. The mobile towers, the backhaul connections from the towers to Internet backbones, network equipment, and Internet backbone are almost all exclusively or predominantly funded through private investment—much of it first to provide mobile voice, which was then upgraded to provide mobile Internet. Where there is no mobile voice network to upgrade, after this many years, it is likely because it is uneconomical to build there, and it is important to identify the reason for that.

First, on the supply side, it may be uneconomical in certain parts of a country because the terrain is challenging and the remaining communities are hard to reach. Where it is mountainous, on an island, or frozen half the year, the cost of deploying the network and maintaining it can be significant. Second, on the demand side, the returns from deployment may be quite low if the community reached is small, dispersed, or low-income. Where these two factors overlap—high costs and low demand—it should be no surprise that there is no commercial network.

In this case, governments have a number of options before opening their own purses, which may be the final outcome. First, they can remove any possible barriers to the private sector addressing the remaining locations to make it as economical as possible; second, they can take actions to help promote new investment.

There can be any number of barriers to deploying mobile networks in remote areas. Following the path from the city outward, often it is very expensive to have access to the rights of way needed to build the backhaul or put up the towers. Without an electric grid, the cost of operating diesel generators to power the networks is also high. And there may be high costs for importing the necessary equipment and barriers to investors. These issues can be resolved by removing the barriers to increase private investment.

To further promote deployment, governments can also help stimulate investment. For instance, instead of auctioning off spectrum at the highest possible prices to maximize government revenues, the governments can include coverage requirements in the licenses. This will lower the value of the spectrum in the auctions, but the outcome may be more efficient. The operators will lower what they pay for spectrum because of the need to meet the coverage requirements but may invest that money much more efficiently in the new coverage than the government would have.

The government can also promote new business plans, technologies, and investment. Approaches such as enabling operators to share towers, or even spectrums, can lower the cost of investment. Allowing new approaches such as Alphabet's Project Loon may also work, by using balloons to beam down the signals from above rather than building the network over hard-to-reach terrain. It is being used in Kenya to provide rural access and was used in Puerto Rico to provide emergency connectivity after Hurricane Maria. And providing community access points or letting communities build their own networks is also useful to increase deployment.

If all else fails, the government may have to provide financial assistance. This could involve building infrastructure, such as extending a backbone to reach the remote areas and making it available to all the mobile operators at an affordable cost. This could also involve providing subsidies so that services can become affordable for residents of the unserved areas.

The money could be funded from general tax revenues, or it could be funded from the revenues of the providers themselves. Often a tax is levied on licensed telecommunications operators to create a universal service fund (USF), which is used to fund projects to increase the deployment of network. Often the telecommunications operators themselves are contracted to build the networks with the USF, which is effectively redirected from their own revenues.

Affordability

Affordability is impacted by a number of factors. First, though mobile services are basically a necessity to many, a number of governments tax the services as if they were luxuries. That can include taxes on all aspect of mobile ownership—handsets, services, and even a tax on activating service in some countries, all on top of general taxes. In some countries, taxes exceed 30 percent of the cost of mobile ownership, and this does not include additional taxes on mobile operators.[12] Given the benefits of Internet usage, these higher taxes can be counterproductive in terms of growing—and then taxing—the new digital economy.

It is understandably hard for governments to give up sure revenue today in favor of likely revenue tomorrow. Lowering the tax on Internet access would increase usage, which should increase economic benefits, which then might be taxed—but that is a hard trade-off for many politicians to make. Sometimes, though, the evidence of the negative effect of taxes presents itself quickly. A few countries have started to impose taxes on social media, such as Uganda—partly to raise revenues and partly to reduce perceived negative social impacts.

You may reasonably ask how it is possible to impose a tax on a service that is free to users. For a free service, you can't charge a percent of the cost, as with many sales taxes, and of course companies such as Facebook have no means in place to charge the tax because they are not charging for their services. Instead, the mobile operators in Uganda were asked to collect the money and block access to social media sites for any subscriber who did not pay.

As noted in the introduction, free is a special price. If something is free and you impose a charge of even one cent, it shifts the whole perception, and demand can fall a lot. Indeed, in the first three months after the tax in Uganda, the number of Internet subscribers fell by 15 percent, reducing taxes from Internet subscriptions and lowering the expected revenues from taxing the social media, not to mention the impact of lower usage on students, businesses, and others who used social media and had to decide whether to pay the tax.[13] To be fair, while the social media tax in Uganda was the equivalent of USD 0.05 per day, Internet access was already unaffordable to many—the decrease in usage was based on not just the changed perception, but also the changed affordability.

Internet access also faces significant intrinsic costs. To start, think about how our Internet usage has changed over time. Early Internet use was largely text-based, for emails and file transfers, and then as the World Wide Web rolled out, for accessing information—all at relatively low traffic volumes. As discussed, this fit well with the prevailing dial-up technology at the time and would not overly tax capacity today.

Soon, however, text gave way to multimedia websites, and in particular video became available. Video requires a lot of bandwidth, and it soon became the majority of Internet traffic and one of the main sources of growth. Within overall Internet traffic, which itself is multiplying, the share of video traffic is growing to over 70 percent of the total. In the United States, during prime time, Netflix alone accounts for over 30 percent of all traffic, as users move from traditional television to streaming videos.

Given the bandwidth of video, it can cause significant congestion, which slows down transmissions. It can also cost a fair amount to access—particularly if it is accessed across borders, more so across oceans. That is partly because of the distance and partly because there are few economies of scale given the relatively low traffic quantities.

As noted in chapter 3, ISPs purchase Internet transit according to the capacity. For instance, one megabit per second (Mbps) of wholesale Internet access can be purchased in some developing countries for USD 200 or more per month. This megabit per second of international traffic might be spread over fifty or more users, allowing them to surf the Internet at very low speeds. To be clear, that would cost four dollars per user to share 1 Mbps of international traffic, although this is definitely on the high end of countries. The faster the speeds sold to users, who are unlikely to demand just 1 Mbps, the higher the cost.

On the other hand, in some hubs in Europe or the United States, the price of wholesale Internet access might be as low as USD 0.30 per megabit per second (if purchased in bulk). In other words, the users in the United States and Europe get noticeably faster download speeds at a fraction of the cost.

The problem is compounded by the fact that in some developing countries, most content is accessed overseas. For instance, up to 80 percent of content accessed in a number of sub-Saharan African countries is hosted outside the continent, mostly in Europe. Likewise, in Latin America a significant amount of the traffic comes from the United States, and in developing Asia the traffic comes from the large hubs of the developed Asia-Pacific region, such as Hong Kong and Singapore. This includes, by the way, websites that were created locally for local audiences but are hosted abroad, typically to save a bit of money. As a result, though, ISPs in those countries face high costs for providing access to the content that sits abroad, which they pass on to their subscribers.

There are solutions, and they have the happy property that not only do they lower the cost of accessing the Internet, but they also increase the quality. Using the international links is the bottleneck: it has a high cost, and because it has a high cost too little is bought, so it is often congested. Therefore, the key is to localize traffic within the country as much as possible. The first issue to be addressed is that the ISPs were using their international links to exchange traffic with each other, in the same country. This exchange is often called *tromboning* because the content leaves the country and returns according to the shape of the musical instrument.

By way of background, it was inefficient for ISPs to connect with each other directly. Each ISP would have to arrange individual lines to connect to every other one, which is a costly spider web of connections. Instead, the industry developed the concept of *Internet exchange points* (IXPs). In an IXP would sit a switch, and each ISP had a point of presence there and could connect to each other ISP through that switch or directly.[14] The result was that each ISP needed only one line to connect to the IXP and then could connect to all the other ISPs through the IXP.

This concept of common exchange points developed in the United States and was so efficient that many European ISPs exchanged their traffic through the United States in the early days of the Internet. This traffic effectively went from an ISP in the United Kingdom, for instance, to a large exchange on the East Coast of the United States, and then to a different ISP in the United Kingdom. Eventually, IXPs were developed in Europe, which saved the cost of tromboning traffic through the United States and also made the Internet work faster—in technical terms, it reduced the *latency*—by not sending it under the ocean and back.

Now, today, many ISPs in developing countries are exchanging their traffic at IXPs in the United States or Europe, which is also not efficient. As a result, IXPs are increasingly being deployed in every country. For instance, an early IXP—called KIXP—was put in place in 2000 in Nairobi. It turned out that very quickly 30 percent of the total traffic in Kenya could be exchanged that way, and it significantly lowered the latency—delay—in exchanging the traffic: from up to two seconds, which on the Internet is an eternity, to a level that is barely perceptible. At the same time, it significantly lowered the cost of bandwidth by relying less on international transit.[15] An IXP is one of the most effective and efficient ways to lower costs and improve the quality of the Internet in a country, and efforts are ongoing to make sure that every country has at least one.[16]

With the rise of content, particularly videos, IXPs evolved from enabling connections between ISPs to enabling access to content. As the Internet globalized and as content moved from text to videos, providers started to move their content closer to users to save on the cost and time of delivering it across oceans and continents each time someone had a request. Data centers began to arise around the world, and specialized companies called content-delivery networks (CDNs) began to store popular content in caches connected to IXPs so that it could be delivered closer to the end users.

A *cache* stores popular content closer to users. Content can be pushed into the cache by the CDN, anticipating that it will be popular, or can be pulled into the cache by the first user who asks for it. Either way, the next time someone nearby asks for it, it does not need to be brought again from its original location; it can be served from the cache. Eventually it will make its way to caches throughout the world.

Using a CDN can lower the latency for delivering the content, making it more responsive to users, and also reduce the need for using international networks to deliver the traffic. A number of CDNs are independent, while some of the largest Internet content companies are developing their own CDNs, including Google, Facebook, and Netflix. In many countries, the IXP provides a critical stepping-stone to providing a cache in the country by connecting the cache to the ISPs in the country. As demand grows in a region, eventually data centers will be built closer, to house the content and services closer to the users.

It turns out that attracting a data center, and content to fill it, is a challenging issue, however—more so than putting together an IXP. Part of this has to do with costs, and part of it has to do with the nature of content and the issue of intermediary liability for content that is not acceptable in a particular country. Google executives, for instance, have been convicted in Italy over a YouTube video posted by users. The executives were not based in Italy and not extradited, and the sentence was suspended in any case. However, liability for content hosted locally can clearly play a factor going into other countries as well.[17] Assuming the legal issues can be overcome, there are other issues.

With respect to costs, there is an economic externality that is difficult to solve. Given the scale of large data centers in hubs such as London, it is much cheaper for a content provider from an African country to host its content there than in data centers in its own country. On the other hand, it is the ISPs who pay more to collect the content in London. So in moving the content back home, the content provider would pay a bit more, while the ISP saves a fair amount of money. The content provider has little incentive to pay more to benefit the ISP—which is a classic economic externality, and one that is difficult to resolve.[18] The ISP could subsidize the local hosting for the content provider to save on international transit. That is particularly true when the ISP also owns a data center and thus could provide a cross subsidy, but I am not aware of a situation in which that has occurred.

The one swing factor is the quality of access. When the content is hosted locally, it loads much faster—particularly large files, such as videos. That is partly because there is less distance, so by the laws of physics, it takes less time to arrive (even over high-speed fiber connections) and the transmission also avoids expensive congested international lines. Local capacity is much cheaper and thus less prone to congestion. When content loads faster, it is used more often, which is good for content and a good reason to host it locally.[19] This creates demand for data centers and hopefully launches a virtuous cycle of growth.

Relevant Content

Ultimately, it is important not just to create a local home for content and make it attractive to use, but also to create local content to fill the home. To attract new users and increase usage, the content should be locally relevant, in a locally relevant language, and meet gaps in demand. There are four potential sources for such content, all of which should be encouraged.

First, and perhaps easiest, is user-generated content. Using existing platforms such as Facebook, WhatsApp, YouTube, and others, users can communicate with one another, post updates on themselves, and create content to share. Likewise, Wikipedia allows the development of content of local relevance in the local language. However, after English, availability tails off quickly; while there are almost six million Wikipedia articles in English, there are just fifty thousand in Swahili, and many languages have far fewer.[20]

Second, and related, is to make existing international content and services available locally. This can include Google Search, Netflix, Spotify, mail services, and many, many, others. They are already popular, many have network effects, and they are relatively easy to supply. Sometimes content needs to be translated into local languages, at least the instructions, and in other cases the local rights must be secured for content such as videos, which is not always trivial. But Netflix, for instance, has a virtually global offering covering 190 countries, and Google Search is now available in 149 languages.[21] Indeed, automatic translation is getting more and more powerful with artificial intelligence (AI) and will help localize international content.

Third is developing a new source of content: government services. These are obviously very relevant and useful as a means for citizens to interact with their government in an efficient manner. Popular services include birth registrations, health and educational services, and appointments, while other services, such as income tax filing, may be less popular but nevertheless efficient to do online. And another large, but often less visible, segment is government-to-business services, such as for clearing customs and business applications. In addition, by creating online services, governments can stimulate the entire ecosystem, acting as a strong anchor tenant for a new data center, a large customer of connectivity, and a generator of local ICT jobs.

Last is a category with perhaps the greatest opportunity and the greatest challenges, and that is local entrepreneurs innovating new services that meet local needs. I would guess that no one in Silicon Valley ever pondered how to make life easier for Kenyan dairy farmers. It's not to say they would not be concerned about their challenges, but it would not occur to them. But a farmer in Kenya did think about this dilemma, and she created the iCow app to help other farmers manage their herds.[22] Other locally developed services, such as Twiga, help food stalls in Nairobi manage their stocks and lower costs.

The Internet itself can provide many means to help entrepreneurs. Entrepreneurs can help train themselves online and reach out to potential collaborators and employees, and there are even platforms to connect entrepreneurs to mentors.[23] Money can be raised through crowdfunding services such as Kickstarter or Indiegogo—if such services work in the country, as discussed ahead. And then, of course, the finished product can be sold through the Internet, allowing entrepreneurs to tap into a local, national, or global market.

However, there are still challenges. Take simply the issue of payments. In many developing countries, people are unbanked, although mobile money services are spreading to enable online payments. But they have not spread fast enough. A ride-hailing app called Yassir in Algeria uses cash, rather than the automatic payments familiar with Uber. And many people are more comfortable with cash on delivery, whereby they order something online and pay when it is delivered, and they can see what they are getting. This is a trust issue and adds a significant cost and risk to e-commerce businesses in many countries.

More generally, imagine you write an app for Google Play, to be used with Android smartphones, which in most developing countries are the most popular phones. In almost forty countries, it is not possible for the developer to register a merchant account, meaning that they cannot sell their apps or receive revenues from advertising for free apps, in their own country or internationally.[24] This is a general banking issue, related to compliance with rules about knowing customers and preventing money laundering and other ills; it is not specific to Google; and the number of countries affected is falling. Yet in those countries, it can hinder the ability to successfully innovate.

Governments can help in a number of ways. Governments can facilitate digital financial services such as mobile money to help with payments; they can help support venture capital funds and encourage crowdfunding; they can support tech hubs where entrepreneurs can gather, support each other, and meet potential funders or employees. And they can increase trust by issuing digital identification so that people can authenticate themselves online, and create laws around privacy and security and consumer protection to promote online sales.

Crowdfunding is an interesting twist, taking advantage of the Internet to raise funds among a potentially global pool of individual funders. Often, the reward to the funder is in the form of the product or service being funded—but a perhaps even more interesting form is equity crowdfunding, where the funder receives shares in the firm and thus might help fund promising firms even if they are not personally interested in the product or service (which is often the case with investors), with the possibility of a higher return. However, with equities involved, the crowdfunding services may be subject to financial regulations that can limit or prevent their usage.

But the final piece is the spark of creativity to come up with the idea, the drive to turn the inspiration into innovation, and the wherewithal to turn the innovation into income. It is not as straightforward as any of the other pieces of the puzzle, such as building a new data center, for which the results of investment are more linear and foreseeable. But the more people are encouraged to try to innovate, and the more support they receive, the better the outcomes.

Digital Skills

Finally, digital skills are critical to bring users online and enable them to engage in a meaningful way. These skills should encompass not just the basics of going online and using a browser or apps, but also being able to create content and, for budding entrepreneurs, create services. Literacy is of course an important precursor, although with new touchscreen devices, some functions can be performed without advanced literacy. Voice messages and voice-to-text dictation also help significantly with literacy challenges for users. WhatsApp, for instance, easily allows users to record a message to send.

An e-Skills Pyramid was developed in a report for the European Commission to describe the varying levels of digital skills needed to participate in the digital economy at various levels. At the base are user skills, which cover digital literacy—namely, the ability to go online and access the Internet at a good comfort level. Above that level are practitioner skills, required to work on developing and supporting ICT systems, and at the top are e-business skills, to establish and grow new businesses, among other things.[25] A simple way to think about it is that everyone should be able to use tools such as Google effectively; a smaller group needs to be able to work at Google, developing its services; and two Stanford students at the top of the pyramid created the idea and built it into a company.

A wide variety of organizations are helping with digital skills programs, including governments through schools and other programs, nonprofits providing materials and trainers, and universities and companies with online training and courses. And there are a wide variety of means, including using the devices to provide the training on how to use the devices, with tutorials that take advantage of the touch screens to teach how to proceed. Other means include training a group of trainers from the targeted communities, who in turn go out and train others.

As with entrepreneurship, there is no one clear path to success in developing digital skills, creativity is required, and there is significant experimentation in trying new ideas. The dividends are clear, however, because digital skills are the bridge between having Internet access on the one hand and using content and services on the other. With no ability or confidence to go online, all other work is for naught and opportunities lie fallow.

T-Shaped Policy

To address the supply side and the demand side of Internet access and adoption, a T-shaped public policy is required. The T-shaped concept became popular in describing desirable employees, who increasingly need deep knowledge in one area (the vertical part of the T), but also must be able to make connections across other areas (the horizontal part of the T). Here, to develop a digital country, the government must have policy deep in telecoms, to foster the supply side, but also have broad policy across ministries, to develop the demand side.

When the bottleneck for getting users online was the fixed network, the locus of government policy was the ministry that encompassed telecommunications either on its own or with the rest of ICT, which would make the policy. When the incumbent was still owned by the government, the policy would be implemented directly. As the market began to liberalize, most countries developed an independent regulator of telecommunications, which was responsible for implementing telecom laws and government policy. This is necessary, but not sufficient, to develop the digital sector.

As a result of the increased importance of promoting the demand side to take advantage of widespread mobile broadband availability, the locus of regulation needs to shift from one focused primarily on the telecom ministry and regulator to one that brings in the rest of the government. The Ministry of Finance has the tools to increase affordability by lowering taxes and import duties. The Ministry of Finance is also likely to be required to pave the way for mobile money and the financial inclusion that results. The Ministry of Education can address digital skills, the Ministry of Health can address digital health services, the Ministry of Trade can address e-commerce issues, and so on.

This T-shaped policy can enable a continued focus on lowering the cost of deployment and filling in gaps for broadband, with a broader focus on content availability and creation.[26] This approach overall will help create a digital infrastructure as the foundation for the desired digital economy, while also spreading digital technologies throughout the economy.

Another broad policy to help promote digital development is to create a single digital market among like countries in a region. Think of the advantages that the United States has in terms of developing the Internet: a large, relatively homogenous market with harmonized laws, enabling scale economies and network effects. That is important for the operators deploying infrastructure, but perhaps even more so for entrepreneurs developing new content and services. Start-ups have a significant single market to start in, speaking the same language and with a shared background and culture, not to mention single set of laws and regulations, before beginning an international expansion.

One might argue that a big factor explaining the success in the United States is the relative wealth of the country, helpful both to be able to afford access and as an attractive market for online advertising. However, it is worth comparing the experiences of China and the European Union. China, in spite of a far lower per capita income, has a large unified market, resulting in companies such as Alibaba that are among the most valuable Internet companies—albeit its own market is protected from competition.

For the EU, on the other hand, despite higher per capita income, and a Digital Single Market initiative, which provides better access for individuals and businesses to digital goods and services across the EU countries, no European company is among the most valuable Internet companies worldwide. There can be many reasons for this, of course, but an inescapable one is language and culture, which are not unified, sometimes even within a country. Someone creating an Internet platform within any European country would quickly have to begin to translate and adapt it to the next country to build up scale, instead of focusing on building scale and learnings for its algorithms before making any international moves.

That said, the EU is clearly a more attractive market for innovation and investment with the digital single market than it would be without it, and other regions are beginning to explore similar groupings. For instance, a grouping of countries in East Africa already have a regional intergovernmental organization, the East Africa Community, and regional cooperation in telecommunications, such as removing roaming charges between the countries, upon which a broader single digital market could be built.[27] Likewise, the countries of the Association of Southeast Asian Nations (ASEAN) are working toward an economic community that would include a single digital market.[28]

Challenges

Of course, there are still significant challenges. Building out to remote areas, developing relevant local content, teaching people digital skills all take time, creativity, and resources. However, the trajectory is going in the right direction, albeit far too slowly for anyone's comfort. I do have several points to raise about the destination, however, which may fall short of more advanced economies.

First, I worry that the outcome will be more geared toward consumption than production. Mobile networks are geared toward mobile usage, not sitting in an office getting work done—although the technology is getting better, and when the fifth generation of mobile service (5G) arrives, it will rival many fixed network speeds. There can also be fixed wireless solutions, which work better for providing access in buildings than mobile networks. The bigger issue is the devices—smartphones and even tablets—being more geared toward consuming content and apps than toward creating them. There are enough issues with the cost of mobile phones without worrying about buying personal computers or advanced tablets for small businesses.

Second, with all the attention on individuals and bringing them online—as important as that is—small businesses seem to be afterthoughts at best. There has been relatively little study of how many businesses are online and what the barriers are to bring the rest of them online. Is it enough to bring individuals online, who can then integrate the Internet into their businesses, or is more needed? What are the requirements for devices, access, services, and training, and how best to meet them? There does not seem to be enough focus on driving these small to medium enterprises (SMEs) online and the economic opportunities that would result.

Even with the focus on increasing Internet access and promoting entrepreneurs, direct revenues from the Internet economy are likely to be no more than 10 percent of total GDP, at least for the near future, in most countries. Today in the United States, home of the largest and most valuable global Internet companies, the total digital economy by one measure is under 7 percent of GDP.[29] And because of the economies of scale of Internet companies, the job impacts are not enormous. The biggest bang comes from bringing the rest of the economy online, to benefit from productivity increases and access to new markets.

This is not a new phenomenon, either. General-purpose technologies such as electricity never themselves made up a large part of any economy; indeed, as utilities they were regulated to actually restrict their direct earnings. Instead, the greatest impact came from electrification. The same holds for oil, transportation, and other fundamental inputs, although of course many of the providers, particularly as trusts in the gilded age, were not shy about maximizing their own revenues. Any country would like to have the next Facebook or Google, of course—but far better to leverage the underlying Internet to the benefit of the rest of the economy. SMEs in particular cannot be left behind because in many countries they make up a large share of the economy.

Finally, with all the issues around data, including privacy and security concerns in developed countries, might developing countries fall prey to the opposite issue—too little data? Looking at sub-Saharan Africa, for instance, there is a bit of a data funnel. First, there are fewer Internet users than in other regions, so fewer people from whom to gather data. Second, not everyone online is online with a smartphone, so there is less of the rich data that such phones can gather, in combination with the fact that not everyone can purchase all apps, particularly paid or advertising-supported apps.

Part of this is an indicator, of course, of current demographics that make smartphones and Internet less affordable and attract less advertising. But it is also a precursor of a less data-rich future. With fewer smartphones, less information is gathered about movements and locations, among many things. With fewer online services used, there is less learning about preferences, and less tailoring of content and services to users. With fewer users, there is less advertising, and less incentive to offer content or create new services that could benefit from advertising. And there is less data available for machine learning.

For instance, consider voice assistants, such as Amazon Alexa, Google Assistant, and Apple Siri. Each can understand no more than a handful of languages, with Siri ahead at twenty-one languages.[30] If you have ever had the frustration of talking into a voice recognition system in the right language but with the wrong accent, then you know that it is not even enough to have English, for instance; it must be adapted to the English of each of a number of countries, and the voice assistants do now support a number of the most widely spoken dialects. Unfortunately, it almost goes without saying that the current offerings cover the major languages in the Americas, Europe, and Asia and have not started to touch the many languages of Africa.

These voice assistants use machine learning to develop, and without a large selection of users, there is little commercial incentive to learn a particular language—and little data to be able to train the voice assistant in any case. It will also be difficult for local companies to enter because they face the same commercial challenges, and in addition they would have to build up the basic algorithms and develop the devices to offer such services locally. This data divide is likely to get worse in the future, when data is used to train machines for AI, and the companies and countries with an advantage today will see that advantage multiplied tomorrow, as we will examine in the next chapter.

Conclusion

There are a number of studies of the economic impact of increased Internet access, which often take the form of illustrating how a 10 percent increase in Internet broadband penetration will increase GDP growth by 1 percent or more. An appreciable bump in GDP growth is nothing to minimize, of course. But that seems to be the floor of the benefits that will be brought by increased Internet access and meaningful use.

The first of these studies came from the World Bank, back when a number of countries had nowhere near 10 percent broadband penetration and Internet access was not fully on the radar of many countries.[31] Today, on the other hand, according to the Broadband Commission for Sustainable Development, over 160 countries in the world have national broadband plans to increase broadband, and many are part of broader digital development strategies to leapfrog ahead.[32]

I can remember a time when I was apartment hunting in Washington, DC, and buildings would boast of having fast Internet connections. Today, you would not benefit from such a boast—because such connections are expected—and indeed, raising the topic at all may raise suspicions. Not having broadband in a building, on the other hand, would be quite a negative.

It is always dangerous to compare the choices of individuals, households, or, in this case buildings to nations—but the point is that today, increasing Internet access in a country is no longer a bonus, or even an option: it is a necessity—in part because with the Internet, jobs and resources can migrate quickly to countries with better Internet access.

In any case, free services enabled by Internet access do not show up in GDP, or at least the direct revenues from using the services, and this leads to some potential measurement problems (setting aside other challenges with using GDP as a measure of the economy). If people stop making paid calls and instead use free online calls, which they have done, GDP will fall because there are fewer call revenues. Likewise with the use of other free services, some of which may replace paid services. But the benefits of free services are not directly showing up in GDP.[33]

In addition, and I say this as an economist, the economic benefits of the Internet are not the only benefit. Staying in touch with family and friends, feeling more connected to communities or creating one's own, having the chance to create and enjoy the creations of others—all are benefits of using the Internet that will not show up in any national accounting. These benefits could not have been better demonstrated than during the tragic (and ongoing) COVID-19 crisis. And yes, there is a flip side, but I firmly believe that the cup is more than half full.

And, finally, there is innovation and growth. When US professional basketball (the NBA) started to cast a global net to recruit players, it seemed as if Americans were suddenly short. In the first few years, the average height of the international players was over seven feet, a good four inches taller than the average US players.[34] Of course, there are far more people outside the United States than inside, so far more men over seven feet. They just needed access to the game and the lure of NBA stardom.

Wilfred Mworia created an app without an iPhone—something inconceivable to most of us—but imagine what he might have done with an iPhone and with an innovation ecosystem around him. As more people around the world find themselves in the right place at the right time to develop their human potential, as Bill Gates was, or Larry Page, Sergey Brin, Mark Zuckerberg, or Jack Ma, founder of Alibaba, then, inevitably, we will see the rise of new innovative companies outside the United States. It will look like the developed regions have fallen behind, but in fact it will just be the rest of the world catching up.

III **The Future of Free**

9 Trust the Future

An economist is an expert who will know tomorrow why the things he predicted yesterday didn't happen today.

—Evan Esar, American humorist

If you took the modern Internet back in time to an early Starbucks in the 1980s, handed the nearest patron an iPad, and explained what it could do, he or she would be amazed. You would explain that from the comfort of the café they could use the device to communicate with their work, pay some bills, check their portfolio, choose a new car, read the news, brush up on a foreign language, and on and on, and most people would be speechless. And then you tell them it is all free (except the car).

I would submit that no one's first reaction would be, "But what about my privacy, the security of my data, the potential power of the companies?" It took us many years and a few hard knocks to get to this reaction. It is not that we had any greater faith in human nature back then—not at all. In the mid-1980s, the United States was not more than ten years away from Watergate; the Bhopal gas leak killed thousands; the accident at Chernobyl had just occurred. A previous generation of tech companies with market power were in the news. And so on.

But these events occurred in the physical world. We understood that world and had institutions in place to address the problems. Not all perfect, again, but the Watergate burglars were caught and a president resigned. The antitrust case against IBM had just closed; the Bell System was broken up. It is quite a leap from there to the privacy, security, and market power issues being raised today. How could one have conceived of Cambridge Analytica back then; the virtual robbery of the Central Bank of Bangladesh, yielding almost $100 million; almost the entire adult population of Bulgaria's tax records breached and released; and that a few online companies started by students would quickly become among the most valuable in the world?

Knowing all this today, we understand the risks, yet continue to use the Internet. Chapter 5 addressed the privacy paradox—that people who express concerns about their privacy still put their personal information into websites. The bigger paradox is that people continue to use the Internet even after being directly or indirectly impacted by a security breach or privacy violation or despite concerns about the size of the company: that is a trust paradox.

The Trust Paradox

In 1996, eight climbers died trying to reach the summit of Mount Everest in one storm. A journalist, Jon Krakauer, had himself reached the summit that day while reporting for *Outside Magazine*, and he wrote a harrowing book, *Into Thin Air*, about the experience.[1] One would think the attention to the tragedy would have reduced demand to climb the mountain, but not at all. Instead, the widespread coverage of the tragedy let people know that almost anyone could join a commercial expedition if they could afford it, and demand went up, as did the number of deaths per climbing season.[2]

I thought about this story when researching the aftermath of the Ashley Madison data breach raised in chapter 6. Again, the website was meant to enable adultery, and thus privacy and security were supposed to be paramount. But they were nevertheless breached, and all thirty-seven million members were exposed. One would think that would put people off using Ashley Madison, but apparently the lesson some took from it was "There's a website for cheating? Sign me up!" It might be safer than climbing Mount Everest, after all. And now the service has more members than when it was breached—although to be fair, it has upped its security as well, or so it says.

That is largely true about other data breaches. Consumers might stop using a site, but I cannot think of an example of a company that has gone under as a result, and most thrive after a few years. That is true for Target, Home Depot, Uber, LinkedIn, and others that had large data breaches. And if people give up on those, they likely simply choose another similar site or service. That seems an extension of the privacy paradox, where we achieve comfort in numbers and become accustomed to the risks, even after the risks are realized.

However, what about the future? Many of the new services just around the corner will, if anything, have a greater privacy element, increase our need for security, and likely increase our reliance on large companies. That includes the Internet of Things, new financial technology (fintech) applications, healthcare (including genetic data), and wider use of AI.

One can, however, already feel some reticence to adopt some new technologies. Not everyone is interested in the idea of having a voice assistant whose role is to listen to what is being said. Even if you have one in your kitchen, would you put one in your bedroom? Self-driving cars are receiving a lot of attention, but would everyone get in one? Think about a trust curve, as in figure 9.1, that tracks individuals' trust levels against their willingness to use an Internet product or service: as trust increases, so does the willingness to use a particular service, and the converse as trust falls.

The trust curve may have a bend in it, however. At the current level of trust, individuals have a certain willingness to use a service. Of course, like almost everything, there are differences among individuals in their perception of trust, with some more forgiving and others more wary. But they may all react to changes in perceived trust levels in similar ways.

As trust levels fall based on new events, usage may not fall very much. There is a certain level of built-in comfort in numbers, and also an unwillingness to give up on existing products and services. For instance, there have been a number of stories about companies monitoring the speech

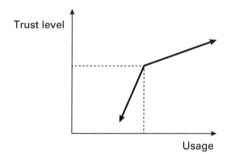

Figure 9.1
Trust curve. *Source:* Michael Kende, 2020.

coming in through their smart speaker offerings. But has anyone who heard those stories thrown away their smart speaker, or are they just a bit more careful about their speech? On the other hand, it may keep some already wary about buying one from doing so.

What about increases in perceived trust? It is possible that increases in trust levels will release a significant amount of demand, once people who are on the fence about a new product or service are convinced of the safety. This may clear the way particularly for these new technologies for which there is no comfort level yet, that we are not used to yet, and that we can clearly get by without so far.

This can help explain a paradox—that there seems to be relatively little impact on existing companies or services when there is a demonstrated breach of trust, but that an increase in trust could have a significant impact on demand and pave the way for new products and services.

The Future of Trust

We understand exponential growth through the story of the rice and the chessboard, in which the inventor of chess asked as his reward from the Emperor of China one grain of rice on the first square of the chessboard, two on the second, four on the third, and to keep doubling with each square. The King does not do the math forward, and of course runs out of rice far before the end of the board—in fact, the amount needed would cover the land on earth. The key is that the huge growth begins towards the second half of the board.[3]

Well, Moore's law predicted that computing power would double every eighteen to twenty-four months, and we have all seen that growth, with our smartphones having more power than the computers guiding the Apollo missions. And now we are probably in the second half of the chessboard and starting to see what is possible.[4] Here is a very high-level view of a few coming attractions. They will all be much more accepted, and acceptable, if they are trusted.

Big Data

As we all know by now, political polls in the run-up to elections can be wrong—sometimes in the level of support and sometimes in the outcome. That is understandable because polls are based on samples, and samples must be adjusted to reflect the population using statistical tools and probabilities. The vote is the final answer because it counts everyone who voted. If a pre-election poll could duplicate that—survey everyone who will vote—it would eliminate sampling bias and surprises. That is the promise of big data in a nutshell.

Taking a census is an early form of big data: rather than sampling the population, everyone is counted. In the United States, it is done every ten years and impacts congressional representation, among other critical government allocations. But the 1880 census took eight years to analyze, at which point the results were outdated. For the 1890 census, which would have taken even longer, the government contracted with an inventor of tabulating machines and punch cards, Herman Hollerith. That census took just a few months to analyze with his tabulators, and his company became IBM.[5]

With the decreasing cost of computer storage and the increasing number of sensors in the world, there is a rise in big data. And many of us, possibly without realizing it, have an incredibly sophisticated sensor with us at all times: our smartphones, which can generate big data. They are not just for communications, entertainment, and photos. They have barometers, accelerometers, a compass, GPS, and more. And crowdsourcing the data from these sensors shows the benefits of big data.

How does Google Maps know where there is traffic? It used to get traffic information from traffic sensors and cameras along the roads, but that was just a sample, on major roads, and not always in real time. Now, it gets info from all users who have turned on location functionality in their apps. It knows how many users are on any particular road and their speed, to deliver real-time traffic information: big data in action. Although the system can be hacked. An artist in Germany recently loaded ninety-nine smartphones in a cart and pulled them down the street, which quickly showed up as congested; as cars avoided his traffic jam, he soon had the road to himself.

A key question revolves around consent. If users are asked to consent to give their data and not everyone agrees, then the result will be a sample of data. It may also be biased toward those willing to give their consent. If all data is made available, the result is big data, which might yield much better insights. Trust is required to move toward the latter situation—trust in the provider of the data, trust in the user of the data, trust that the results will deliver corresponding benefits, and trust that the data will be protected.

Internet of Things

If you were in poor health, but high wealth, you could hire a nurse to help you monitor your health at home and make recommendations and work with your doctor. You might see his or her hovering presence as a barely acceptable intrusion on your personal privacy but would not need to worry about the nurse gossiping about your habits. Patient confidentiality is strictly protected, and the nurse would be fired for any indiscretions.

On the other hand, if you could not afford a nurse, would you buy or rent a device to monitor your health at home? One that would count your trips to the bathroom, monitor your sleep, detect if you fell, and possibly communicate with your doctor or hospital?[6] You would likely have the opposite concerns as with the nurse; you might prefer having the device watching you to a nurse doing so, but you would definitely worry more about the privacy of the data. If the data is shared or breached, it can spread much farther than a nurse's gossip, and there is little recourse today.

Voice assistants are now basically just a hands-free way of interacting with our apps, allowing us to search for information, play games, and order from Amazon. If you assume they are only listening when they are supposed to listen, then they may not add much personal information to our storehouses that would not have been entered on a device. But even if the vendor only listens when asked, what about a hacker? There are already reports of hackers taking over online baby monitors, creepily moving the camera to track a parent, and even talking to them.[7]

Other devices raise other security concerns. There are smart locks on doors that use a phone to enter, Wi-Fi-enabled security cameras, apps to open your car, and so on. All these devices can increase safety, as well as convenience, but at what cost? If a website can be hacked, what about your online door lock? Yes, of course, they can and have been hacked.

As IoT devices spread, they will introduce new vulnerabilities, not just for our privacy, but for our physical security. Early negative examples generally come from traditional manufacturers who add an Internet element to their existing products, seemingly without any idea about security. We already covered what happened when Jeep added Internet access to their entertainment system and security researchers took over a car. The list goes on.

A gun manufacturer created a self-aiming rifle: set the sight on the target and the rifle will aim itself. Setting aside the fundamental question of whether this is a good idea, a Wi-Fi connection was included so that it was possible to stream the shot. Anyone who made it to this point in the book might not be surprised that some hackers figured out how to remotely commandeer the rifle so that it aims at something other than where the sight is pointing; in other words, the owner would have no idea this is happening.

Fortunately, many of these early hacks have been done by the good guys—*white hats*—who report the vulnerabilities rather than exploit them. But that will not always be the case, and all manufacturers will be vulnerable if they are not careful. If trust does not develop, then uptake of a host of IoT products will be impacted throughout our homes, offices, and cities. Looking forward, trust in security will be one of the many hurdles that self-driving cars will have to overcome, not to mention self-flying passenger drones that are already in prototype.

Artificial Intelligence

Artificial intelligence is a very broad topic because of its possible implications, fueled in no small part by the depictions of robots in movies and books. It is worth noting that robots may be one outcome of artificial intelligence, but the other will be more hidden, with perhaps more widespread impacts, and that is embedding artificial intelligence into services.[8] For instance, allowing AI to make decisions on whether to put a suspect in pretrial detention, identify fraud in financial transactions, diagnose patients, or identify people on the streets using facial recognition.

Artificial intelligence can develop through machine learning, as we saw with the example of differentiating cats and dogs discussed earlier. More broadly, machines can be fed with training data to teach them how to make decisions—for instance, learning from known outcomes to decisions that were made. First, they analyze existing inputs that lead to particular outcomes and develop an algorithm to explain those outcomes. Then they use that information to predict outcomes and make decisions in new situations. And finally, they continue to iterate and learn from the outcomes to those decisions.

Think about the relatively simple example of movie recommendations we looked at earlier. One option is to analyze the preferences of all customers in terms of how they rate movies. Then a service can find customers similar to me based on my ratings and recommend movies that those customers like which I have not seen. At the end, it will find out if it is correct based on whether I finish the movie and what rating I give it, and it can adjust its algorithm and my recommendations going forward.

Of course, this depends on the data that the organization already has. With big data, it would have all preferences of all people who have watched movies and have a pretty good idea, but with a more limited sample it may not have enough people like me. This leads us to several general issues with machine learning, which can be much more serious than making a bad film recommendation.

First, as noted in chapter 7, those with existing datasets have an advantage— not just in the present, but also as a bridge to the future. It would be very hard to compete with Netflix without its dataset on movie ratings. Going forward, that algorithm could be applied to new services, or the underlying dataset could be applied to new services. Netflix already uses its data when choosing or developing its original content, starting with the TV series *House of Cards*, which its analysis was so sure would be a hit that it ordered two full seasons before any scene was shot, at a reported cost of over USD 100 million.[9]

Second is a broader trust issue. As AIs begin to make decisions in place of individuals, the key question is how they make these decisions? Was the AI trained on a broad enough dataset? There are already serious questions about facial-recognition software with respect to accuracy identifying women and people of color. And if there is bias in training data, then that bias will extend to the decision-making. Say you wanted to train a system to identify the best job candidates, to streamline the process and remove bias. But if the training data includes bias—such as too few women applying or being accepted—then the machine will learn the same bias and dismiss female candidates.[10]

Connected to that is the question of what is sometimes referred to as *algorithmic governance*. Can the system explain why a decision was made? What movies that I liked led it to recommend this one? What in my financial portfolio led an algorithm to deny me a loan? Without this level of clarity, there will be worries about bias in the training dataset or in the model itself. And it will be hard to determine what could be done to change the situation, what information was missing.

Finally, these three future trends will converge as big data is used to train AI in IoT devices. Those devices may be integrated into everyday things, from cars to refrigerators; they may be strewn throughout a smart city. They may be incorporated into the price of new purchases; they may offer services for free. Ways to help protect privacy are being explored. Because if the new tools are not trusted, if we do not learn from our current challenges with respect to privacy, security, and market power, then they will not be accepted or will magnify today's problems as they impact our lives and livelihoods.

Solutions

To some degree, the concerns we might have overlap; steps to improve privacy may increase security and lessen the extent or impact of market power. We will first examine the three concerns separately, and then step back and look at the combination.

Privacy

It is clear that privacy is being reset. The GDPR in Europe was implemented in 2018. California—home of many of the largest online companies—passed a similar bill in response to a citizen referendum, and there is talk of the US federal government following.[11] CEOs are taking note: Facebook's Mark Zuckerberg has been stressing privacy and the need to change Facebook services, Alphabet's Sundar Pichai wrote an opinion piece for the *New York Times* on privacy, and Apple's Tim Cook is stressing Apple's own privacy protections as a differentiator.[12]

None of this is surprising. Given the concerns about privacy, increased regulation was inevitable, and it in turn helps promote self-regulation to limit the extent of government regulation. Self-regulation can backfire, though, when the companies that ostensibly benefit from the lack of regulation end up going too far. For instance, deregulation leading effectively to self-regulation was an important element leading up to the 2008 financial crisis.

What is clear to me, however, is that increasing privacy will not necessarily increase trust. In other words, our privacy may improve as new laws and business models are put in place; since that is their goal, it should hopefully be their outcome. But it will only increase our level of trust if we have a tangible sense of a change for the better. And the key to that, I would argue, is to introduce transparency alongside simplicity.

Today, it is difficult to determine, maintain, confirm, and change one's level of privacy protection for any one service, much less a broad set of services. There are potentially two sets of privacy controls—one set for websites and one set for apps. Websites—Amazon, Facebook, Google, and so on—all have their own privacy policies for users and settings that users can choose. At the same time, the browsers users are using will also have their own privacy settings, which cover features across all websites—such as the use of cookies—or govern for particular websites what features of the computer can be accessed, such as location.

Likewise for apps. Each app can have its own privacy policy and settings, and there are settings in the device that allow or disallow access to each component of the device, such as, again, location, or the camera or the microphone. Of course, if you are using multiple devices, such settings have to be set per device. And if you are using the website on a computer and the app on a phone for the same underlying service, it can start to become complicated as there may be differences in how the settings are laid out.

In chapter 4, I discussed the location history feature on Apple devices. People are still surprised today when I lead them through to this function because they were not aware that it was introduced a number of years ago, and the default was set to be on. And it is not clear how the settings on the different services interact with the settings on the browsers or devices. Nor is it clear—or at least verifiable—where the data are kept or where they go.

One solution to complexity is to use a smart agent—artificial intelligence—to learn about our preferences and make the settings for us. An example is the Carnegie Mellon University Personalized Privacy Assistant Project, which would create "intelligent agents capable of learning the privacy preferences of their users over time, semi-automatically configuring many settings, and making many privacy decisions on their behalf." This agent could alert users about questionable practices and nudge them toward different choices.[13]

Such a privacy assistant works best, however, if users have knowledge about how their information is being shared. In one study at Carnegie Mellon, subjects were given a permission manager, and all but one participant used it to review and set their permissions on multiple apps. Then, however, the participants learned how their data was being shared. One person learned that their location had been shared 5,398 times with ten apps over the past fourteen days. These notifications led the participants to quickly further modify their permissions and adjust their privacy settings.[14]

Laws cannot mandate the use or choice of a privacy agent. However, they can include requirements on transparency, for instance, that give us confidence that a privacy agent is able to determine what information is shared. At the same time, companies are beginning to offer their own privacy solutions that make it easier to implement privacy settings. The result will not be that no information is shared, but rather that users have more confidence in what is shared and have more trust as a result.

Security

The early hacks of IoT devices are canaries in the coal mine, signaling what can happen when our physical world is Internet enabled. One could argue that this resulted from traditional manufacturers adding in Internet as a supplement, rather than building it in from the beginning. What happened to the Jeep might never happen to a fully self-driving car, designed and built by an Internet company.

But ultimately these security gaps illustrate that, to date, the lessons of Internet security have not made their way to IoT, where the results could be even worse. The market failures described in chapter 6 included externalities—the company being hacked did not bear the full cost of the hack—and asymmetric information—it was not possible for users to assess the security levels of online services. These market failures are already present in IoT.[15]

First, there are externalities. As noted earlier, after a Jeep was hijacked via its entertainment system, the company argued, successfully, that the security breach was not a defect—such as a bad airbag—for which they would have liability, but was rather an act of vandalism. In general, as software begins to be added to existing devices, there seems to be a trend that the exemption from liability typical of software applies, rather than the stricter liability that goes with traditional products such as automobiles, baby monitors, and others. When it is "just" software, that is one issue, and a debatable one given the privacy risks, but when it is a product such as a car, it is a serious safety issue. The same reasoning that led to product standards should apply to products connected to the Internet.

Second, there is asymmetric information: there would be no way for the average buyer to know the vulnerability of their new Jeep. After all, it admittedly took skilled professionals quite a bit of effort to pull off the hack. On the other hand, the same is true for a car airbag or the quality of the brakes. But there is no need for the average consumer to test those safety features; there are standards, and there are ratings. While the test for cybersafety is clearly not as straightforward as putting a crash test dummy in a car and directing it at a wall, there has to be some improvement to build trust.[16]

But ultimately, this lack of incentive to increase security expresses itself often in designs that are easy to hack—such as using a default password that many users do not change—and making it difficult to patch the security. Some devices cannot be patched at all; they might not be accessible, or they do not have the possibility to enable updates.[17] The Jeep was hacked remotely, but the patch had to be installed physically with a USB drive, which no doubt limited the number of installations; people who are afraid of toying with their familiar computers are unlikely to update the software on their car.

Principles or standards have been proposed to address these issues in order to build in security up front, rather than as an afterthought. These include making sure all IoT devices have certain security measures by default—for instance, not using default passwords, making the devices patchable, and making vendors commit to creating patches when needed.[18] We must learn our lessons from today, particularly when our safety is in the mix tomorrow.

Market Power
Earlier, we discussed the risk that large companies leverage their way into new markets horizontally—adding on a new service to complement an existing service—or vertically—into an upstream input or downstream market. That can also take place temporally. In other words, the companies may be able to leverage their existing market position into these new markets—not on the basis of necessarily having the best new service, which of course they might, but on the basis of having the best dataset upon which to train their AI.

In other words, data may be the bridge to the next generation of services, enabling the current holders to extend their advantages. Let's take Uber as a relatively simple example. If, or when, self-driving cars emerge, they could clearly rival Uber for taxi services by providing passenger rides with no driver, which may be safer and of lower cost even than Uber's current model.

Such a self-driving model could be a disruptive innovation allowing a new company or companies to displace Uber, but Uber itself is developing its own self-driving car.[19] In any competition between Uber and an entrant for self-driving taxi services, however, Uber has one perhaps insurmountable advantage—big data. Uber has three million drivers in six hundred cities across sixty-five countries, having provided a total of fifteen billion rides, all tracked and stored. In other words, Uber already knows where people are likely to be on a Friday evening in Mexico City, where they like to go, and information about routes and road conditions. Even with better cars and algorithms, an entrant might not be able to overcome the advantage with which Uber would start.

There must no doubt be other examples such as this one—but many of the innovative uses for this data are unknown today and in the current situation may be unknowable. Just as it was difficult to predict that a company such as Uber or Airbnb would be successful, there may be other new examples that may not be able to emerge or compete based on the big data gap that they face. There are several ways to address this.

First would be a competition policy approach. This would go to the crux of the issue and, if successful, enable some form of data sharing from the largest companies to the smaller ones, as discussed in chapter 7. However, this might require a more proactive role for competition policy than has been taken to date, with a view to increasing future competition rather than addressing current harms. This would require new laws to implement new standards or new standards for enforcement of existing laws. Either approach is likely to be slow.

Another approach would come from a privacy angle. The data portability section of the GDPR already reflects this; by allowing users to control their own data, they also give them agency to move to a competing company. More broadly, the idea would be that allowing data to be shared would increase consumer choice in other companies. It may allow consumers to choose companies with better privacy, but it may not make enough data available for new companies to emerge with new ideas. Other ideas for data sharing are explored in the next chapter.

The key is to ensure that future entry is possible to increase competition and innovation by removing entry barriers, with access to big data perhaps being the key barrier.

The Data Divide

Looking forward, the digital divide in developing countries is being addressed. Much of the broadband supply is being provided by commercial mobile operators, upgrading their networks to offer mobile broadband in response to increases in demand. New submarine cables are being built, fiber backhaul is being deployed, and data centers constructed. Closing the digital divide is a moving target, of course, as advanced countries are also investing continuously in new and updated infrastructure. However, leapfrogging is possible; for instance, the speed of 5G approaches or surpasses fixed broadband speeds.

At the same time, governments, international organizations, nonprofits, and others are all working to help promote the demand side, and these efforts will continue to pay off. The children learning at schools will grow up and continue to use the Internet, the prices of devices will fall, new content and services are being created, and Internet access and usage will continue to grow and spread through the economy and society.

As the traditional digital divide—based on access to the Internet and usage—begins to close, a new one may open that may be more difficult to close. While developed countries are worried about too much data and corresponding privacy and security concerns, might developing countries fall prey to the opposite issue—too little data? Looking at sub-Saharan Africa, for instance, the problems cascade today. First, there are fewer Internet users than in other regions, so there are fewer people from whom to gather data. Second, not everyone online is online with a smartphone, so there is less of the rich data that such phones can gather, in combination with the fact that not everyone can purchase apps, particularly paid or advertising-supported apps.

Part of this is an indicator, of course, of current demographics that make smartphones and Internet use less affordable and attract less advertising. But it is also a precursor for a less data-rich future. Using Uber again as an example, as of this writing it is available in only twenty-two cities in Africa, of which most are in countries in North Africa and South Africa, and only nine in between. So less data is being gathered about those cities, meaning less chance of having self-driving cars and other new technologies based on such data. The same is true with voice assistants, as we saw in the previous chapter.

And when such services do come to those areas, they are likely to be international service providers applying their general expertise to specific regions and users, rather than local providers, which have less data upon which to grow new services. Thus, even as the digital divide slowly erodes, there may be a data divide that persists. As if any more urgency were needed, policymakers should account for the future impacts of efforts to address current needs in the industry.

Conclusion

I recently came across the picture of a prototype of a self-driving Audi oil tanker. It turns out that it was a concept created by two independent designers, unaffiliated with Audi, but it made me think—first about all the things that could go wrong with this somewhat remarkable idea, and second about who would be in a position to stop it if someone actually produced one. The same holds true, of course, for self-driving cars and single-passenger drones that are already in prototype.

Specifically, what standards would they have to conform to, and who would do the testing? All vehicles today undergo rigorous testing, are subject to product liability, and must be insured. But would the same organizations that test cars test autonomous cars? Do they understand algorithms and cybersecurity? Would the software elements be subject to the same product liability as the vehicles themselves? And would insurance companies take on the risk? If not, would they cast the ultimate negative vote?

Similar questions hold true for many of the new systems that are coming into being these days. When a judge makes a decision on sentencing, the judge is accountable for that decision—but what if the judge simply agrees with the AI agent that makes the recommendation based on machine learning? What if the AI agent was trained on biased data, resulting in biased decisions? And what if anonymized big data is given to urban planners without the subjects' explicit consent and it is not correctly anonymized?

That these questions are being asked at all is a question of trust. The lack of trust may be based on a doomsday scenario from a movie about robots or on a lack of understanding or on a fear of the impact on jobs. But there is good reason to raise the issue when seeing the market failures taking place today with cybersecurity, sometimes based on the most easily avoidable mistakes, and the lack of efforts to fix them. If we cannot protect ourselves today, what about tomorrow?

Ultimately, what say does society have over the adoption of new technologies? Today it seems like they are inevitable, with all their potential impact on income equality, jobs, trade, privacy, and security. And I am the last person to argue against technological progress. But someone has to raise the questions, and someone has to be accountable, to make sure the problems of the past do not become the disasters of the future.

10 The Need for Change

Some people don't like change, but you need to embrace change if the alternative is disaster.

—Elon Musk

There are over one hundred thousand commercial airline flights per day, but on the vast majority of days when all land safely, that is not front-page news. Of course, when disaster strikes, it captures and holds our attention because of the number of casualties and our empathy for the victims and survivors. The Internet is like this: billions of social interactions, millions of financial transactions, and untold government inactions going unnoticed, save for the days when something goes wrong. When accounts are hacked, identities are stolen, or money pilfered, we empathize with the victims, briefly wonder if we should be more careful online, and then generally move on.

On most days, we focus on the positive impact of the Internet. Every day new users come online, and existing users find new wonders. We find old friends online and make new ones. Young tech wizards become millionaires; millionaires become billionaires. Politicians successfully harness the power of social media to seemingly come from nowhere to win elections, and we discover or become the next generation of entertainers. And this reliance, and its impact, were magnified during the COVID-19 crisis.

This growth, and optimism, is powered by a virtuous circle built on the foundation of free. Users discover and use a seemingly endless array of free content and services. The use of the free services is fostered by unmetered online usage in many cases. And new and interesting devices and services are created based on open standards, which in turn attract more users and usage. Now something has changed, and the ratio of attention is starting to flip, even if our actions are not always following. Now it seems like no day goes by without some evidence of techlash.[1]

As I was writing this book, there was an endless stream of news articles to clip, expressing concerns about online privacy, plans to rein in or break up companies, worries about the impact of social media on society, and highlighting a steady stream of data breaches and cyberattacks. Policymakers are taking notice. Record fines have been announced, plans to break up tech companies are floated, arguments made on how to filter content and protect elections. But it all feels a bit like closing the barn door after the cows have escaped.

At the heart of the growth—and the challenges—of the Internet is data. Data is being generated by existing and new users and existing and new uses in exponential leaps. Privacy regulations aim to limit the use of data; cybersecurity measures aim to protect data; data is a basis for market power; lack of data is the hidden danger of the digital divide; and data will train the algorithms of the future AI. Data is changing the nature of economies, and this in turn will change Internet governance.

The Acoustic Guitar

When new variations of existing things are introduced, the variation has to be identified. Often, this is when something goes electric or digital—electric guitar, digital watch, smartphone. Then, eventually, if the new variation becomes more popular, it becomes the default and the old one needs to be identified—acoustic guitar, analog watch, feature phone. This is so common that it has a name—adding *acoustic* to what used to be called just a guitar is a *retronym*. And it is not just from electronics: milk is now whole milk, and sometimes even cow milk, and if you don't want to pay for water in a restaurant you have to ask for tap water.

The same shift is likely to take place as the Internet continues to spread and become pervasive. Most countries have plans to create digital economies, and we measure what percentage of economic GDP comes from the digital economy.[2] Amazon is clearly a part of the digital economy, but Walmart, known for its old-fashioned brick-and-mortar stores (another retronym), may not seem to all customers to be part of the digital economy. But in fact, savvy readers will know that Walmart not only sells an enormous amount online, at least in absolute terms, but has also pioneered the use of information technology throughout its supply chain. Does that not also make it part of the digital economy?

The same process is likely to take place throughout the economy. Agriculture, one of the oldest economic activities, is going digital as well with connected machinery, IoT sensors, and integrated supply chains. Soon, the entire economy will be digital, and we may need a retronym for the analog components of the new digital world, if any survive. This change will in turn spill over to Internet governance.

As online activities begin to expand to cover an increasing range of activities, the government role will continue to grow. Take, just for one example, online finance. Eventually cash will be displaced by online currency. But governments will still need to stop or punish theft, there will need to be a central bank for currencies, and governments will still want to tax income and certain transactions. And who but governments could address market power and privacy violations and respond to state-sponsored attacks against their citizens or institutions?

As governments increasingly begin to intervene, they are now often using traditional tools for traditional problems. And this may very well be appropriate in many cases. Laws on protecting medical records need to be enforced, competition policy applied, political advertising controlled. As a result, governance on the Internet may increasingly resemble governance off the Internet; government involvement will not differentiate between online and offline issues. As a result, the concept of Internet governance may largely apply just to governance of the Internet—to standards, names and numbers, and other areas critical to the operation of the Internet that are working well. We may soon need a retronym for regulation that only applies offline.

But this cannot mean a return to business as usual for the role of government, nor a diminution of the vital role of all stakeholders. Companies are making changes to their own policies, and Microsoft has even called on governments to regulate facial-recognition technology. The Online Trust Alliance, an Internet Society initiative, is proposing a trust framework for securing the Internet of Things so that it has better security from the beginning. When certain governments see Internet access as a threat and turn it off, civil society will continue to work on highlighting human rights issues.

As governments continue to determine how to address old issues as they arise online, new issues arise and new approaches are required. The ultimate issue going forward may be data governance because data is ultimately what differentiates the analog economy from a digital one.

Data Governance

Going back in time, the most valuable companies were a reflection of the stage of the industrial revolution. One hundred years ago, in the United States, the largest companies mainly provided inputs—oil and steel—with AT&T the exception. Fifty years ago, there was a shift to outputs, including General Motors and Kodak, and IBM joined AT&T on the list as the ICT sector began to form. All of these companies made and sold tangible products or services.

Today, two of the most valuable companies in the world, Facebook and Alphabet (Google's parent company), offer free services. The others are all also Internet related, with Apple, Microsoft, and Amazon in the mix, although these companies make the bulk of their revenues through selling hardware, software, and, in the case of Amazon, almost everything.[3] All of them rely on data and the insights provided by data.

It has been fashionable to think of data as the new oil, fueling the information revolution the way oil literally fueled the industrial revolution. And on the downside, when oil spills, it is an environmental catastrophe, costing companies and countries billions to clean up. Likewise, when data is used improperly, when it is breached, it can have significant negative impacts. Nonetheless, the analogy is misleading, for reasons that explain why data governance is unique.

First, oil is physical: it can only be in one place at one time, and it can only be used once. Indeed, oil is the classic nonrenewable resource and will need to be replaced as an energy source on that basis alone. And of course, when oil is consumed it is intrinsically bad for the environment and contributes to climate change. Government efforts to clean it and tax it can only make it less bad.

Data, on the other hand, can have many uses at the same time—it can be perfectly copied, used with no cost, and my usage does not take away from your usage. Put differently, it is *nonrival*; one use does not impact another. Indeed, if or when data is released, it becomes a public good, which anyone can use. It can be repurposed, and it may become more valuable over time as more accumulates. Further, it is *generative*; the more it is used, the more is generated.

Thus, energy policy has to increasingly balance the economic necessity of using oil with the unavoidable short- and long-term negative impacts, and thus the focus is to use it more efficiently and find alternatives. Data policy does not intrinsically incorporate a balancing act. Yes, of course, privacy and data protection must be assured, but the goal should be to do that without sacrificing gathering and using data beneficially. Here data governance can learn a useful lesson from oil policy—the Deepwater Horizon oil spill cost BP at least USD 65 billion—and Internet companies should likewise bear greater liability for their own breaches. But other lessons do not necessarily translate.

For instance, as a result of market power, Standard Oil was ordered broken up into thirty-four independent companies after an early antitrust case in the United States in 1911. While parts of the company reformed into ExxonMobil, that was through mergers and acquisitions, rather than any intrinsic propensity to grow organically. On the other hand, we discussed earlier some of the intrinsic characteristics of Internet platforms that lead to growth, such as network effects and economies of scale. As a result, a breakup of an Internet company could deprive consumers of benefits, and one of the resulting companies may organically grow back to its old position anyway.

So the question for data governance is how to leverage the unique features of data and avoid the costs: how to generate positive good while protecting privacy and security for personal data; how to maintain appropriate property rights to reward innovation and investment while checking market power; how to enable machine learning while allowing new companies strong on innovation and short on data to flourish; how to ensure that the digital divide is not replaced by a data divide.

Do No Harm

First, the increased amount of data, and the increase in the breadth and depth of its usage, requires increased vigilance. We have to learn from what has gone wrong to date with privacy and security and try to anticipate the new problems that will arise, as AI will create its own set of challenges.

Back to automobile safety, there are two general categories of safety measures in modern cars—active and passive. The active ones are those that help avoid a crash—lane departure and collision-warning systems, and antilock braking and traction control, among others. The passive ones are those that protect you in a crash—seat belts, airbags, crumple zones. While some of these are required by law, others are optional ones over which manufacturers compete, with testing to rate the car safety and bearing the liability if a measure fails.

In data terms, active measures are means to prevent a data breach, such as firewalls, automatic updating of software, antivirus software, employee training, and others, while passive measures include data minimization, to reduce the data that is stored, and encryption, to protect what is stored. We have already run through the challenges of determining and signaling the level of security and the limited liability if there is a breach. These areas can all be strengthened, as happened with car safety, so that companies can credibly signal their current levels of security and have an incentive to compete over new ones.

But AI also introduces new sets of data challenges, and we can stick with the automobile example further. A self-driving car must be trained, which introduces two new sets of issues. Has it been trained on a sufficient set of data? There is already evidence that self-driving cars have bias in terms of recognizing certain pedestrians, and other cases of cars with autopilot not seeing or avoiding trucks. Researchers recently put a bit of tape on a 35 MPH speed limit sign to make it look like 85, making Teslas automatically accelerate to the higher limit. We may know from experience that when a ball is bouncing out from between several parked cars, a small child may follow, but does a self-driving car know that?

And then, what is it trained to do based on what it does see? This is a variation of the classic trolley problem—a hypothetical ethical challenge where a trolley is heading for five people on the main track who it will kill, but someone has the chance to divert it to the side track where it would "only" kill one person, but at the hand of the person who diverted the trolley. Here, the trolley problem is built into the software: When there is an unavoidable crash, what is the car programmed to do? Does it avoid the child chasing the ball to crash into a bike coming the other way? As drivers, we would have to make a tragic split-second decision, which is hard to blame after the fact, but the car has the decision built in. Who bears liability for the results of the decision?

Data for the Public Good

The other issue is to harness data—particularly big data—for good. In chapter 7 we discussed sharing data in the context of addressing market power, and in chapter 9 we discussed big data. This could be more fundamental. Here any form of data sharing could focus on categories of data, creating big data, and not just focus on the data from one company, which would be the case in a competition review. It would not be in response to market power, although it might prevent it, and would help promote other social objectives, including innovation, on topics that can include monitoring traffic or developing weather forecasts.

A *data pool* is one approach to provide aggregated data—in which all companies, large and small, share certain data in a common pool, enabling all of them to compete using the same data. Of course, one might argue that this would enable the larger companies to benefit from the data gathered from the smaller companies, thus cementing their advantages rather than giving a leg up to the smaller companies. However, this could make sense where the data provide a public good, as well as a private one. For instance, ridesharing data help not only companies such as Uber, but also cities working on congestion and public transportation. Likewise, data from fitness trackers can help health researchers and insurance companies, beyond the benefits to the tracking companies.

One example of developing a data pool is a data commons approach being pioneered in Barcelona. The idea is that the data would come from people, sensors and devices, regarding urban problems such as noise levels or air quality. Individuals can control the privacy of the data they provide using technologies including blockchain, created by a European project called DECODE (Decentralized Citizen Owned Data Ecosystem). The data would be treated similarly to a public infrastructure, such as roads and water, and made accessible to organizations to develop data-driven services for the public good.[4] Here consumers would opt-in to share their data.

As part of a Data for Development initiative, the telephone company Orange (formerly France Telecom) made available 2.5 billion records from five million mobile phones in the Ivory Coast. For Orange, it was an example of *data philanthropy*—making data available for the public good—and its partners in the initiative, including UN Global Pulse, MIT Media Lab, and World Economic Forum, challenged researchers to determine the value of the data for development. One winner of the challenge was IBM Research, which used the data to analyze urban commutes and redesign the bus system to cut down travel time.

The data made available by Orange was anonymized, so consent was not asked—but that must be done carefully, as we saw earlier with the AOL search data. One study using anonymized location data showed that it was relatively easy to identify people based on a few known locations. In other words, if someone knew my location four times in a day, they could identify me in the dataset and determine where I was the rest of the day.[5] Knowing this, Orange gave the dataset to several researchers to test whether it was truly anonymous data and, after adjustments, made it available to the researchers under agreed upon terms and conditions for its usage.

The form and nature of any such data for a public good initiative is at heart a multistakeholder issue. It will involve those who hold data and those who could benefit from the data. It will involve national governments setting regulations and international organizations governing cross-border uses and abuses. It will involve the technical community to set or update appropriate standards and civil society to represent users and amplify their concerns. But ultimately, users should understand the benefits and the trade-offs, particularly when it is sensitive data or when they have to opt-in to the program.

Conclusion

This book started by showing the benefits of free Internet. Much of the Internet is built on free standards, enabling an endless stream of new innovations. Many of the services and much of the content we access on the Internet are free. And while we are using these services or enjoying the content, often our usage is not metered. This has fueled the adoption and usage of the Internet. But the data gathered in the course of this growth has a flip side.

A number of unexpected paradoxes have come up in the digital age. There is the privacy paradox—the gulf between what users say about the privacy of their personal data and what they do about it. There is a security paradox—that companies are not doing enough to protect their own customers from breaches of their data. After a breach, there is a related trust paradox—that actual cyberevents do not seem to reduce online activities. And there is the paradox of market power—that despite the ease of entering online markets, existing companies have grown large.

We examined the proximate causes of these paradoxes. We looked at behavioral economics, which can help explain seemingly irrational choices by individuals that help explain the privacy paradox, and we discussed the market failures that expose users to companies' lack of security. We also looked at the market forces that have led to the growth of the Internet market leaders. And we examined the multistakeholder model in which government was but one of the stakeholders engaged in Internet governance, rather than claiming any primacy.

The bigger picture is that our mental map of how the world worked could not chart the path that the new forces unleashed. Those of us used to paying for content and services took time to realize the downside of free services, and likewise, if you ever had to watch your minutes when using a telephone connected to the wall, it was hard to picture any downside of unmetered access. And from an age of costly entry barriers—retail required brick-and-mortar stores; newspapers required presses and journalists—it took time to recognize the new online entry barriers that replaced those traditional barriers.

Likewise the digital divide. The pessimism of bringing people online by trying to expand the fixed network in many countries was soon replaced by the optimism of widespread mobile networks. It was easy to understand that affordability would be a big issue, but many of us assumed that demand would otherwise be a given. How could everyone not be as interested in the Internet as we are? So it took time to come to the realization that Internet availability was necessary, but not sufficient—that awareness and relevance would be a significant issue to bring new users online.

But maybe this was the reaction of the generation (including me) that could remember life as an adult before the Internet, when we would go to a Starbucks and buy a newspaper, pay in cash, and use a pay phone. Or use *TV Guide* to choose what to watch and have to be in front of the TV at the right time or wait for the rerun to show. The digital natives—surely another retronym in the making—are not burdened with comparisons before the

Internet and after the Internet, but rather with comparisons between good experiences online and bad ones. We are clearly catching up, however, as everyone focuses on the challenges of online life and how to address them.

The lessons to be drawn from the past are twofold. First, government policy must adapt to address the current issues raised in a way that maintains the positive characteristics of the Internet and the multistakeholder model that characterizes Internet governance. This is clearly underway and, if anything, the risk now is that the pendulum has swung too far, from blissful focus on the upside to panicked attacks on the downside.

But also, the second lesson is to not repeat the same mistakes of the past. It is important to acknowledge and recognize that old models of behavior—whether users, markets, or governments—did not anticipate the problems that arose—for good reason, given the novelty and immediate benefits. But that will not excuse not anticipating some of the new challenges. Big data, machine learning, and the Internet of Things will generate more data that needs to be protected, that can be breached, that will underlie market power, and that will further the digital divide. The difference is that we can anticipate and regulate at least some of the issues before they arise and become entrenched.

Many of these new services will continue to be free, be built on open standards, and be accessed through unmetered access, which will drive growth and usage. There is, of course, a flip side, and it does need to be addressed. The traditional way to address negative harms was with a tax or other means to raise the price, to lower usage. That is not the solution for the Internet, and certainly not one that is intended by the thesis of this book. Many of the benefits of the Internet arise from the unique economics of things being free. The solution must focus on anticipating and reducing the flip side. I remain ever optimistic that this can be done.

Acknowledgments

Several years ago, I developed a course for the Graduate Institute of International and Development Studies in Geneva, entitled Internet Economics and Governance, and I thank former director Philippe Burrin and Damien Neven for their support. As I put together the syllabus for the course, I could not find a book that covered all the topics of interest, which set me thinking. After teaching and refining the course a few times, I began to write this book and submitted it to the press of my graduate alma mater.

The book brings together many years of my experience that tracked the emergence of the Internet and its related issues: researching network economics at INSEAD business school while the Internet was still a limited academic and research network; working at the US Federal Communications Commission as the Internet was emerging as a commercial force; working as a partner at Analysys Mason advising countries and companies developing Internet policies, networks, and services, as the Internet went global; and serving as Chief Economist at the Internet Society, ensuring that global access was universal, affordable, and secure. Throughout this career I had the pleasure and privilege of working with colleagues, clients, and partners whose insights helped develop the framework for this book.

While writing this book, I benefited from insights and assistance from Richard Baldwin, Vint Cerf, Jane Coffin, Jorge Contreras, Alissa Cooper, Steve Crocker, Carl Gahnberg, Neil Gandal, Geoff Huston, Michuki Mwangi, Mike Nelson, Robert Pepper, Carlo Rossotto, Nermine El Saadany, Tim Unwin, David Weinberger, Robin Wilton, Alex Wong, and Peter Zemsky. David Abecassis, Dale Hatfield, Richard Hill, Bill Lehr, Bastiaan Quast, Roxana Radu, and Karen Rose reviewed chapters and provided invaluable comments, in addition to what I learned from them as colleagues over the years.

I am very grateful to the team at the MIT Press, including Emily Taber, the acquisitions editor who helped shape the book in many important ways, and manuscript editor Kathleen Caruso and copyeditor Melinda Rankin, for their care and attention to the finishing touches. I would also like to thank the anonymous reviewers who provided helpful comments on the drafts.

I finalized and reviewed the book while confined at home during the COVID-19 pandemic, a period that increased everyone's appreciation of the Internet and crystalized the issues raise here. What would we have done without it? Final thanks go to my family for their love and support. The book is dedicated to the memory of my father.

Notes

1 Introduction

1. "Starbucks Privacy Statement," January 1, 2020.

2. Rana Foroohar, "Year in a Word: Techlash," *Financial Times*, December 16, 2018.

3. Andrew Blum, *Tubes: A Journey to the Center of the Internet* (New York: Harper-Collins, 2012).

4. This address uses the legacy Internet protocol known as IPv4. There is a total of roughly 4.3 billion IPv4 addresses; that once seemed an unattainable number to use, but it has now been attained. The new version IPv6 has been introduced, with a total number of addresses that likely is unattainable. However, the two versions are incompatible, so IPv4 is still being used while adoption and use of IPv6 is advancing.

5. Vinton G. Cerf, "Ownership vs. Stewardship," *Communications of the ACM* 62, no. 3 (March 2019): 6.

6. Stephen W. Hawking, *A Brief History of Time: From the Big Bang to Black Holes* (New York: Bantam Books, 1988), vi–vii.

7. For a further discussion of the business model behind free services, see Chris Anderson, *Free: The Future of a Radical Price* (New York: Hyperion, 2009).

8. Dan Ariely, *Predictably Irrational: The Hidden Forces That Shape Our Decisions* (New York: HarperCollins, 2008), chap. 3.

9. NPR, "The Cost of Free Doughnuts," *Planet Money*, January 8, 2020, https://www.npr.org/transcripts/794592539.

10. Explanation provided by Professor Uri Simonsohn, "The Cost of Free Doughnuts."

11. "The Story of Svalbarði," Svalbarði Polar Iceberg Water, accessed July 22, 2019, https://svalbardi.com/pages/the-story.

12. The following example is based on the Coase theorem. Ronald Coase, "The Problem of Social Cost," *Journal of Law and Economics* 3 (October 1960): 1–44.

13. Institute on Governance, "Defining Governance," accessed September 1, 2019, http://iog.ca/what-is-governance/.

14. John Perry Barlow, "A Declaration of the Independence of Cyberspace," Electronic Frontier Foundation, February 8, 1996, https://www.eff.org/cyberspace-independence.

15. "Resolution Adopted by the General Assembly 56/183, World Summit on the Information Society, Pub. L. No. United Nations A/RES/56/183, January 31, 2002, https://www.itu.int/net/wsis/docs/background/resolutions/56_183_unga_2002.pdf.

16. World Summit on the Information Society, "Basic Information: About WSIS," accessed July 24, 2019, https://www.itu.int/net/wsis/basic/about.html.

17. *Report of the Working Group on Internet Governance*, Bogis-Bossey, Switzerland: Working Group on Internet Governance, June 2005, http://www.wgig.org/WGIG -Report.html. This definition is repeated in the Tunis Agenda, which followed the second phase of the WSIS, at "Tunis Agenda for the Information Society," Document WSIS-05/TUNIS/DOC/6(Rev. 1)-E, ITU, November 18, 2005, https://www.itu .int/net/wsis/docs2/tunis/off/6rev1.html, sec. 34.

18. "Tunis Agenda for the Information Society," sec. 35.a.

19. Andy Greenberg, "It's Been 20 Years since This Man Declared Cyberspace Independence," *Wired*, February 8, 2016, https://www.wired.com/2016/02/its-been-20 -years-since-this-man-declared-cyberspace-independence/.

20. Personal communication with the author.

21. Michael Kende, "The Digital Handshake: Connecting Internet Backbones, " Office of Plans and Policy Working Paper Series (Washington, DC: Federal Communications Commission, September 1, 2000), https://www.fcc.gov/reports-research/working-papers /digital-handshake-connecting-internet-backbones.

2   The Global Standard

1. This refers to the technical standards, not to whether all content can be accessed from all countries, due to copyright restrictions or filtering.

2. William Lehr et al., *Whither the Public Internet?*, SSRN scholarly paper (Rochester, NY: Social Science Research Network, March 16, 2018), https://papers.ssrn.com /abstract=3141969.

3. For more details, see https://en.wikipedia.org/wiki/Internet_protocol_suite.

4. Joseph Farrell and Timothy Simcoe, "Four Paths to Compatibility," in *The Oxford Handbook of the Digital Economy*, ed. Martin Peitz and Joel Waldfogel (New York: Oxford University Press, 2012), 38.

5. Stanley M. Besen and George Sadowsky, "The Economics of Internet Standards," in *Handbook on the Economics of the Internet*, ed. Johannes M. Bauer and Michael Lazer (Cheltenham, UK: Edward Elgar Publishing, 2016), 214–217, https://www .elgaronline.com/view/edcoll/9780857939845/9780857939845.00018.xml.

6. Barry M. Leiner et al., *Brief History of the Internet* (Internet Society, 1997), https:// www.internetsociety.org/wp-content/uploads/2017/09/ISOC-History-of-the -Internet_1997.pdf.

7. Leiner et al., 9; Janet Abbate, *Inventing the Internet* (Cambridge, MA: MIT Press, 1999), 143.

8. Leiner et al., *Brief History of the Internet*, 5.

9. Leiner et al.; Katie Hafner and Matthew Lyon, *Where Wizards Stay Up Late: The Origins of the Internet* (New York: Simon & Schuster, 1996); Abbate, *Inventing the Internet*.

10. Internet Society, *Internet Invariants: What Really Matters* (Internet Society, October 18, 2016), https://www.internetsociety.org/wp-content/uploads/2017/08/Internet 20Invariants-20What20Really20Matters.pdf.

11. See National Research Council, *Realizing the Information Future: The Internet and Beyond* (Washington, DC: National Academies Press, 1994), 51–53, https://doi.org /10.17226/4755.

12. William Grimes, "Raymond Tomlinson, Who Put the @ Sign in Email, Is Dead at 74," *New York Times*, March 7, 2016, https://www.nytimes.com/2016/03/08/technology /raymond-tomlinson-email-obituary.html.

13. Andrew Sullivan, "Avoiding Lamentation: To Build a Future Internet," *Journal of Cyber Policy* 2, no. 3 (September 2, 2017): 323–337, https://doi.org/10.1080 /23738871.2017.1400083.

14. Ole J. Jacobsen, ed., *ConneXions: The Interoperability Report* 2, no. 11 (November 1988): 7, http://www.cbi.umn.edu/hostedpublications/Connexions/ConneXions02_ 1988/ConneXions2-11_Nov1988.pdf.

15. Leiner et.al., *Brief History of the Internet*, 15.

16. Email from Vint Cerf, February 7, 2019.

17. William Lehr, "Compatibility Standards and Interoperability: Lessons from the Internet," in *Standards Policy for Information Infrastructure*, ed. Brian Kahin and Janet Abbate (Cambridge, MA: MIT Press, 1995), 121–147.

18. Lehr.

19. David D. Clark, "A Cloudy Crystal Ball—Visions of the Future," in *Proceedings of the Twenty-Fourth Internet Engineering Task Force*, ed. Meagan Davies, Cynthia Clark,

and Debra Legare (Reston, VA: Corporation for National Research Initiatives, 1992), 539–543, https://www.ietf.org/proceedings/24.pdf.

20. Pete Resnick, "On Consensus and Humming in the IETF," Requests for Comments, Internet Engineering Task Force, June 2014, https://tools.ietf.org/html/rfc7282 #ref-Clark.

21. See https://open-stand.org.

22. Jorge Contreras, *Patents and Internet Standards*, Global Commission on Internet Governance Paper Series, GCIG paper no. 29 (Waterloo, Canada, and London: CIGI and Chatham House, April 15, 2016), https://www.cigionline.org/publications/patents -and-internet-standards.

23. Ann Armstrong, Joseph Mueller, and Tim Syrett, *The Smartphone Royalty Stack: Surveying Royalty Demands for the Components within Modern Smartphones*, SSRN scholarly paper (Rochester, NY: Social Science Research Network, May 29, 2014), https:// papers.ssrn.com/abstract=2443848.

24. The $400 price for the smartphone is what the mobile carriers pay the vendors, not the end price for consumers. Armstrong, Mueller, and Syrett.

25. For one list of cases, see https://en.wikipedia.org/wiki/Smartphone_patent_wars.

26. Contreras, *Patents and Internet Standards*, 4.

27. Jorge Contreras, "Why We Need a Global FRAND Rate-Setting Tribunal," Research Institute of Econony, Trade and Industry, *Perspectives from Around the World* (blog), June 6, 2019, https://www.rieti.go.jp/en/special/p_a_w/128.html.

28. See https://en.wikipedia.org/wiki/Open-source_software.

29. See https://en.wikipedia.org/wiki/Free_and_open-source_software.

30. CERN, "The Birth of the Web," accessed June 11, 2019, https://home.cern/science /computing/birth-web.

31. Brian McCullough, *How the Internet Happened: From Netscape to the iPhone* (New York: Liveright Publishing Corporation, 2018), 26.

32. Stacey Leasca, "People Would Rather Have the Internet than a Cure for Cancer, Study Says," *Elite Daily* (blog), May 11, 2016, https://www.elitedaily.com/envision /internet-obsession-cure-for-cancer/1490852.

33. According to one study, the open-source Linux kernel has far fewer bugs than commercial software. *Wired* Staff, "Linux: Fewer Bugs than Rivals," *Wired*, December 14, 2004, https://www.wired.com/2004/12/linux-fewer-bugs-than-rivals/.

3 Why Is Wi-Fi Free?

1. Martin Campbell-Kelly, "Pioneer Profiles: Donald Davies," *Computer Resurrection* 44 (Autumn 2008), http://www.computerconservationsociety.org/resurrection/res44.htm.

2. Kende, *The Digital Handshake*.

3. Harry McCracken, "A History of AOL, as Told in Its Own Old Press Releases," *Technologizer—A Smarter Take on Tech* (blog), May 24, 2010, https://www.technologizer.com/2010/05/24/aol-anniversary/.

4. "Industry: ISPs," *Cybertelecom* (blog), accessed July 2, 2020, https://www.cybertelecom.org/industry/isp.htm. Citing *Boardwatch Magazine*, Directory of Internet Service Providers, 13th ed., Spring 2001, p. 4.

5. Jason Oxman, "The FCC and the Unregulation of the Internet," Office of Plans and Policy Working Paper no. 31 (Washington, DC: Federal Communications Commission, July 1999), https://transition.fcc.gov/Bureaus/OPP/working_papers/oppwp31.pdf.

6. Telecommunications Development Sector, *Regulating Broadband Prices*, Broadband Series (Geneva: International Telecommunication Union, April 2012), 28, https://www.itu.int/ITU-D/treg/broadband/ITU-BB-Reports_RegulatingPrices.pdf.

7. This is based on my research in Africa. See, for instance, Michael Kende and Karen Rose, *Promoting Local Content Hosting to Develop the Internet Ecosystem* (Internet Society, January 12, 2015), https://www.internetsociety.org/resources/doc/2015/promoting-local-content-hosting-to-develop-the-internet-ecosystem/.

4 Something for Nothing

1. Simon Hill, "Why Do We Call It Spam? Blame Spiced Ham Shoulder, Monty Python and Usenet," *Digital Trends* (blog), February 8, 2015, https://www.digitaltrends.com/web/why-junk-email-is-spam/.

2. Chris Kanich et al., "Spamalytics: An Empirical Analysis of Spam Marketing Conversion," in *Proceedings of the 15th ACM Conference on Computer and Communications Security*, CCS '08 (New York: ACM, 2008), https://doi.org/10.1145/1455770.1455774.

3. McCullough, *How the Internet Happened*, 76–79.

4. Don Roy King, "SNL Transcripts: Tom Hanks: 10/08/18: First Citiwide Change Bank I," SNL Transcripts Tonight, October 8, 2018, https://snltranscripts.jt.org/88/88achangebank1.phtml.

5. Floyd Norris and Lawrence M. Fisher, "Offspring Outweighs Parent as Offering Hits the Market," *New York Times*, March 3, 2000, https://www.nytimes.com/2000/03/03/business/offspring-outweighs-parent-as-offering-hits-the-market.html.

6. Geoff Huston, "Where Is the Content Economy?," *ISP Column* (blog), June 2001, http://www.potaroo.net/ispcol/2001-06/2001-06-content.html; Geoff Huston, "Carriage vs. Content," *ISP Column* (blog), July 2012, http://www.potaroo.net/ispcol/2012-07/carriagevcontent.html.

7. Chris Anderson, *The Long Tail: Why the Future of Business Is Selling Less of More* (New York: Hyperion, 2008).

8. John Battelle, *The Search: How Google and Its Rivals Rewrote the Rules of Business and Transformed Our Culture* (New York: Portfolio, 2005), chap. 6.

9. Elisa Gabbert, "The 25 Most Expensive Keywords in AdWords—2017 Edition!," *WordStream* (blog), June 10, 2019, https://www.wordstream.com/blog/ws/2017/06/27/most-expensive-keywords.

10. Google Ads Help, "About Ad Position and Ad Rank," accessed June 11, 2019, https://support.google.com/google-ads/answer/1722122?hl=en.

11. Michael Barbaro and Tom Zeller Jr., "A Face Is Exposed for AOL Searcher No. 4417749," *New York Times*, August 9, 2006, https://www.nytimes.com/2006/08/09/technology/09aol.html.

12. Christopher Rowland, "With Fitness Trackers in the Workplace, Bosses Can Monitor Your Every Step—and Possibly More," *Washington Post*, February 16, 2019, https://www.washingtonpost.com/business/economy/with-fitness-trackers-in-the-workplace-bosses-can-monitor-your-every-step--and-possibly-more/2019/02/15/75ee0848-2a45-11e9-b011-d8500644dc98_story.html.

13. Alex Hern, "Fitness Tracking App Strava Gives Away Location of Secret US Army Bases," *Guardian*, January 28, 2018, https://www.theguardian.com/world/2018/jan/28/fitness-tracking-app-gives-away-location-of-secret-us-army-bases.

14. Ben Gilbert, "There's a Simple Reason Your New Smart TV Was So Affordable: It's Collecting and Selling Your Data, and Serving You Ads," *Business Insider*, April 5, 2019, https://www.businessinsider.com/smart-tv-data-collection-advertising-2019-1.

15. Mark Bergen and Jennifer Surane, "Google and Mastercard Cut a Secret Ad Deal to Track Retail Sales," *Bloomberg*, August 30, 2018, https://www.bloomberg.com/news/articles/2018-08-30/google-and-mastercard-cut-a-secret-ad-deal-to-track-retail-sales.

5   Did We Give Away Our Privacy?

1. United Nations, *The Universal Declaration of Human Rights*, 1948, http://www.un.org/en/universal-declaration-human-rights/.

2. UN General Assembly, The Right to Privacy in the Digital Age: Resolution Adopted by the General Assembly on 18 December 2013, United Nations, December 2013.

3. Internet Society, *An Introduction to Privacy on the Internet: An Internet Society Public Policy Briefing* (Internet Society, October 30, 2015), https://www.internetsociety.org /wp-content/uploads/2015/10/ISOC-PolicyBrief-Privacy-20151030-nb-1.pdf.

4. Internet Society, *An Introduction to Privacy on the Internet*. The European Union defines personal data as follows: "'personal data' shall mean any information relating to an identified or identifiable natural person ('data subject'); an identifiable person is one who can be identified, directly or indirectly, in particular by reference to an identification number or to one or more factors specific to his physical, physiological, mental, economic, cultural or social identity." See Directive 95/46/EC of the European Parliament and of the Council of 24 October 1995 on the Protection of Individuals with Regard to the Processing of Personal Data and on the Free Movement of Such Data (1995), http://data.europa.eu/eli/dir/1995/46/oj, Article 2a.

5. Ellen Pan et al., "Panoptispy—Characterizing Audio and Video Exfiltration from Android Applications," *Proceedings of Privacy Enhancing Technologies Symposium* 18, no. 4 (2018), https://recon.meddle.mobi/panoptispy/.

6. David Goldman, "Your Samsung TV Is Eavesdropping on Your Private Conversations," CNN Business, February 10, 2015, https://money.cnn.com/2015/02/09 /technology/security/samsung-smart-tv-privacy/index.html.

7. See Spyros Kokolakis, "Privacy Attitudes and Privacy Behavior: A Review of Current Resesearch on the Privacy Paradox Phenomenon," *Computer Security* 64 (2017); and Susanne Barth and Menno D. T. de Jong, "The Privacy Paradox—Investigating Discrepancies between Expressed Privacy Concerns and Actual Online Behavior—A Systematic Literature Review," *Telematics and Informations* 34 (2017).

8. Dr. Alan Westin used this term in the context of a number of surveys he conducted to develop privacy indexes. For a summary of those surveys, see Ponnurangam Kumaraguru and Lorrie Faith Cranor, *Privacy Indexes: A Survey of Westin's Studies* (Pittsburgh: School of Computer Science, Carnegie Mellon University, December 2005), http://reports-archive.adm.cs.cmu.edu/anon/isri2005/CMU-ISRI-05-138.pdf.

9. See Julie Bort, "Eric Schmidt's Privacy Policy Is One Scary Philosophy," *Network World* (blog), December 11, 2009, https://www.networkworld.com/article/2232821 /eric-schmidt-s-privacy-policy-is-one-scary-philosophy.html.

10. Jay R. Corrigan et al., "How Much Is Social Media Worth? Estimating the Value of Facebook by Paying Users to Stop Using It," *PLOS ONE* 13, no. 12 (December 19, 2018), https://doi.org/10.1371/journal.pone.0207101.

11. Erik Brynjolfsson, Avinash Collis, and Felix Eggers, "Using Massive Online Choice Experiments to Measure Changes in Well-Being," *Proceedings of the National Academy of Sciences* 116, no. 15 (April 2019).

12. William D. Nordhaus, *Schumpeterian Profits and the Alchemist Fallacy*, Yale Economic Applications and Policy Discussion paper no. 6 (Rochester, NY: Yale University, April 2, 2005), https://papers.ssrn.com/abstract=820309.

13. For more details, see Alessandro Acquisti and Jens Grossklags, "Privacy and Rationality in Individual Decision Making," *IEEE Security and Privacy* 3, no. 1 (January 2005), https://doi.org/10.1109/MSP.2005.22.

14. Ros Page, "Beware the Hidden Conditions in Your User Agreement," CHOICE, March 15, 2017, https://www.choice.com.au/shopping/consumer-rights-and-advice /your-rights/articles/end-user-licence-agreement-hidden-conditions-and-risks.

15. See Katharine Schwab, "How Widely Do Companies Share User Data? Here's A Chilling Glimpse," *Fast Company*, January 19, 2018, https://www.fastcompany .com/90157501/how-widely-do-companies-share-user-data-heres-a-chilling -glimpse.

16. Jennifer Valentino-DeVries et al., "Your Apps Know Where You Were Last Night, and They're Not Keeping It Secret," *New York Times*, December 10, 2018, https://www .nytimes.com/interactive/2018/12/10/business/location-data-privacy-apps.html.

17. See, for instance Barth and de Jong, "The Privacy Paradox": "To our knowledge, there is not one unilaterally accepted theory used to explain the online behavior of users when it comes to information disclosure, nor is there a consensus on the mental processes users rely upon when deciding whether to disclose information or not" (1040).

18. Mark Zuckerberg, "A Privacy-Focused Vision for Social Networking," Facebook, March 6, 2019, https://www.facebook.com/notes/mark-zuckerberg/a-privacy -focused-vision-for-social-networking/10156700570096634/.

19. Geoffrey A. Fowler, "What If We Paid for Facebook—Instead of Letting It Spy on Us for Free?," *Washington Post*, April 5, 2018, https://www.washingtonpost.com /news/the-switch/wp/2018/04/05/what-if-we-paid-for-facebook-instead-of-letting-it -spy-on-us-for-free/.

20. Sam Harrison, "Can You Make Money Selling Your Data?," BBC, September 21, 2018, https://www.bbc.com/worklife/article/20180921-can-you-make-money-selling -your-data.

21. Charles Duhigg, "How Companies Learn Your Secrets," *New York Times Magazine*, February 16, 2012, https://www.nytimes.com/2012/02/19/magazine/shopping -habits.html.

22. Uri Gneezy and Aldo Rustichini, "A Fine Is a Price," *Journal of Legal Studies* 29, no. 1 (January 2000).

23. Richard H. Thaler and Cass R. Sunstein, *Nudge: Improving Decisions about Health, Wealth, and Happiness* (New Haven: Yale University Press, 2008).

24. DuckDuckGo, "DuckDuckGo Privacy," accessed August 6, 2019, https://duckduckgo .com/privacy.

25. DuckDuckGo, "DuckDuckGo Traffic," accessed August 6, 2019, https://duckduckgo .com/traffic.

26. Internet Live Stats, "1 Second—Internet Live Stats," accessed August 6, 2019, https://www.internetlivestats.com/one-second/#google-band.

27. Paul Hitlin and Lee Rainie, "Facebook Algorithms and Personal Data," Pew Research Center, January 16, 2019, https://www.pewinternet.org/2019/01/16/facebook -algorithms-and-personal-data/.

28. Regulation (EU) 2016/679 of the European Parliament and of the Council of 27 April 2016 on the Protection of Natural Persons with Regard to the Processing of Personal Data and on the Free Movement of Such Data, and Repealing Directive 95/46/EC (General Data Protection Regulation), 2016, http://data.europa.eu/eli/reg /2016/679/2016-05-04.

29. Regulation (EU) 2016/679, Articles 34 and 83(2)(c).

30. Tom Fox-Brewster, "TRUSTe Fined $200,000 for Misleading Web Security Seal," *Guardian*, November 18, 2014, https://www.theguardian.com/technology/2014/nov /18/truste-fine-web-security-seals.

31. Jeffrey Chester, executive director of the Center for Digital Democracy, quoted in Aliya Ram and Madhumita Murgia, "Data Brokers: Regulators Try to Rein in the 'Privacy Deathstars,'" *Financial Times*, January 8, 2019.

32. Natasha Singer, "Mapping, and Sharing, the Consumer Genome," *New York Times*, June 16, 2012, https://www.nytimes.com/2012/06/17/technology/acxiom-the-quiet-giant -of-consumer-database-marketing.html.

33. Joana Moll and Tactical Tech, "The Dating Brokers: An Autopsy of Online Love," Tactical Tech, October 2018, https://datadating.tacticaltech.org/viz.

6 Is Our Data Secure?

1. National Inventors Hall of Fame, "Featured Exhibit: Experience Automotive Innovation with the Ford Mustang," accessed August 6, 2019, https://www.invent .org/blog/innovation-display/featured-exhibit-ford-mustang.

2. Ralph Nader, *Unsafe At Any Speed* (New York: Grossman Publishers, 1965).

3. Craig Timberg, "A Flaw in the Design," *Washington Post*, May 30, 2015, http:// www.washingtonpost.com/sf/business/2015/05/30/net-of-insecurity-part-1/.

4. Tom Lamont, "Life after the Ashley Madison Affair," *Guardian*, February 28, 2016, https://www.theguardian.com/technology/2016/feb/28/what-happened-after-ashley -madison-was-hacked.

5. Online Trust Alliance, *2018 Cyber Incident & Breach Trends Report* (Reston, VA: Internet Society, July 9, 2019), https://www.internetsociety.org/wp-content/uploads /2019/07/OTA-Incident-Breach-Trends-Report_2019.pdf.

6. Michael Kassner, "Anatomy of the Target Data Breach: Missed Opportunities and Lessons Learned," ZDNet, February 2, 2015, https://www.zdnet.com/article /anatomy-of-the-target-data-breach-missed-opportunities-and-lessons-learned/.

7. Adam Segal, "Using Incentives to Shape the Zero-Day Market," *Cyber Brief* (blog), September 19, 2016, https://www.cfr.org/report/using-incentives-shape-zero -day-market.

8. In this study, for the first half of 2018, there were 944 breaches involving over 3.3 billion records, and only 1 percent of the breaches involved encrypted data. "Data Breaches Compromised 3.3 Billion Records in First Half of 2018" (Amsterdam: Gemalto | Thales Group, October 23, 2018), https://www.thalesgroup.com/en /markets/digital-identity-and-security/press-release/data-breaches-compromised-3-3 -billion-records-in-first-half-of-2018.

9. This section draws on a report that I authored for the Internet Society. See Internet Society, *Global Internet Report 2016: The Economics of Building Trust Online: Preventing Data Breaches* (Internet Society, 2016), https://www.internetsociety.org /globalinternetreport/2016/.

10. Paul Rubens, "Open Source Code Contains Fewer Defects, but There's a Catch," *CIO* (blog), November 18, 2014, https://www.cio.com/article/2847880/open-source -code-contains-fewer-defects-but-theres-a-catch.html.

11. For more on this, see Bruce Schneier, *Click Here to Kill Everybody: Security and Survival in a Hyper-connected World* (New York: W. W. Norton & Company, 2018), chap. 7.

12. Leslie Scism, "Insurers Creating a Consumer Ratings Service for Cybersecurity Industry," *Wall Street Journal*, March 26, 2019, https://www.wsj.com/articles/insurers -creating-a-consumer-ratings-service-for-cybersecurity-industry-11553592600.

13. Andy Greenberg, "Hackers Remotely Kill a Jeep on the Highway—With Me in It," *Wired*, July 21, 2015, https://www.wired.com/2015/07/hackers-remotely-kill-jeep -highway/.

14. KPMG, *Protecting the Fleet . . . and the Car Business* (KPMG's US Manufacturing Institute Automotive Center, 2017), https://advisory.kpmg.us/content/dam/advisory /en/pdfs/protecting-the-fleet-web1.pdf.

7 Platform Power

1. The scene did not involve James Bond creating a market in taxi rides, of course. It was a scene from the 2006 movie *Casino Royale*, in which James Bond sees his

car moving on a mobile phone map toward his nemesis. Because this was before the iPhone and widespread use of map apps, it stood out as a scene for Uber founder Garrett Camp. Brad Stone, *The Upstarts: How Uber, Airbnb, and the Killer Companies of the New Silicon Valley Are Changing the World* (New York: Little, Brown and Company, 2017), 40.

2. Stone, 52.

3. John R. Hicks, "Annual Survey of Economic Theory: The Theory of Monopoly," *Econometrica* 3, no. 1 (January 1935).

4. *U.S. v. Aluminum Co. of America et al.*, 148 F. 2d 416 427 (1945).

5. *U.S. v. Aluminum Co. of America et al.*, 430.

6. Matt Flegenheimer, "$1 Million Medallions Stifling the Dreams of Cabdrivers," *New York Times*, November 14, 2013, https://www.nytimes.com/2013/11/15/nyregion/1-million-medallions-stifling-the-dreams-of-cabdrivers.html.

7. Brian M. Rosenthal, "'They Were Conned': How Reckless Loans Devastated a Generation of Taxi Drivers," *New York Times*, May 19, 2019, https://www.nytimes.com/2019/05/19/nyregion/nyc-taxis-medallions-suicides.html.

8. For more details, see Stone, *The Upstarts*.

9. For instance, Section 230 of the US Communications Decency Act (1996) states that "no provider or user of an interactive computer service shall be treated as the publisher or speaker of any information provided by another information content provider." The EU e-Commerce Directive (2000) plays a similar role in Europe. The US Digital Millennium Copyright Act (1998) and the EU Copyright Directive (2001) created a safe harbor for copyright material, with the requirement to takedown infringing material upon notice from the rightsholder.

10. The Wainwright office building was named after John Wainwright, who purchased a book on April 3, 1995. Quentin Fottrell, "Meet Amazon's First Customer—This Is the Book He Bought," *MarketWatch* (blog), May 15, 2017, https://www.marketwatch.com/story/meet-amazons-first-ever-customer-2015-04-22.

11. John D. Wells, Joseph S. Valacich, and Traci J. Hess, "What Signal Are You Sending? How Website Quality Influences Perceptions of Product Quality and Purchase Intentions," *MIS Quarterly* 35, no. 2 (June 2011).

12. Justin Smith, "ECommerce Website Pricing: What Affects Cost in an ECommerce Build," *OuterBox* (blog), January 22, 2020, https://www.outerboxdesign.com/web-design-articles/ecommerce_website_pricing.

13. Kit Eaton, "How One Second Could Cost Amazon $1.6 Billion In Sales," *Fast Company*, March 15, 2012, https://www.fastcompany.com/1825005/how-one-second-could-cost-amazon-16-billion-sales.

14. David Abecassis, Richard Morgan, and Shahan Osman, *Infrastructure Investment by Online Service Providers*, white paper (London: Analysys Mason, December 2018), https://www.analysysmason.com/globalassets/infrastructure-investment-by-online -service-providers---20-dec-2018---web.pdf.

15. The Stop Enabling Sex Traffickers Act (SESTA) and Allow States and Victims to Fight Online Sex Trafficking Act (FOSTA), together known as FOSTA-SESTA, became law on April 11, 2018. The bills exclude enforcement of sex-trafficking laws from the Section 230 safe harbors of the US Communications Decency Act.

16. The Directive on Copyright in the Digital Single Market was passed on March 26, 2019, and the draft Article 13 requires intermediaries hosting user-generated content to prevent users from violating copyright using "effective and proportionate measures." This would seemingly require platforms to filter material being uploaded and to limit or remove the safe harbor that had been in place. Countries will have two years to implement the directive with legislation.

17. Cedric Manara, "Protecting What We Love about the Internet: Our Efforts to Stop Online Piracy," *Google Public Policy* (blog), November 7, 2018, https://www .blog.google/outreach-initiatives/public-policy/protecting-what-we-love-about -internet-our-efforts-stop-online-piracy/.

18. Privacy team, "GDPR—What Happened?," *Whotracks.Me* (blog), September 3, 2018, https://whotracks.me/blog/gdpr-what-happened.html.

19. See, for instance, Google Chairman Eric Schmidt's testimony to a Senate anti-trust panel, in which "Mr. Schmidt described the online economy as highly competitive, with users 'one click away' from other sources of information." Steve Lohr, "Google's Competitors Square Off against Its Leader," *New York Times*, September 21, 2011, https://www.nytimes.com/2011/09/22/technology/google-takes-the-hot-seat -in-washington.html.

20. Craig Timberg, "FTC: Google Did Not Break Antitrust Law with Search Practices," *Washington Post*, January 3, 2013, https://www.washingtonpost.com/business /technology/ftc-to-announce-google-settlement-today/2013/01/03/ecb599f0-55c6 -11e2-bf3e-76c0a789346f_story.html.

21. Natasha Lomas, "Google Fined $2.7BN for EU Antitrust Violations over Shopping Searches," *TechCrunch* (blog), June 27, 2017, http://social.techcrunch.com /2017/06/27/google-fined-e2-42bn-for-eu-antitrust-violations-over-shopping -searches/.

22. United States Department of Justice, "Assistant Attorney General Makan Delrahim Delivers Keynote Address at Silicon Flatirons Annual Technology Policy Conference at the University of Colorado Law School," Boulder, CO, February 11, 2019, https://www.justice.gov/opa/speech/assistant-attorney-general-makan-delrahim -delivers-keynote-address-silicon-flatirons.

23. See Tim Wu, *The Curse of Bigness: Antitrust in the New Gilded Age* (New York: Columbia Global Reports, 2018), 15.

24. Lina Khan, "Amazon's Antitrust Paradox," *Yale Law Journal* 126 (2017): 780–783.

25. Jean Tirole, *Economics for the Common Good* (Princeton, NJ: Princeton University Press, 2017), 405–408, https://press.princeton.edu/titles/10919.html.

26. "Frequently Asked Questions: What Is a Pod?," accessed July 2, 2020, https://solidproject.org/faqs.

27. For one vision of how competition policy can evolve, which discusses how competition policy should be applied to platforms and data, see Jacques Crémer, Yves-Alexandre de Montjoye, and Heike Schweitzer, *Competition Policy for the Digital Era*, European Commission, Directorate-General for Competition (Luxembourg: Publication Office of the European Union, 2019), http://publications.europa.eu/publication /manifestation_identifier/PUB_KD0419345ENN. See also Digital Competition Expert Panel, *Unlocking Digital Competition, Report of the Digital Competition Expert Panel* (London: HM Treasury, United Kingdom, March 13, 2019), https://www.gov.uk/govern ment/publications/unlocking-digital-competition-report-of-the-digital-competition -expert-panel.

8   The Digital Divide

1. G. Pascal Zachary, "Inside Nairobi, the Next Palo Alto?," *New York Times*, July 20, 2008, https://www.nytimes.com/2008/07/20/business/worldbusiness/20ping.html.

2. Trading Economics, "Tanzania—Unmet Demand," accessed August 7, 2019, https:// tradingeconomics.com/tanzania/unmet-demand-percent-of-waiting-list-to-number -main-fixed-telephone-lines-in-operation-wb-data.html.

3. Rwanda Utilities Regulatory Authority, *Statistics Report for Telecom, Media, and Broadcasting Sector as of the Fourth Quarter of the Year 2019* (Kigali: Rwanda Utilities Regulatory Authority, December 2019), https://www.rura.rw/fileadmin/Documents /ICT/statistics/Report_for_quarterly_telecom_statistics_report_as_of_December _2019.pdf.

4. For instance, Brazil has been conducting surveys of nonusers for many years, with very valuable insights based on gender, education levels, and other demographic factors, via the Regional Center for Studies to the Development of the Information Society; see https://cetic.br/publicacoes/indice/. For a summary of recent reasons users do not go online, see Gustavo Ribeiro, "How Brazilians Connect to the Internet," *Brazilian Report* (blog), July 26, 2018, https://brazilian.report/society/2018/07 /26/brazilians-connect-internet/.

5. An entry-level broadband package is considered to be 1 GB of data per month. See Broadband Commission for Sustainable Development, *The State of Broadband:*

Broadband as a Foundation for Sustainable Development (Geneva: International Tele-communication Union and United Nations Educational, Scientific, and Cultural Organization, September 2019), https://www.itu.int/dms_pub/itu-s/opb/pol/S-POL -BROADBAND.20-2019-PDF-E.pdf.

6. The Alliance for Affordable Internet has focused on increasing affordability of broadband for a number of years. It first introduced the goal of 2 percent of income, which was adopted by the Broadband Commission. For a broad list of affordability rates by country, see Alliance for Affordable Internet, "Mobile Broadband Pricing: Data for Q4 2018," A4AI.com, 4, https://a4ai.org/extra/mobile_broadband_pricing_ gnicm-2018Q4.

7. See "Data Test: How Much Is 1GB?," *Lowdown* (blog), Carphone Warehouse, June 1, 2017, https://lowdown.carphonewarehouse.com/how-to/data-test-how-much-is-1gb /29283/.

8. Kofi Annan, "Address by UN Secretary-General to the World Summit on the Infor-mation Society," Geneva, December 10, 2003, https://www.itu.int/net/wsis/geneva /coverage/statements/opening/annan.html.

9. See W3Techs, "Historical Trends in the Usage of Content Languages for Websites, August 2019," W3Techs, accessed August 7, 2019, https://w3techs.com/technologies /history_overview/content_language.

10. Leo Mirani, "Millions of Facebook Users Have No Idea They're Using the Inter-net," *Quartz* (blog), February 9, 2015, https://qz.com/333313/milliions-of-facebook -users-have-no-idea-theyre-using-the-internet/.

11. See "Survey on the Use of Information and Communication Technologies in Brazilian Households: ICT Households 2018" (São Paulo: Brazilian Internet Steering Committee, 2018), tables A10 and A10A, 273–277, https://www.cetic.br/media/docs /publicacoes/2/12225320191028-tic_dom_2018_livro_eletronico.pdf.

12. GSMA Intelligence, "Rethinking Mobile Taxaton to Improve Connectivity," GSMA, 2019, sec. 5, https://www.gsmaintelligence.com/research/?file=8f36cd1c58c 0d619d9f165261a57f4a9&download.

13. Michael Kende, David Abecassis, and Elena Korsukova, "Impact of Taxation on Social Media in Africa" (London: Analysys Mason, May 15, 2019), https://www .analysysmason.com/consulting-redirect/reports/impact-of-taxation-on-social -media-africa-may2019/.

14. When the Internet first commercialized in the United States, peering took place at Network Access Points, which were soon replaced by IXPs. For more details, see Michael Kende, *Overview of Recent Changes in the IP Interconnection Ecosystem*, white paper (London: Analysys Mason, January 23, 2011), https://www.google.com/url?sa=t &rct=j&q=&esrc=s&source=web&cd=1&ved=2ahUKEwjsuejyqMnjAhUIVhoKHUtY Do4QFjAAegQIBRAC&url=https%3A%2F%2Fwww.analysysmason.com%2FAbout

-Us%2FNews%2FInsight%2FInternet_exchange_points_Feb2011%2FRelated-report
-download%2F&usg=AOvVaw1ljdYCYnI94ou2uzrN8nc0.

15. TESPOK, "KIXP Background," Technology Service Providers of Kenya, September 30, 2015, https://www.tespok.co.ke/?page_id=11651; Michael Kende and Charles Hurpy, *Assessment of the Impact of Internet Exchange Points—Empirical Study of Kenya and Nigeria* (Analysys Mason and Internet Society, April 2012), https://www.internetsociety.org/wp-content/uploads/2017/09/Assessment-of-the-impact-of-Internet-Exchange-Points-—empirical-study-of-Kenya-and-Nigeria.pdf.

16. See, for instance, Internet Society, "Internet Exchange Points (IXPs)," accessed August 7, 2019, https://www.internetsociety.org/issues/ixps/.

17. See Kashmir Hill, "The Downside of Being a Google Executive," *Forbes*, September 27, 2012, https://www.forbes.com/sites/kashmirhill/2012/09/27/the-downside-of-being-a-google-executive/.

18. Kende and Rose, *Promoting Local Content Hosting*.

19. Michael Kende and Bastiaan Quast, *The Benefits of Local Content Hosting: A Case Study* (Internet Society, April 11, 2017), https://www.internetsociety.org/wp-content/uploads/2017/08/ISOC_LocalContentRwanda_report_20170505.pdf.

20. Wikimedia, "List of Wikipedias by Language Group—Meta," accessed August 7, 2019, https://meta.wikimedia.org/wiki/List_of_Wikipedias_by_language_group.

21. The increase in language availability makes Google more accessible, leading to more usage and even employment opportunities. See Bastiaan Quast, "Making the Next Billion Demand Access," working paper 01 (Geneva: Graduate Institute Geneva, Centre for Finance and Development, 2016), http://repec.graduateinstitute.ch/pdfs/cfdwpa/CFDWP01-2016.pdf.

22. Sudarsan Raghavan, "New Apps Transforming Remote Parts of Africa," *Washington Post*, March 31, 2013, https://www.washingtonpost.com/world/africa/new-apps-transforming-remote-parts-of-africa/2013/03/31/2149f93a-9646-11e2-8764-d42c128a01ef_story.html.

23. See Michael Kende, "ICTs for Inclusive Growth: E-Entrepreneurship on the Open Internet," in *Global Information Technology Report 2015* (Geneva: World Economic Forum, 2015), http://wef.ch/1Fqc6Ej.

24. For a full list of countries where merchants are not eligible for merchant accounts, see "Supported Locations for Developer & Merchant Registration—Play Console Help," Google Support, accessed August 7, 2019, https://support.google.com/googleplay/android-developer/answer/9306917?hl=en.

25. Desirée van Welsum and Bruno Lanvin, "E-Leadership Skills," Vision Report, The European Commission, October 2012, http://leadership2017.eu/fileadmin/eSkills Vision/documents/Vision%20report.pdf.

26. Michael Kende, *Promoting the African Internet Economy* (Internet Society, November 22, 2017), https://www.internetsociety.org/wp-content/uploads/2017/11 /AfricaInternetEconomy_111517.pdf.

27. World Bank, "A Single Digital Market for East Africa: Presenting Vision, Strategic Framework, Implementation Roadmap, and Impact Assessment" (working paper, Washington, DC: World Bank, May 8, 2019), http://documents.worldbank.org/curated /en/809911557382027900/A-Single-Digital-Market-for-East-Africa-Presenting-Vision -Strategic-Framework-Implementation-Roadmap-and-Impact-Assessment.

28. The members of ASEAN are Indonesia, Thailand, Singapore, Malaysia, Philippines, Vietnam, Cambodia, Brunei, Myanmar, and Laos.

29. Richard Baldwin, *The Globotics Upheaval: Globalisation, Robotics and the Future of Work* (New York: Oxford University Press, 2019).

30. Globalme, "Language Support in Voice Assistants Compared," Globalme, May 13, 2020, https://www.globalme.net/blog/language-support-voice-assistants-compared.

31. Christine Zhen-Wei Qiang, Carlo M. Rossotto, and Kaoru Kimura, "Economic Impacts of Broadband," in *Information and Communications for Development 2009: Extending Reach and Increasing Impact* (Washington, DC: World Bank Group, 2009), 35–50. http://siteresources.worldbank.org/EXTIC4D/Resources/IC4D_Broadband_35_50 .pdf.

32. Broadband Commission for Sustainable Development, *The State of Broadband*.

33. Brynjolfsson, Collis, and Eggers, "Using Massive Online Choice Experiments."

34. Dimitrije Curcic, "67 Years of Height Evolution in the NBA—In-Depth Research," *RunRepeat* (blog), May 14, 2019, https://runrepeat.com/height-evolution-in-the-nba.

9 Trust the Future

1. Jon Krakauer, *Into Thin Air* (New York: Villard Books, 1997).

2. Jacob Bogage, "How Mount Everest Became a Tourist Destination," *Washington Post*, May 31, 2019, https://www.washingtonpost.com/sports/2019/05/31/how-mount -everest-became-tourist-destination/.

3. Ray Kurzweil, "The Law of Accelerating Returns," *Kurzweil* (blog), March 7, 2001, https://www.kurzweilai.net/the-law-of-accelerating-returns. In other tellings of the fable, it is wheat, not rice, and takes place in India, not China. But this is the way Ray Kurzweil tells it.

4. Kurzweil; Erik Brynjolfsson and Andrew McAfee, *The Second Machine Age: Work, Progress, and Prosperity in a Time of Brilliant Technologies*. (New York: W. W. Norton & Company, 2014).

5. Viktor Mayer-Schönberger and Kenneth Cukier, *Big Data: A Revolution That Will Transform How We Live, Work, and Think* (New York: Houghton Mifflin Harcourt, 2013), chap. 2.

6. Chris Welch, "Comcast Is Reportedly Developing a Device That Would Track Your Bathroom Habits," The *Verge* (blog), May 21, 2019, https://www.theverge.com /2019/5/21/18634466/comcast-health-monitoring-speaker-amazon-echo.

7. Amy B. Wang, "'I'm in Your Baby's Room': A Hacker Took over a Baby Monitor and Broadcast Threats, Parents Say," *Washington Post*, December 20, 2018, https:// www.washingtonpost.com/technology/2018/12/20/nest-cam-baby-monitor-hacked -kidnap-threat-came-device-parents-say/.

8. See, for instance, Baldwin, *The Globotics Upheaval*.

9. Roberto Baldwin, "Netflix Gambles on Big Data to Become the HBO of Streaming," *Wired* (blog), November 29, 2012, https://www.wired.com/2012/11/netflix-data -gamble/.

10. Karen Hao, "This Is How AI Bias Really Happens—and Why It's So Hard to Fix," *MIT Technology Review*, February 4, 2019, https://www.technologyreview.com/s/612876 /this-is-how-ai-bias-really-happensand-why-its-so-hard-to-fix/.

11. Editorial Board, "Why Is America So Far Behind Europe on Digital Privacy?," *New York Times*, June 8, 2019, https://www.nytimes.com/2019/06/08/opinion/sunday /privacy-congress-facebook-google.html.

12. Zuckerberg, "A Privacy-Focused Vision for Social Networking"; Sundar Pichai, "Google's Sundar Pichai: Privacy Should Not Be a Luxury Good," *New York Times*, May 7, 2019, https://www.nytimes.com/2019/05/07/opinion/google-sundar-pichai -privacy.html; Natalia Drozdiak and Stephanie Bodoni, "'This Is Surveillance': Apple CEO Tim Cook Slams Tech Rivals over Data Collection," *Time*, October 24, 2018, https://time.com/5433499/tim-cook-apple-data-privacy/.

13. See https://www.privacyassistant.org.

14. Byron Spice, "Carnegie Mellon Study Shows People Act to Protect Privacy when Told How Often Phone Apps Share Personal Information," Carnegie Mellon School of Computer Science, March 23, 2015, https://www.cs.cmu.edu/news/carnegie-mellon -study-shows-people-act-protect-privacy-when-told-how-often-phone-apps-share -personal-information.

15. For an application of the market failures described in chapter 6 to IoT, see Schneier, *Click Here to Kill Everybody*, chap. 7.

16. Schneier, chap. 7.

17. Schneier, chap. 2.

18. "IoT Trust by Design," Online Trust Alliance, May 22, 2018, https://www
.internetsociety.org/resources/doc/2018/iot-trust-by-design; Schneier, *Click Here to Kill
Everybody*, chap. 6.

19. Joseph L. Bower and Clayton M. Christensen, "Disruptive Technologies: Catching the Wave," *Harvard Business Review* 73, no. 1 (January-February 1995).

10   The Need for Change

1. See Rana Foroohar, *Don't Be Evil: How Big Tech Betrayed Its Founding Principles—
and All of Us* (New York: Currency, 2019).

2. See, for instance, National Telecommunications and Information Administration,
"Digital Economy Accounted for 6.9 Percent of GDP in 2017," *National Telecommunications and Information Administration* (blog), April 5, 2019, https://www.ntia.doc
.gov/blog/2019/digital-economy-accounted-69-percent-gdp-2017.

3. Jeff Desjardins, "Most Valuable U.S. Companies Over 100 Years," *Visual Capitalist*
(blog), November 14, 2017, https://www.visualcapitalist.com/most-valuable-companies
-100-years/.

4. Francesca Bria, "Our Data Is Valuable: Here's How We Can Take That Value
Back," *Guardian*, April 5, 2018, https://www.theguardian.com/commentisfree/2018
/apr/05/data-valuable-citizens-silicon-valley-barcelona.

5. Kim Zetter, "Anonymized Phone Location Data Not So Anonymous, Researchers
Find," *Wired*, March 27, 2013, https://www.wired.com/2013/03/anonymous-phone
-location-data/.

Bibliography

Alliance for Affordable Internet. "Mobile Broadband Pricing: Data for Q4 2018." Accessed July 1, 2010. A4AI.com. https://a4ai.org/extra/mobile_broadband_pricing_gnicm-2018Q4.

Abbate, Janet. *Inventing the Internet*. Cambridge, MA: MIT Press, 1999.

Abecassis, David, Richard Morgan, and Shahan Osman. *Infrastructure Investment by Online Service Providers*. White paper. London: Analysys Mason, December 2018. https://www.analysysmason.com/globalassets/infrastructure-investment-by-online-service-providers---20-dec-2018---web.pdf.

Acquisti, Alessandro, and Jens Grossklags. "Privacy and Rationality in Individual Decision Making." *IEEE Security and Privacy* 3, no. 1 (January 2005): 26–33. https://doi.org/10.1109/MSP.2005.22.

Anderson, Chris. *Free: The Future of a Radical Price*. New York: Hyperion, 2009.

Anderson, Chris. *The Long Tail: Why the Future of Business Is Selling Less of More*. New York: Hyperion, 2008.

Annan, Kofi. "Address by UN Secretary-General to the World Summit on the Information Society," December 10, 2003. https://www.itu.int/net/wsis/geneva/coverage/statements/opening/annan.html.

Ariely, Dan. *Predictably Irrational: The Hidden Forces That Shape Our Decisions*. New York: HarperCollins, 2008.

Armstrong, Ann, Joseph Mueller, and Tim Syrett. *The Smartphone Royalty Stack: Surveying Royalty Demands for the Components within Modern Smartphones*. SSRN scholarly paper. Rochester, NY: Social Science Research Network, May 29, 2014. https://papers.ssrn.com/abstract=2443848.

Baldwin, Richard. *The Globotics Upheaval: Globalisation, Robotics and the Future of Work*. New York: Oxford University Press, 2019.

Baldwin, Roberto. "Netflix Gambles on Big Data to Become the HBO of Streaming." *Wired* (blog), November 29, 2012. https://www.wired.com/2012/11/netflix-data -gamble/.

Barbaro, Michael, and Tom Zeller Jr. "A Face Is Exposed for AOL Searcher No. 4417749." *New York Times*, August 9, 2006. https://www.nytimes.com/2006/08/09 /technology/09aol.html.

Barlow, John Perry. "A Declaration of the Independence of Cyberspace." Electronic Frontier Foundation, February 8, 1996. https://www.eff.org/cyberspace-independence.

Barth, Susanne, and Menno D. T. de Jong. "The Privacy Paradox—Investigating Discrepancies between Expressed Privacy Concerns and Actual Online Behavior—A Systematic Literature Review." *Telematics and Informations* 34 (2017): 1038–1058.

Battelle, John. *The Search: How Google and Its Rivals Rewrote the Rules of Business and Transformed Our Culture*. New York: Portfolio, 2005.

Bergen, Mark, and Jennifer Surane. "Google and Mastercard Cut a Secret Ad Deal to Track Retail Sales." *Bloomberg*, August 30, 2018. https://www.bloomberg.com/news /articles/2018-08-30/google-and-mastercard-cut-a-secret-ad-deal-to-track-retail-sales.

Besen, Stanley M., and George Sadowsky. "The Economics of Internet Standards." In *Handbook on the Economics of the Internet*, edited by Johannes M. Bauer and Michael Latzer, 211–228. Cheltenham, UK: Edward Elgar Publishing, 2016. https://www.elga ronline.com/view/edcoll/9780857939845/9780857939845.00018.xml.

Blum, Andrew. *Tubes: A Journey to the Center of the Internet*. New York: HarperCollins, 2012.

Bogage, Jacob. "How Mount Everest Became a Tourist Destination." *Washington Post*, May 31, 2019. https://www.washingtonpost.com/sports/2019/05/31/how-mount-eve rest-became-tourist-destination/.

Bort, Julie. "Eric Schmidt's Privacy Policy Is One Scary Philosophy." *Network World* (blog), December 11, 2009. https://www.networkworld.com/article/2232821/eric -schmidt-s-privacy-policy-is-one-scary-philosophy.html.

Bower, Joseph L., and Clayton M. Christensen. "Disruptive Technologies: Catching the Wave." *Harvard Business Review* 73, no. 1 (January-February 1995): 43–53.

Bria, Francesca. "Our Data Is Valuable: Here's How We Can Take That Value Back." *Guardian*, April 5, 2018. https://www.theguardian.com/commentlsfree/2018/apr/05 /data-valuable-citizens-silicon-valley-barcelona.

Broadband Commission for Sustainable Development. *The State of Broadband: Broad-band as a Foundation for Sustainable Development*. Geneva: International Telecommuni-cation Union and United Nations Educational, Scientific, and Cultural Organization,

September 2019. https://www.itu.int/dms_pub/itu-s/opb/pol/S-POL-BROADBAND.20 -2019-PDF-E.pdf.

Brynjolfsson, Erik, Avinash Collis, and Felix Eggers. "Using Massive Online Choice Experiments to Measure Changes in Well-Being." *Proceedings of the National Academy of Sciences* 116, no. 15 (April 2019): 7250–7255.

Brynjolfsson, Erik, and Andrew McAfee. *The Second Machine Age: Work, Progress, and Prosperity in a Time of Brilliant Technologies*. New York: W. W. Norton & Company, 2014.

Campbell-Kelly, Martin. "Pioneer Profiles: Donald Davies." *Computer Resurrection* 44 (Autumn 2008). http://www.computerconservationsociety.org/resurrection/res44 .htm.

Cerf, Vinton G. "Ownership vs. Stewardship." *Communications of the ACM* 62, no. 3 (March 2019): 6.

CERN. "The Birth of the Web." Accessed June 11, 2019. https://home.cern/science /computing/birth-web.

Clark, David D. "A Cloudy Crystal Ball—Visions of the Future." In *Proceedings of the Twenty-Fourth Internet Engineering Task Force*, edited by Meagan Davies, Cynthia Clark, and Debra Legare, 539–543. Reston, VA: Corporation for National Research Initiatives, 1992. https://www.ietf.org/proceedings/24.pdf.

Coase, Ronald, "The Problem of Social Cost." *Journal of Law and Economics* 3 (October 1960): 1–44.

Contreras, Jorge. *Patents and Internet Standards*. Global Commission on Internet Governance Paper Series, GCIG paper no. 29. Waterloo, Canada, and London: CIGI and Chatham House, April 15, 2016. https://www.cigionline.org/publications/patents -and-internet-standards.

Contreras, Jorge. "Why We Need a Global FRAND Rate-Setting Tribunal." Research Institute of Economy, Trade and Industry. *Perspectives from around the World* (blog), June 6, 2019. https://www.rieti.go.jp/en/special/p_a_w/128.html.

Corrigan, Jay R., Saleem Alhabash, Matthew Rousu, and Sean B. Cash. "How Much Is Social Media Worth? Estimating the Value of Facebook by Paying Users to Stop Using It." *PLOS ONE* 13, no. 12 (December 19, 2018): 1–11. https://doi.org/10.1371 /journal.pone.0207101.

Crémer, Jacques, Yves-Alexandre de Montjoye, and Heike Schweitzer. *Competition Policy for the Digital Era*. European Commission, Directorate-General for Competition. Luxembourg: Publication Office of the European Union, 2019. http://publications.europa.eu/publication/manifestation_identifier/PUB_KD0419 345ENN.

Curcic, Dimitrije. "67 Years of Height Evolution in the NBA—In-Depth Research." *RunRepeat* (blog), May 14, 2019. https://runrepeat.com/height-evolution-in-the-nba.

"Data Breaches Compromised 3.3 Billion Records in First Half of 2018." Amsterdam: Gemalto | Thales Group, October 23, 2018. https://www.thalesgroup.com/en /markets/digital-identity-and-security/press-release/data-breaches-compromised-3-3 -billion-records-in-first-half-of-2018.

"Data Test: How Much Is 1GB?" *Lowdown* (blog). Carphone Warehouse, June 1, 2017. https://lowdown.carphonewarehouse.com/how-to/data-test-how-much-is-1gb/29283/.

Desjardins, Jeff. "Most Valuable U.S. Companies Over 100 Years." *Visual Capitalist* (blog), November 14, 2017. https://www.visualcapitalist.com/most-valuable-compa nies-100-years/.

Digital Competition Expert Panel. *Unlocking Digital Competition, Report of the Digital Competition Expert Panel*. London: HM Treasury, United Kingdom, March 13, 2019. https://www.gov.uk/government/publications/unlocking-digital-competition-report -of-the-digital-competition-expert-panel.

Directive 95/46/EC of the European Parliament and of the Council of 24 October 1995 on the Protection of Individuals with Regard to the Processing of Personal Data and on the Free Movement of Such Data. 1995. http://data.europa.eu/eli/dir/1995/46/oj.

Drozdiak, Natalia, and Stephanie Bodoni. "'This Is Surveillance': Apple CEO Tim Cook Slams Tech Rivals over Data Collection." *Time*, October 24, 2018. https://time .com/5433499/tim-cook-apple-data-privacy/.

DuckDuckGo. "DuckDuckGo Privacy." Accessed August 6, 2019. https://duckduckgo .com/privacy.

DuckDuckGo. "DuckDuckGo Traffic." Accessed August 6, 2019. https://duckduckgo .com/traffic.

Duhigg, Charles. "How Companies Learn Your Secrets." *New York Times Magazine*, February 16, 2012. https://www.nytimes.com/2012/02/19/magazine/shopping-habits .html.

Eaton, Kit. "How One Second Could Cost Amazon $1.6 Billion In Sales." *Fast Company*, March 15, 2012. https://www.fastcompany.com/1825005/how-one-second-could -cost-amazon-16-billion-sales.

Editorial Board. "Why Is America So Far Behind Europe on Digital Privacy?" *New York Times*, June 8, 2019. https://www.nytimes.com/2019/06/08/opinion/sunday/privacy -congress-facebook-google.html.

Farrell, Joseph and Timothy Simcoe, "Four Paths to Compatibility." In *The Oxford Handbook of the Digital Economy*, edited by Martin Peitz and Joel Waldfogel, 34–58. New York: Oxford University Press, 2012.

Flegenheimer, Matt. "$1 Million Medallions Stifling the Dreams of Cabdrivers." *New York Times*, November 14, 2013. https://www.nytimes.com/2013/11/15/nyregion/1 -million-medallions-stifling-the-dreams-of-cabdrivers.html.

Foroohar, Rana. *Don't Be Evil: How Big Tech Betrayed Its Founding Principles—and All of US*. New York: Currency, 2019.

Foroohar, Rana. "Year in a Word: Techlash." *Financial Times*, December 16, 2018.

Fottrell, Quentin. "Meet Amazon's First Customer—This Is the Book He Bought." *MarketWatch* (blog), May 15, 2017. https://www.marketwatch.com/story/meet-amazons-first -ever-customer-2015-04-22.

Fowler, Geoffrey A. "What If We Paid for Facebook—Instead of Letting It Spy on Us for Free?" *Washington Post*, April 5, 2018. https://www.washingtonpost.com/news /the-switch/wp/2018/04/05/what-if-we-paid-for-facebook-instead-of-letting-it-spy -on-us-for-free/.

Fox-Brewster, Tom. "TRUSTe Fined $200,000 for Misleading Web Security Seal." *Guardian*, November 18, 2014. https://www.theguardian.com/technology/2014/nov /18/truste-fine-web-security-seals.

"Frequently Asked Questions: What Is a Pod?" Accessed July 2, 2020. https://solidpro ject.org/faqs.

Gabbert, Elisa. "The 25 Most Expensive Keywords in AdWords—2017 Edition!" *WordStream* (blog), June 10, 2019. https://www.wordstream.com/blog/ws/2017/06 /27/most-expensive-keywords.

Gilbert, Ben. "There's a Simple Reason Your New Smart TV Was So Affordable: It's Collecting and Selling Your Data, and Serving You Ads." *Business Insider*, April 5, 2019. https://www.businessinsider.com/smart-tv-data-collection-advertising-2019-1.

Globalme. "Language Support in Voice Assistants Compared." Globalme. May 13, 2020, https://www.globalme.net/blog/language-support-voice-assistants-compared.

Gneezy, Uri, and Aldo Rustichini. "A Fine Is a Price." *Journal of Legal Studies* 29, no. 1 (January 2000): 1–17.

Goldman, David. "Your Samsung TV Is Eavesdropping on Your Private Conversations." CNN Business, February 10, 2015. https://money.cnn.com/2015/02/09/tech nology/security/samsung-smart-tv-privacy/index.html.

Google Ads Help. "About Ad Position and Ad Rank." Accessed June 11, 2019. https:// support.google.com/google-ads/answer/1722122?hl=en.

Greenberg, Andy. "Hackers Remotely Kill a Jeep on the Highway—With Me in It." *Wired*, July 21, 2015. https://www.wired.com/2015/07/hackers-remotely-kill-jeep -highway/.

Greenberg, Andy. "It's Been 20 Years since This Man Declared Cyberspace Independence." *Wired*, February 8, 2016. https://www.wired.com/2016/02/its-been-20-years -since-this-man-declared-cyberspace-independence/.

Grimes, William. "Raymond Tomlinson, Who Put the @ Sign in Email, Is Dead at 74." *New York Times*, March 7, 2016. https://www.nytimes.com/2016/03/08/technology /raymond-tomlinson-email-obituary.html.

GSMA Intelligence. "Rethinking Mobile Taxation to Improve Connectivity." GSMA, 2019. https://www.gsma.com/publicpolicy/wp-content/uploads/2019/02/Rethinking -mobile-taxation-to-improve-connectivity_Feb19.pdf.

Hafner, Katie, and Matthew Lyon. *Where Wizards Stay Up Late: The Origins of the Internet*. New York: Simon & Schuster, 1996.

Hao, Karen. "This Is How AI Bias Really Happens—and Why It's So Hard to Fix." *MIT Technology Review*, February 4, 2019. https://www.technologyreview.com/s/612876 /this-is-how-ai-bias-really-happensand-why-its-so-hard-to-fix/.

Harrison, Sam. "Can You Make Money Selling Your Data?" BBC, September 21, 2018. https://www.bbc.com/worklife/article/20180921-can-you-make-money-selling-your -data.

Hawking, Stephen W. *A Brief History of Time: From the Big Bang to Black Holes*. New York: Bantam Books, 1988.

Hern, Alex. "Fitness Tracking App Strava Gives Away Location of Secret US Army Bases." *Guardian*, January 28, 2018. https://www.theguardian.com/world/2018/jan /28/fitness-tracking-app-gives-away-location-of-secret-us-army-bases.

Hicks, John R. "Annual Survey of Economic Theory: The Theory of Monopoly." *Econometrica* 3, no. 1 (January 1935): 1–20.

Hill, Kashmir. "The Downside of Being a Google Executive." *Forbes*, September 27, 2012. https://www.forbes.com/sites/kashmirhill/2012/09/27/the-downside-of-being -a-google-executive/.

Hill, Simon. "Why Do We Call It Spam? Blame Spiced Ham Shoulder, Monty Python and Usenet." *Digital Trends* (blog), February 8, 2015. https://www.digitaltrends.com /web/why-junk-email-is-spam/.

Hitlin, Paul, and Lee Rainie. "Facebook Algorithms and Personal Data." Pew Research Center, January 16, 2019. https://www.pewinternet.org/2019/01/16/facebook-algori thms-and-personal-data/.

Huston, Geoff. "Carriage vs. Content." *ISP Column* (blog), July 2012. http://www .potaroo.net/ispcol/2012-07/carriagevcontent.html.

Huston, Geoff. "Where Is the Content Economy?" *ISP Column* (blog), June 2001. http://www.potaroo.net/ispcol/2001-06/2001-06-content.html.

"Industry: ISPs," *Cybertelecom* (blog). Accessed July 2, 2020. https://www.cybertelecom .org/industry/isp.htm.

Institute on Governance. "Defining Governance?" Accessed on September 1, 2019. http://iog.ca/what-is-governance/.

Internet Live Stats. "1 Second—Internet Live Stats." Accessed August 6, 2019. https:// www.internetlivestats.com/one-second/#google-band.

Internet Society. *Global Internet Report 2016: The Economics of Building Trust Online: Preventing Data Breaches.* Internet Society, 2016. https://www.internetsociety.org /globalinternetreport/2016/.

Internet Society. "Internet Exchange Points (IXPs)." Accessed August 7, 2019. https:// www.internetsociety.org/issues/ixps/.

Internet Society. *Internet Invariants: What Really Matters.* Internet Society, October 18, 2016. https://www.internetsociety.org/wp-content/uploads/2017/08/Internet20Invari ants-20What20Really20Matters.pdf.

Internet Society. *An Introduction to Privacy on the Internet: An Internet Society Public Policy Briefing.* Internet Society, October 30, 2015. https://www.internetsociety.org /wp-content/uploads/2015/10/ISOC-PolicyBrief-Privacy-20151030-nb-1.pdf.

"IoT Trust by Design." Online Trust Alliance, May 22, 2018. https://www.internetsociety .org/resources/doc/2018/iot-trust-by-design.

Jacobsen, Ole J., ed. *ConneXions: The Interoperability Report* 2, no. 11 (November 1988). http://www.cbi.umn.edu/hostedpublications/Connexions/ConneXions02_1988 /ConneXions2-11_Nov1988.pdf.

Kanich, Chris, Christian Kreibich, Kirill Levchenko, Brandon Enright, Geoffrey M. Voelker, Vern Paxson, and Stefan Savage. "Spamalytics: An Empirical Analysis of Spam Marketing Conversion." In *Proceedings of the 15th ACM Conference on Computer and Communications Security,* 3–14. CCS '08. New York: ACM, 2008. https://doi.org /10.1145/1455770.1455774.

Kassner, Michael. "Anatomy of the Target Data Breach: Missed Opportunities and Lessons Learned." ZDNet, February 2, 2015. https://www.zdnet.com/article/anatomy -of-the-target-data-breach-missed-opportunities-and-lessons-learned/.

Kende, Michael. "The Digital Handshake: Connecting Internet Backbones." Office of Plans and Policy Working Paper Series. Washington, DC: Federal Communications Commission, September 1, 2000. https://www.fcc.gov/reports-research/working-papers /digital-handshake-connecting-internet-backbones.

Kende, Michael. "ICTs for Inclusive Growth: E-Entrepreneurship on the Open Internet." In *Global Information Technology Report 2015.* Geneva: World Economic Forum, 2015. http://wef.ch/1Fqc6Ej.

Kende, Michael. *Overview of Recent Changes in the IP Interconnection Ecosystem*. White paper. London: Analysys Mason, January 23, 2011. https://www.analysysmason.com /globalassets/x_migrated-media/media/analysys_mason_international_ip_interconnec tion_23_feb_20113.pdf.

Kende, Michael. *Promoting the African Internet Economy*. Internet Society, November 22, 2017. https://www.internetsociety.org/wp-content/uploads/2017/11/AfricaInter netEconomy_111517.pdf.

Kende, Michael, David Abecassis, and Elena Korsukova. *Impact of Taxation on Social Media in Africa*. London: Analysys Mason, May 15, 2019. https://www.analysysmason .com/consulting-redirect/reports/impact-of-taxation-on-social-media-africa-may 2019/.

Kende, Michael, and Charles Hurpy. *Assessment of the Impact of Internet Exchange Points—Empirical Study of Kenya and Nigeria*. Analysys Mason and Internet Society, April 2012. https://www.internetsociety.org/wp-content/uploads/2017/09/Assessment -of-the-impact-of-Internet-Exchange-Points---empirical-study-of-Kenya-and-Nigeria .pdf.

Kende, Michael, and Bastiaan Quast. *The Benefits of Local Content Hosting: A Case Study*. Internet Society, May 2017. https://www.internetsociety.org/wp-content/uploads /2017/08/ISOC_LocalContentRwanda_report_20170505.pdf.

Kende, Michael, and Karen Rose. *Promoting Local Content Hosting to Develop the Internet Ecosystem*. Internet Society, January 12, 2015. https://www.internetsociety .org/resources/doc/2015/promoting-local-content-hosting-to-develop-the-internet -ecosystem/.

Khan, Lina. "Amazon's Antitrust Paradox." *Yale Law Journal* 126 (2017): 710–805.

King, Don Roy. "SNL Transcripts: Tom Hanks: 10/08/88: First Citiwide Change Bank I." SNL Transcripts Tonight, October 8, 2018. https://snltranscripts.jt.org/88 /88achangebank1.phtml.

King, Don Roy. "SNL Transcripts: Tom Hanks: 10/08/88: First Citiwide Change Bank II." SNL Transcripts Tonight, October 8, 2018. https://snltranscripts.jt.org/88 /88achangebank2.phtml.

Kokolakis, Spyros. "Privacy Attitudes and Privacy Behavior: A Review of Current Research on the Privacy Paradox Phenomenon." *Computer Security* 64 (2017): 122–134.

KPMG. *Protecting the Fleet … and the Car Business*. KPMG's US Manufacturing Institute Automotive Center, 2017. https://advisory.kpmg.us/content/dam/advisory/en /pdfs/protecting-the-fleet-web1.pdf.

Krakauer, Jon. *Into Thin Air*. New York: Villard Books, 1997.

Kumaraguru, Ponnurangam, and Lorrie Faith Cranor. *Privacy Indexes: A Survey of Westin's Studies*. Pittsburgh: School of Computer Science, Carnegie Mellon University, December 2005. http://reports-archive.adm.cs.cmu.edu/anon/isri2005/CMU-ISRI -05-138.pdf.

Kurzweil, Ray. "The Law of Accelerating Returns." *Kurzweil* (blog), March 7, 2001. https://www.kurzweilai.net/the-law-of-accelerating-returns.

Lamont, Tom. "Life after the Ashley Madison Affair." *Guardian*, February 28, 2016. https://www.theguardian.com/technology/2016/feb/28/what-happened-after -ashley-madison-was-hacked.

Leasca, Stacey. "People Would Rather Have the Internet than a Cure for Cancer, Study Says." *Elite Daily* (blog), May 11, 2016. https://www.elitedaily.com/envision /internet-obsession-cure-for-cancer/1490852.

Lehr, William. "Compatibility Standards and Interoperability: Lessons from the Internet." In *Standards Policy for Information Infrastructure*, edited by Brian Kahin and Janet Abbate, 121–147. Cambridge, MA: MIT Press, 1995.

Lehr, William, David D. Clark, Steven Bauer, Arthur Berger, and Philipp Richter. *Whither the Public Internet?* SSRN scholarly paper. Rochester, NY: Social Science Research Network, March 16, 2018. https://papers.ssrn.com/abstract=3141969.

Leiner, Barry M., Vinton G. Cerf, David D. Clark, Robert E. Kahn, Leonard Kleinrock, Lynch, Daniel C., Jon Postel, Larry G. Roberts, and Stephen Wolff. *Brief History of the Internet*. Internet Society, 1997. Last updated September 13, 2017. https://www .internetsociety.org/wp-content/uploads/2017/09/ISOC-History-of-the-Internet_1997 .pdf.

Lohr, Steve. "Google's Competitors Square Off against Its Leader." *New York Times*, September 21, 2011. https://www.nytimes.com/2011/09/22/technology/google-takes -the-hot-seat-in-washington.html.

Lomas, Natasha. "Google Fined $2.7BN for EU Antitrust Violations over Shopping Searches." *TechCrunch* (blog), June 27, 2017. http://social.techcrunch.com/2017/06 /27/google-fined-e2-42bn-for-eu-antitrust-violations-over-shopping-searches/.

Manara, Cedric. "Protecting What We Love about the Internet: Our Efforts to Stop Online Piracy." *Google Public Policy* (blog), November 7, 2018. https://www .blog.google/outreach-initiatives/public-policy/protecting-what-we-love-about -internet-our-efforts-stop-online-piracy/.

Mayer-Schönberger, Viktor, and Kenneth Cukier. *Big Data: A Revolution That Will Transform How We Live, Work, and Think*. New York: Houghton Mifflin Harcourt, 2013.

McCracken, Harry. "A History of AOL, as Told in Its Own Old Press Releases." *Technologizer: A Smarter Take on Tech* (blog), May 24, 2010. https://www.technologizer.com/2010/05/24/aol-anniversary/.

McCullough, Brian. *How the Internet Happened: From Netscape to the iPhone*. New York: Liveright Publishing Corporation, 2018.

Mirani, Leo. "Millions of Facebook Users Have No Idea They're Using the Internet." *Quartz* (blog), February 9, 2015. https://qz.com/333313/milliions-of-facebook-users-have-no-idea-theyre-using-the-internet/.

Moll, Joana, and Tactical Tech. "The Dating Brokers: An Autopsy of Online Love." Tactical Tech, October 2018. https://datadating.tacticaltech.org/viz.

Nader, Ralph. *Unsafe at Any Speed*. New York: Grossman Publishers, 1965.

National Inventors Hall of Fame. "Featured Exhibit: Experience Automotive Innovation with the Ford Mustang." Accessed August 6, 2019. https://www.invent.org/blog/innovation-display/featured-exhibit-ford-mustang.

National Research Council. *Realizing the Information Future: The Internet and Beyond*. Washington, DC: National Academies Press, 1994. https://doi.org/10.17226/4755.

National Telecommunications and Information Administration. "Digital Economy Accounted for 6.9 Percent of GDP in 2017." *National Telecommunications and Information Administration* (blog), April 5, 2019. https://www.ntia.doc.gov/blog/2019/digital-economy-accounted-69-percent-gdp-2017.

Nordhaus, William D. *Schumpeterian Profits and the Alchemist Fallacy*. Yale Economic Applications and Policy Discussion paper no. 6. Rochester, NY: Yale University, April 2, 2005. https://papers.ssrn.com/abstract=820309.

Norris, Floyd, and Lawrence M. Fisher. "Offspring Outweighs Parent as Offering Hits the Market." *New York Times*, March 3, 2000. https://www.nytimes.com/2000/03/03/business/offspring-outweighs-parent-as-offering-hits-the-market.html.

NPR. "The Cost of Free Doughnuts." *Planet Money*, January 8, 2020. Episode originally aired in 2012. https://www.npr.org/transcripts/794592539.

Online Trust Alliance. *2018 Cyber Incident & Breach Trends Report*. Reston, VA: Internet Society, July 9, 2019. https://www.internetsociety.org/wp-content/uploads/2019/07/OTA-Incident-Breach-Trends-Report_2019.pdf.

Oxman, Jason. "The FCC and the Unregulation of the Internet." Office of Plans and Policy Working Paper no. 31. Washington, DC: Federal Communications Commission, July 1999. https://transition.fcc.gov/Bureaus/OPP/working_papers/oppwp31.pdf.

Page, Ros. "Beware the Hidden Conditions in Your User Agreement." CHOICE, March 15, 2017. https://www.choice.com.au/shopping/consumer-rights-and-advice/your-rights/articles/end-user-licence-agreement-hidden-conditions-and-risks.

Pan, Ellen, Jingjing Ren, Martina Lindorfer, Christo Wilson, and David Choffnes. "Panoptispy—Characterizing Audio and Video Exfiltration from Android Applications." *Proceedings of Privacy Enhancing Technologies Symposium* 18, no. 4 (2018):1–18. https://recon.meddle.mobi/panoptispy/.

Peitz, Martin, and Joel Waldfogel, eds. *The Oxford Handbook of the Digital Economy*. New York: Oxford University Press, 2012.

Pichai, Sundar. "Google's Sundar Pichai: Privacy Should Not Be a Luxury Good." *New York Times*, May 7, 2019. https://www.nytimes.com/2019/05/07/opinion/google -sundar-pichai-privacy.html.

Privacy team. "GDPR—What Happened?" *Whotracks.Me* (blog), September 3, 2018. https://whotracks.me/blog/gdpr-what-happened.html.

Qiang, Christine Zhen-Wei, Carlo M. Rossotto, and Kaoru Kimura. "Economic Impacts of Broadband." In *Information and Communications for Development 2009: Extending Reach and Increasing Impact*, 35–50. Washington, DC: World Bank Group, 2009. http://documents1.worldbank.org/curated/en/645821468337815208/pdf/487 910PUB0EPI11010Official0Use0Only1.pdf.

Quast, Bastiaan. "Making the Next Billion Demand Access." Working paper 01. Geneva: Graduate Institute Geneva, Centre for Finance and Development, 2016. http://repec.graduateinstitute.ch/pdfs/cfdwpa/CFDWP01-2016.pdf.

Raghavan, Sudarsan. "New Apps Transforming Remote Parts of Africa." *Washington Post*, March 31, 2013. https://www.washingtonpost.com/world/africa/new-apps-trans forming-remote-parts-of-africa/2013/03/31/2149f93a-9646-11e2-8764-d42c128a01ef _story.html.

Ram, Aliya, and Madhumita Murgia. "Data Brokers: Regulators Try to Rein in the 'Privacy Deathstars.'" *Financial Times*, January 8, 2019.

Regulation (EU) 2016/679 of the European Parliament and of the Council of 27 April 2016 on the Protection of Natural Persons with Regard to the Processing of Personal Data and on the Free Movement of Such Data, and Repealing Directive 95/46/EC (General Data Protection Regulation), 2016. http://data.europa.eu/eli/reg/2016/679 /2016-05-04.

Report of the Working Group on Internet Governance. Bogis-Bossey, Switzerland: Working Group on Internet Governance, June 2005. http://www.wgig.org/WGIG-Report.html.

Resnick, Pete. "On Consensus and Humming in the IETF." Requests for Comments. Internet Engineering Task Force, June 2014. https://tools.ietf.org/html/rfc7282#ref -Clark.

Resolution Adopted by the General Assembly 56/183. World Summit on the Information Society, Pub. L. No. United Nations A/RES/56/183. January 31, 2002. https:// www.itu.int/net/wsis/docs/background/resolutions/56_183_unga_2002.pdf.

Ribeiro, Gustavo. "How Brazilians Connect to the Internet." *Brazilian Report* (blog), July 26, 2018. https://brazilian.report/society/2018/07/26/brazilians-connect-internet/.

Rosenthal, Brian M. "'They Were Conned': How Reckless Loans Devastated a Generation of Taxi Drivers." *New York Times*, May 19, 2019. https://www.nytimes.com /2019/05/19/nyregion/nyc-taxis-medallions-suicides.html.

Rowland, Christopher. "With Fitness Trackers in the Workplace, Bosses Can Monitor Your Every Step—and Possibly More." *Washington Post*, February 16, 2019. https://www.washingtonpost.com/business/economy/with-fitness-trackers-in-the -workplace-bosses-can-monitor-your-every-step--and-possibly-more/2019/02/15 /75ee0848-2a45-11e9-b011-d8500644dc98_story.html.

Rubens, Paul. "Open Source Code Contains Fewer Defects, but There's a Catch." *CIO* (blog), November 18, 2014. https://www.cio.com/article/2847880/open-source-code -contains-fewer-defects-but-theres-a-catch.html.

Rwanda Utilities Regulatory Authority. *Statistics Report for Telecom, Media and Broadcasting Sector as of the Fourth Quarter of the Year 2019*. Kigali: Rwanda Utilities Regulatory Authority, December 2019. https://www.rura.rw/fileadmin/Documents/ICT /statistics/Report_for_quarterly_telecom_statistics_report_as_of_December_2019.pdf.

Schneier, Bruce. *Click Here to Kill Everybody: Security and Survival in a Hyper-connected World*. New York: W. W. Norton & Company, 2018.

Schwab, Katharine. "How Widely Do Companies Share User Data? Here's A Chilling Glimpse." *Fast Company*, January 19, 2018. https://www.fastcompany.com/90157501 /how-widely-do-companies-share-user-data-heres-a-chilling-glimpse.

Scism, Leslie. "Insurers Creating a Consumer Ratings Service for Cybersecurity Industry." *Wall Street Journal*, March 26, 2019. https://www.wsj.com/articles/insurers -creating-a-consumer-ratings-service-for-cybersecurity-industry-11553592600.

Segal, Adam. "Using Incentives to Shape the Zero-Day Market." *Cyber Brief* (blog). Council on Foreign Relations, September 19, 2016. https://www.cfr.org/report/using -incentives-shape-zero-day-market.

Singer, Natasha. "Mapping, and Sharing, the Consumer Genome." *New York Times*, June 16, 2012. https://www.nytimes.com/2012/06/17/technology/acxiom-the-quiet -giant-of-consumer-database-marketing.html.

Smith, Justin. "ECommerce Website Pricing: What Affects Cost in an ECommerce Build." *OuterBox* (blog), January 22, 2020. https://www.outerboxdesign.com/web-design -articles/ecommerce_website_pricing.

Spice, Byron. "Carnegie Mellon Study Shows People Act to Protect Privacy when Told How Often Phone Apps Share Personal Information." Carnegie Mellon School of Computer Science, March 23, 2015. https://www.cs.cmu.edu/news/carnegie-mellon

-study-shows-people-act-protect-privacy-when-told-how-often-phone-apps-share -personal-information.

"Starbucks Privacy Statement," January 1, 2020. https://www.starbucks.com/about -us/company-information/online-policies/privacy-policy.

Stone, Brad. *The Upstarts: How Uber, Airbnb, and the Killer Companies of the New Silicon Valley Are Changing the World*. New York: Little, Brown and Company, 2017.

Sullivan, Andrew. "Avoiding Lamentation: To Build a Future Internet." *Journal of Cyber Policy* 2, no. 3 (September 2, 2017): 323–337. https://doi.org/10.1080/23738871.2017 .1400083.

"Supported Locations for Developer & Merchant Registration—Play Console Help." Google Support. Accessed August 7, 2019. https://support.google.com/googleplay /android-developer/answer/9306917?hl=en.

"Survey on the Use of Information and Communication Technologies in Brazilian Households: ICT Households 2018." São Paulo: Brazilian Internet Steering Committee, 2019. https://www.cetic.br/media/docs/publicacoes/2/12225320191028-tic_dom_2018_ livro_eletronico.pdf.

Svalbarði Polar Iceberg Water. "The Story of Svalbarði." Accessed July 2, 2020. https:// svalbardi.com/pages/the-story.

Telecommunications Development Sector. *Regulating Broadband Prices*. Broadband Series. Geneva: International Telecommunication Union, April 2012. https://www .itu.int/ITU-D/treg/broadband/ITU-BB-Reports_RegulatingPrices.pdf.

TESPOK. "KIXP Background." Technology Service Providers of Kenya, September 30, 2015. https://www.tespok.co.ke/?page_id=11651.

Thaler, Richard H., and Cass R. Sunstein. *Nudge: Improving Decisions about Health, Wealth, and Happiness*. New Haven: Yale University Press, 2008.

Timberg, Craig. "A Flaw in the Design." *Washington Post*, May 30, 2015. http://www .washingtonpost.com/sf/business/2015/05/30/net-of-insecurity-part-1/.

Timberg, Craig. "FTC: Google Did Not Break Antitrust Law with Search Practices." *Washington Post*, January 3, 2013. https://www.washingtonpost.com/business/technology /ftc-to-announce-google-settlement-today/2013/01/03/ecb599f0-55c6-11e2-bf3e -76c0a789346f_story.html.

Tirole, Jean. *Economics for the Common Good*. Princeton, NJ: Princeton University Press, 2017. https://press.princeton.edu/titles/10919.html.

Trading Economics. "Tanzania—Unmet Demand." Accessed August 7, 2019. https:// tradingeconomics.com/tanzania/unmet-demand-percent-of-waiting-list-to-number -main-fixed-telephone-lines-in-operation-wb-data.html.

"Tunis Agenda for the Information Society." Document WSIS-05/TUNIS/DOC/6(Rev. 1)-E. ITU, November 18, 2005. https://www.itu.int/net/wsis/docs2/tunis/off/6rev1 .html.

UN General Assembly. The Right to Privacy in the Digital Age: Resolution Adopted by the General Assembly on 18 December 2013. United Nations, December 2013.

United Nations. *The Universal Declaration of Human Rights*, 1948. http://www.un.org /en/universal-declaration-human-rights/.

United States Department of Justice. "Assistant Attorney General Makan Delrahim Delivers Keynote Address at Silicon Flatirons Annual Technology Policy Conference at the University of Colorado Law School." Boulder, CO, February 11, 2019. https:// www.justice.gov/opa/speech/assistant-attorney-general-makan-delrahim-delivers -keynote-address-silicon-flatirons.

Valentino-DeVries, Jennifer, Natasha Singer, Michael H. Keller, and Aaron Krolik. "Your Apps Know Where You Were Last Night, and They're Not Keeping It Secret." *New York Times*, December 10, 2018. https://www.nytimes.com/interactive/2018/12 /10/business/location-data-privacy-apps.html.

W3Techs. "Historical Trends in the Usage of Content Languages for Websites, August 2019." Accessed August 7, 2019. https://w3techs.com/technologies/history_ overview/content_language.

Wang, Amy B. "'I'm in Your Baby's Room': A Hacker Took over a Baby Monitor and Broadcast Threats, Parents Say." *Washington Post*, December 20, 2018. https:// www.washingtonpost.com/technology/2018/12/20/nest-cam-baby-monitor-hacked -kidnap-threat-came-device-parents-say/.

Welch, Chris. "Comcast Is Reportedly Developing a Device That Would Track Your Bathroom Habits." *Verge* (blog), May 21, 2019. https://www.theverge.com/2019/5/21 /18634466/comcast-health-monitoring-speaker-amazon-echo.

Wells, John D., Joseph S. Valacich, and Traci J. Hess. "What Signal Are You Sending? How Website Quality Influences Perceptions of Product Quality and Purchase Intentions." *MIS Quarterly* 35, no. 2 (June 2011): 373–396.

Welsum, Desirée van, and Bruno Lanvin. "E-Leadership Skills." Vision Report. The European Commission, October 2012. http://leadership2017.eu/fileadmin/eSkillsVision /documents/Vision%20report.pdf.

Wikimedia. "List of Wikipedias by Language Group—Meta." Accessed August 7, 2019. https://meta.wikimedia.org/wiki/List_of_Wikipedias_by_language_group.

Wired Staff. "Linux: Fewer Bugs than Rivals." *Wired*, December 14, 2004. https:// www.wired.com/2004/12/linux-fewer-bugs-than-rivals/.

World Bank. "A Single Digital Market for East Africa: Presenting Vision, Strategic Framework, Implementation Roadmap, and Impact Assessment." Working paper. Washington, DC: World Bank, May 8, 2019. http://documents.worldbank.org/curated /en/809911557382027900/A-Single-Digital-Market-for-East-Africa-Presenting-Vision -Strategic-Framework-Implementation-Roadmap-and-Impact-Assessment.

World Summit on the Information Society. "Basic Information: About WSIS." Accessed July 24, 2019. https://www.itu.int/net/wsis/basic/about.html.

Wu, Tim. *The Curse of Bigness: Antitrust in the New Gilded Age*. New York: Columbia Global Reports, 2018.

Zachary, G. Pascal. "Inside Nairobi, the Next Palo Alto?" *New York Times*, July 20, 2008. https://www.nytimes.com/2008/07/20/business/worldbusiness/20ping.html.

Zetter, Kim. "Anonymized Phone Location Data Not So Anonymous, Researchers Find." *Wired*, March 27, 2013. https://www.wired.com/2013/03/anonymous-phone -location-data/.

Zuckerberg, Mark. "A Privacy-Focused Vision for Social Networking." Facebook, March 6, 2019. https://www.facebook.com/notes/mark-zuckerberg/a-privacy-focused-vision -for-social-networking/10156700570096634/.

Index

3Com, 66–67

9/11 terrorist attacks, 44–46

Ad blockers, 77–78
Advertising
  accounts and, 71–72
  apps and, 12, 90, 102, 164, 169, 188
  banners and, 65, 74, 77
  bubbles and, 65–67, 69
  business models and, 64–72, 74, 78
  consumers and, 65, 67, 72
  cookies and, 71–72
  digital divide and, 150, 164, 167, 169
  Google and, 67, 69–70, 73, 77
  health issues and, 70–71, 73
  Internet economics and, 12
  Internet service providers (ISPs) and,
    68, 79
  keywords and, 70
  mobile, 75–77
  music and, 67, 75, 79
  need for change and, 193
  networks and, 64, 67, 74–75
  online economic growth and, 68–75
  personal data and, 70, 76–79, 90, 139
  platforms and, 122, 128, 131, 133,
    140, 143–144
  privacy and, 70–71, 80, 90–91, 94–96,
    99, 102–103
  programmatic, 74–75

public records and, 71
ranked, 70
regulation and, 72
revenue and, 65–70, 74–79, 94, 128,
  131, 144, 164
search ads and, 69–71
security and, 80, 109, 113
spam and, 16, 62, 64, 139
subscriptions and, 67–71, 75, 77–78
targeted, 70, 76, 78–79, 90, 95–96
television and, 63, 78, 140
third parties and, 72, 76
trust and, 188
videos and, 68–69, 75, 78–79
Wanamaker and, 63–64, 78
Your Ad Preferences and, 99
Airbnb, 121, 128–131, 135, 187
Algeria, 164
Algorithms
  digital divide and, 167, 170
  governance and, 182
  need for change and, 192
  Netflix ratings and, 95
  platforms and, 137, 139–140,
    144–145
  privacy and, 95, 98
  search, 98
  trust and, 181–182, 187, 189
Alibaba, 133, 171
Alliance for Affordable Internet (A4AI),
  216n6

Allow States and Victims to Fight Online Sex Trafficking (FOSTA), 214n15
Alphabet (company), 121, 154, 157, 183, 194
Amazon
  company value of, 67
  competition and, 6
  delivery times and, 69
  digital divide and, 169, 180, 184
  need for change and, 192, 194
  online retail share of, 142
  platforms and, 121–122, 127, 129, 133–136, 142, 144
  privacy and, 73, 184
  response times and, 136
  start of, 127
  user agreements and, 89
  winner-takes-all markets and, 133–136, 142, 144
Amazon Alexa, 135, 169
Amazon Kindle, 89
Amazon Marketplace, 144
Amazon Mechanical Turk, 129
Amazon Prime, 129
Android, 25–26, 35, 37, 42, 58, 135, 140, 164
Annan, Kofi, 18
Anonymity, 70, 85, 87, 90, 94, 189, 198
Antitrust cases, 24, 123, 125, 141–145, 147, 175, 195
AOL, 5, 49–50, 61, 65, 70–71, 198
Apache Web Server, 36
Apple
  Android and, 58
  App Store and, 76, 149
  AT&T and, 58
  company value of, 67
  competition and, 25, 42, 58
  Cook and, 183
  digital divide and, 149, 169
  iOS of, 25, 37
  iPads, 78, 175

iPhones, 26, 57–59, 66, 75–76, 91, 97–98, 149, 171
iPods, 91–92
iTunes, 9, 68–69
Jobs and, 68, 76
need for change and, 194
platforms and, 127, 129
privacy and, 76–77
Siri and, 169
standards and, 25, 37, 42
start of, 127
trust and, 183–184
Apple TV, 129
Apps, 66
  advertising and, 12, 90, 102, 164, 169, 188
  credit cards and, 4
  developers of, 61
  digital divide and, 149, 151, 154, 163–165, 168–169, 171
  fitness, 3, 13
  freemium, 76
  iTunes and, 9
  killer, 27
  location data and, 76, 90–92, 95, 97, 102, 136, 179, 184
  platforms and, 121–122, 128, 133–136
  plethora of, 76
  prices and, 56–57, 61
  privacy and, 3, 6, 84, 90–92, 97, 102, 169, 184
  ride hailing, 121
  standards and, 23–24, 27, 37–38
  trust and, 179–180, 184, 188
  weather, 90
App Store, 76, 149
Arnold, Thelma, 71
ARPANET, 27–28, 64
Artificial intelligence (AI)
  digital divide and, 163, 169–170
  do-no-harm approach and, 195
  machine learning and, 20, 80, 144–148, 169–170, 181–182, 189, 195, 200

need for change and, 195, 200
platforms and, 143–146, 148
recommendation systems and, 94–95, 135, 146, 181–182, 189
trust and, 177, 181–184, 189
Ashley Madison, 109–110, 112, 115–117, 176
Assembly lines, 23
Assistants, 61, 66, 135, 169–170, 177, 180, 184, 188
Asymmetric information, 110, 114–116, 120, 185
AT&T
  advertising and, 65
  Bell System and, 24, 29–30, 35, 43, 51, 143, 175
  data governance and, 194
  iPhone and, 57–58
  proprietary system of, 24
  subscriptions and, 24
  Unix and, 35
Auctions, 58, 70, 129, 151, 157

Baidu, 98, 133
Bandwidth, 31, 48, 50–55, 59–61, 159–161
Bankruptcy, 17, 118–119
Banks
  central, 108, 175, 193
  grandeur of, 136
  online, 88, 108, 116
  privacy and, 83, 88, 90, 99, 101
  security and, 108, 116–117
Banner ads, 65, 74, 77
Baran, Paul, 46
Barlow, John Perry, 17
Bell System, 24, 29–30, 35, 43, 51, 143, 175
Berkeley Software Distribution (BSD), 35
Berners-Lee, Tim, 29, 32, 36, 146
Betamax, 21, 25
Big data, 95–96, 178–179, 182, 187–189, 197–200

Bing, 98
Blackmail, 91, 109, 118
Blogs, 21, 65, 131
Bluetooth, 107
Boycotts, 74
BP, 195
Brandeis, Louis, 142
Brief History of Time, A (Hawking), 10
Brin, Sergey, 171
Broadband
  DSL and, 51–53
  networks and, 10, 15, 39, 42, 49–59, 67, 94, 123–124, 150–156, 166–167, 170–171, 188
  prices and, 51–56
Broadband Commission for Sustainable Development, 153, 170
Broadband Genie, 55
Business models
  advertising and, 64–72, 74, 78
  early online, 64–68
  platforms and, 132, 144–145
  privacy and, 93–96, 98, 103, 105
  regulation and, 19
  revenue and, 65 (*see also* Revenue)
  supply/demand and, 10–11, 60–61, 126, 147, 152, 156, 166, 188
  trust and, 183
  Uber and, 129–131
Bytes, 50, 55

Cable networks, 5
  digital divide and, 150, 152, 156
  DOCSIS and, 52
  platforms and, 137
  prices and, 40, 48, 52–53
  standards and, 21, 28
  television and, 8, 31, 52
  trust and, 188
Caches, 161
California Computer Privacy Act, 103
Cambridge Analytica, 5, 86, 92, 96, 104, 175

Candy Crush (game), 76
Capacity
    bandwidth and, 31, 48, 50–55, 59–61,
        159–161
    networks and, 40–41, 46, 49–55, 59,
        61, 133, 137, 150, 159, 162
Carnegie Mellon University, 184
Case, Steve, 49
Central Bank of Bangladesh, 108,
    175
Cerf, Vint, 27, 32
CERN, 29, 32–33, 36
China, 10, 55, 98, 133, 167, 178,
    218n3
Christchurch shooting, 5, 20
Cisco Systems, 114, 151
Clark, David, 32, 108
CNN, 45
Competition
    Amazon and, 6
    antitrust cases and, 24, 123, 125,
        141–145, 147, 175, 195
    Apple and, 25, 42, 58
    digital divide and, 151, 155, 167
    facilities-based, 52–53
    market power and, 42, 122–127, 133,
        140, 143, 187, 197
    monopolies and, 41–43, 53, 123–126,
        142–143, 151
    need for change and, 193, 197
    Netflix and, 69, 121, 128–129, 159,
        182
    perfect, 11
    platforms and, 122–148
    policy for, 122, 140–143, 148, 187,
        192, 215n27
    prices and, 11, 40–44, 50–53, 55,
        57–58, 122–127, 141, 143, 147
    reputation and, 101
    security and, 114, 116, 119
    standards and, 24, 37
    telecommunications and, 19, 40
    television and, 128–129, 159

trust and, 187
    winner-takes-all markets and,
        133–141, 144
Consent, online, 12, 72, 85, 143–146,
    179, 189, 198
Consent Decree, 143
Consumer Reports, 115
Consumers
    advertising and, 65, 67, 72
    digital divide and, 164
    entry barriers and, 15
    need for change and, 195, 197
    platforms and, 124–126, 130,
        134–135, 141–142, 145, 147
    prices and, 41, 51, 55, 60
    privacy and, 88–89, 100, 104–105
    rational, 12
    security and, 111, 114–118
    trust and, 176, 186–187
Consumer surplus, 88
Contact tracing apps, 6
Content-delivery networks (CDNs),
    161
Content ID, 138, 145
Contention ratio, 54
Cook, Tim, 183
Cookies, 4, 71–72, 91, 102, 184
Copyright, 9, 16, 204n1
    digital rights management (DRM) and,
        68
    Directive on Copyright in the Digital
        Single Market and, 214n16
    Europe and, 138
    Napster and, 65, 68
    piracy and, 65
    platforms and, 128, 132, 145
    user agreements and, 89
    YouTube and, 138–139
Core Infrastructure Initiative, 114
COVID-19 crisis, 5, 171, 191
Craigslist, 128
Creative destruction, 121–122, 124, 128,
    130, 143, 147–148

Credit cards, 4, 13–14, 79, 85, 104, 111, 117, 136
Creep factor, 91–92
Crocker, Steve, 32
Crowdfunding, 163–165
Cyberattacks, 5–6, 110–112, 116, 192. *See also* Security

Data breaches
    extent of, 212n8
    need for change and, 192–196, 199–200
    platforms and, 142
    privacy and, 86, 91, 97, 100
    security and, 109–112, 117–120
    trust and, 176, 178, 180, 185
Data divide, 170, 188–189, 195
Data governance, 194–195
Data over Cable Service Interface Specification (DOCSIS), 52
Data philanthropy, 198
Data plans, 6, 57, 59, 61, 101
Data protection, 62, 80, 100–102, 105, 120, 142, 145, 195
Davies, Donald, 46
Day care paradox, 96
Day traders, 67
Declaration of the Independence of Cyberspace, A (Barlow), 17
DecNET, 26
DECODE (Decentralized Citizen Owned Data Ecosystem), 197
Deepwater Horizon, 195
Defense Advanced Research Projects Agency (DARPA), 27, 35
Demand curve, 11, 14, 126
Democracy, 6, 18, 142, 153
Democratic Republic of Congo, 153
Department of Transportation, 108
Developing countries
    digital divide and, 7, 10, 56, 60, 139, 149–164, 167–171, 188

lack of data in, 7
    platforms and, 139
    prices and, 60
Dial-up access, 49–51
Digital divide
    advertising and, 150, 164, 167, 169
    affordability and, 158–162, 216n6
    algorithms and, 167, 170
    Alliance for Affordable Internet and, 216n6
    Amazon and, 169, 180, 184
    Apple and, 149, 169
    apps and, 149, 151, 154, 163–165, 168–169, 171
    availability and, 156–158
    Broadband Commission for Sustainable Development and, 153, 170
    challenges for, 168–170
    competition and, 151, 155, 167
    consumers and, 164
    crowdfunding and, 163–165
    data usage and, 153
    developing countries and, 7, 10, 56, 60, 139, 149–164, 167–171, 188
    economics and, 152, 156–159, 162, 168–171
    email and, 153–154, 159
    Facebook and, 154–156, 158, 161–162, 169
    fiber optics and, 150, 152, 162
    Google and, 156, 161–165, 169
    government and, 149–151, 155–158, 163–167, 188
    health issues and, 163, 166
    innovation and, 163–167, 171
    International Telecommunications Union (ITU) and, 153
    Internet exchange points (IXPs) and, 160–161, 216n14
    Internet service providers (ISPs) and, 159–162
    lack of interest and, 153–154

Digital divide (cont.)
  language and, 150, 154, 162–163, 167,
    169–170, 217n21
  Latin America and, 149, 159–160
  legal issues and, 162
  mobile networks and, 8, 23, 28–31,
    40, 53, 57–60, 75, 134, 149–152,
    155–157, 168, 188, 199
  music and, 153, 160
  networks and, 149–158, 161, 163,
    166–168
  offloading and, 150–151
  platforms and, 139–140
  privacy and, 155, 164, 169
  Project Loon and, 157
  regulation and, 151, 165–169
  relevant content and, 162–165
  revenue and, 151, 157–158, 164,
    168–169, 171
  security and, 155, 164, 169
  simulators and, 149
  skills and, 165–166
  smartphones and, 150, 155, 169
  social media and, 154, 158
  solutions for, 155–166
  standards and, 149, 154
  subscriptions and, 150, 152–153, 155,
    158, 160
  supply and demand issues and, 152–156
  trust and, 164, 188–189
  T-shaped policy and, 166–168
  universal service fund (USF) and,
    157–158
  videos and, 159, 161–163
Digital Equipment Company (DEC), 26,
  31–33
Digital rights management (DRM), 68
Digital subscriber line (DSL), 51–53
Directive on Copyright in the Digital
  Single Market, 214n16
Disney, 76, 129
Domain names, 8–9, 16, 19, 154
Dot-com bubble, 65–67, 69, 129

Drupal, 36
DuckDuckGo, 98
DVD Forum, 25

Economics
  advertising and, 68
  asymmetric information and, 110,
    114–116, 120, 185
  banks and, 83, 88, 90, 99, 101, 108,
    116–117, 136, 149–150, 155, 164,
    170, 175, 193
  behavioral, 92–93
  consumer surplus and, 88
  creative destruction and, 121–122,
    124, 128, 130, 143, 147–148
  crowdfunding and, 163–165
  data brokers and, 103–105
  day care paradox and, 96
  demand curve and, 11, 14, 126
  developing countries and, 7, 60, 139,
    149–153, 156, 159–160, 164, 169, 188
  digital divide and, 152, 156–158, 162,
    168, 170–171
  efficient outcomes and, 89, 126
  financial crisis of 2008 and, 183
  generative context and, 195
  gig economy and, 129
  Great Depression, 130
  information, 89–92
  Internet and, 10–16 (*see also* Internet)
  lockdown and, 5
  need for change and, 192–195,
    198–200
  network effects and, 134, 141, 147–148,
    167, 195
  nonexcludable context and, 112
  nonrival context and, 112–113,
    194–195
  platforms and, 122–123, 126, 130–134,
    138, 143, 147
  prices and, 42 (*see also* Prices)
  privacy and, 83, 85, 88–93, 96–97, 99,
    103–105

public good and, 112–114, 120, 194,
    197–198
response times and, 136
revenue and, 78 (*see also* Revenue)
scarcity and, 3–4, 60
security and, 112, 114, 116–117
small to medium enterprises (SMEs)
    and, 168–169
standards and, 6, 23
sunk cost fallacy and, 137
supply and demand, 10–11, 60–61,
    126, 147, 152–156, 166, 188
universal coverage and, 150
winner-takes-all markets and, 133–141,
    144
Economies of scale
digital divide and, 159, 169
entry barriers and, 136
market power and, 123
need for change and, 195
platforms and, 123, 134, 136–137,
    141, 147–148
response times and, 136
standards and, 25
winner-takes-all markets and, 136–137
Ecuador, 104
EDGE, 153
Efficient outcomes, 89, 126
Egosurfing, 71
Electronic Frontier Foundation, 17, 103
Email
contact information and, 8
development of, 27, 29, 32
digital divide and, 153–154, 159
early, 5, 50, 64
ease of, 3, 9, 13
impact of, 79
internetworking and, 9
as old-fashioned, 44
platforms and, 139, 142
prices and, 6
privacy and, 85, 88, 97, 101
security and, 108–111

smartphones and, 57
social engineering and, 110
spam and, 16, 62, 64, 139
Encryption, 36, 76, 87, 97, 100, 112,
    120, 196
End-to-end principle, 30, 33
English, 22, 154, 162–163, 170
Entry barriers, 15
economies of scale and, 136
need for change and, 199
platforms and, 122–128, 133–137,
    142, 144, 146
prices and, 43, 50, 52
trust and, 187
Esar, Evan, 175
e-Skills Pyramid, 165
Ethernet, 8, 28, 33–34, 37, 66
European Commission, 165
European New Car Assessment Program,
    115
European Union (EU), 14, 100–104,
    141–142, 167, 209n4
Experian, 102
ExxonMobil, 195

Facebook, 73
Cambridge Analytica and, 86
Christchurch shooting and, 20
cost of, 12–13
digital divide and, 154–156, 158,
    161–162, 169
platform power and, 121, 127,
    133–134, 142, 144
privacy and, 86, 88, 92–94, 98–99,
    103–104, 183–184
Safety Check and, 45
start of, 127
trust and, 183–184
winner-takes-all markets and, 133–134,
    142, 144
Your Ad Preferences and, 99
Zuckerberg and, 93, 97, 171, 183
Facebook Live, 20

Face Time, 3, 39
Facial recognition, 97, 181
Facilities-based competition, 52–53
Fact checking, 138
Fair, reasonable, and nondiscriminatory
    (FRAND) rates, 34
Federal Bureau of Investigation (FBI), 107
Federal Communications Commission
    (FCC), 5, 19, 30, 51–52, 58
Federal Trade Commission (FTC), 100, 141
Fiber-optic networks, 8, 28, 53, 57, 137,
    150, 152, 162, 188
Filofax, 66
Filters, 7, 15, 64, 132, 138–139, 192
Fiorina, Carly, 149
First-party cookies, 72
Ford Motor Company, 23, 107
Foundem, 141
France Telecom, 30, 197
Free and open-source software (FOSS), 35
Free-rider problem, 15, 78, 113
Free Software Foundation, 35

Games, 57, 60–61, 75–76, 79, 134, 149,
    152, 171, 180, 187
Gates, Bill, 171
General Data Protection Regulation
    (GDPR), 100, 103, 139, 146, 183, 187
General Motors, 194
Gig economy, 129
Global Pulse, 198
Gmail, 116, 140
Google
    advertising and, 67, 69–70, 73, 77
    Alphabet and, 121, 154, 157, 183, 194
    Android and, 25–26, 35, 37, 42, 135,
        140, 164
    Brin and, 171
    Chromium and, 36
    company value of, 67
    credit card storage and, 14
    digital divide and, 156, 161–165, 169
    FTC and, 141

    need for change and, 194
    Page and, 171
    platform power and, 121, 124, 127,
        129, 133–145
    privacy and, 87, 95, 98, 184
    response times and, 136
    right to be forgotten and, 17
    Schmidt and, 87, 214n19
    search bias and, 141
    security and, 114
    standards and, 25, 36–37
    start of, 127, 140
    trust and, 179, 184
    winner-takes-all markets and, 133–141,
        144
Google Assistant, 169
Google Chrome, 140
Google Docs, 140
Google Drive, 140
Google Fiber, 53
Google Hangouts, 140
Google Maps, 140–141, 179
Google Play, 164
Google Search, 8, 12, 69, 140, 163
Google Shopping, 141
GoTo.com, 69
Governance
    algorithmic, 182
    data, 194–195
    Internet, 16–20, 192–194, 199–200
    Working Group on Internet
        Governance (WGIG) and, 18
Government
    ARPANET and, 27–28, 64
    digital divide and, 149–151, 155–158,
        163–167, 188
    FCC and, 5, 30, 51–52, 58
    GDPR and, 100, 103, 139, 146, 183, 187
    ICANN and, 9
    intervention by, 15–16
    laissez-faire, 20
    market failure and, 14–15, 43, 92–93,
        99, 113, 115, 126, 139, 199

need for change and, 191–194, 198–200

NSFNET and, 28, 64–65, 108

online role of, 17

platforms and, 6, 123, 125–126, 139

prices and, 13, 15, 43, 61–62

privacy and, 83–86, 93, 99–105, 183

regulation and, 4–5, 14–20, 43, 85, 93,
  99, 101, 103, 166, 183, 193, 198

security and, 109, 113, 115, 117–118,
  120

standards and, 25–27, 31

trust and, 179, 183, 188

GPRS, 153

GPS location, 57, 76, 91, 107, 179

Great Depression, 130

Guardian newspaper, 77–78, 94

Hackers

  Ashley Madison and, 109–110, 112,
    115, 117, 176

  automobiles and, 119, 180, 185–186

  data breaches and, 86, 91, 97, 100,
    109–112, 117–120, 142, 176, 178,
    180, 185, 192–196, 199–200

  Heartbleed bug and, 114

  identity theft and, 91, 111, 118

  passwords and, 110–111, 118, 186

  personal data and, 4, 62

  phishing and, 110–111

  Russian, 62

  safety and, 180, 185–186

  security and, 4, 62, 107–120, 179–181,
    185–186, 191

  social engineering and, 110

  trust and, 179–181, 185

  white hat, 181

  zero-day vulnerabilities and, 111–112

Hand, Learned, 123, 125

Hawking, Stephen, 10

Health issues

  advertising and, 70–71, 73

  digital divide and, 163, 166

  need for change and, 197

platforms and, 136

privacy and, 87, 99

security and, 108–109, 119

trackers and, 73

trust and, 177, 180

Heartbleed bug, 114

Hewlett-Packard, 127

Hicks, John, 123, 140

Hollerith, Herman, 179

Home Depot, 176

Hong Kong, 160

Hopper, Grace, 21

Horizontal mergers, 126

Hotspots, 4, 8, 59, 61, 151

Human rights, 83, 87, 193

Hush-a-Phone, 29–30

IBM

  antitrust case against, 175

  data governance and, 194, 198

  Hollerith and, 179

  platforms and, 125–126, 141, 143

  Systems Network Architecture (SNA)
    and, 26

  standards and, 24, 26, 31–32

ICANN (Internet Corporation for
  Assigned Names and Numbers), 9,
  19, 154

Identity theft, 91, 111, 118

Indiegogo, 163

Information and communications
  technology (ICT), 18–19, 24, 143,
  148, 152, 163, 165–166, 194

Initial public offerings (IPOs),
  66–67

Innovation

  creative destruction and, 121–122,
    124, 128, 130, 143, 147–148

  digital divide and, 163–167, 171

  need for change and, 195, 197–198

  permissionless, 29

  platforms and, 122, 124, 140–141,
    145, 147–148

Innovation (cont.)
  risk and, 7
  self-driving cars and, 120, 181,
    185–189, 196
  standards and, 29–30, 37
  sunk cost fallacy and, 137
  trust and, 187
Institute of Electrical and Electronics
  Engineers (IEEE), 33
Intel, 33
Intellectual property (IP)
  copyright and, 9, 16, 65, 128, 132,
    138, 145
  digital rights management (DRM) and,
    68
  Directive on Copyright in the Digital
    Single Market and, 214n16
  legal issues and, 9, 15, 34
  licenses and, 24, 34, 37, 58–59, 113,
    124, 129, 143, 151, 157
  Napster and, 65, 68
  patents and, 31, 34, 36–37, 124
  piracy and, 65
  user agreements and, 89
  WIPO and, 18
International Labor Organization (ILO),
  18
International Organisation for
  Standardisation (ISO), 26
International Telecommunications
  Union (ITU), 18–19, 153
Internet
  applying economics to, 10–16
  broadband, 10, 15, 39, 42, 49, 51–59,
    67, 94, 123–124, 150–156, 166–167,
    170–171, 188
  capacity and, 40–41, 45–46, 49–55, 59,
    61, 133, 137, 150, 159, 162
  digital divide and, 149–171
  DOCSIS and, 52
  domains names and, 8–9, 16, 19,
    154
  end-to-end principle and, 30, 33

explaining, 7–10
  governance and, 16–20, 192–194,
    199–200
  ICANN and, 9, 19, 154
  interconnection and, 47–48
  mobile, 57–59
  need for change and, 191–200
  network infrastructure and, 28–31
    (see also Networks)
  online economic growth and,
    68–75
  packet switching and, 44–48
  permissionless innovation and, 29–31,
    122
  positive impact of, 191–192
  retronyms and, 192–194
  routers and, 8, 21
  standards and, 8 (see also Standards)
  TCP/ICP protocols and, 22, 26–28,
    31–33, 35, 143
  U.S. influence on, 9–10
  World Wide Web and, 8, 28–29,
    32–33, 36, 93, 103, 159
Internet Architecture Board (IAB), 33
Internet Engineering Task Force (IETF),
  32–34, 72, 113, 154
Internet exchange points (IXPs),
  160–161, 216n14
Internet of Things (IoT), 79, 180–182,
  185, 193, 219n15
Internet service providers (ISPs)
  advertising and, 68, 79
  contention ratio and, 54
  digital divide and, 159–162
  prices and, 8, 46–56
  standards and, 21, 29
  subscription model and, 68
  website retrieval and, 9
Internet Society (ISOC), 5, 33, 85, 93,
  103, 193, 209n4, 212n9
Internetworking, 9, 27
Into Thin Air (Krakauer), 176
iPads, 78, 175

iPhones, 26, 57–59, 66, 75–76, 91, 97–98, 149, 171
iPods, 91–92
IPv4 protocol, 203n4
iTunes, 9, 68–69
Ivory Coast, 198

Japan, 134
Jobs, Steve, 68, 76

Kagame, Paul, 152
Kahn, Bob, 27
Kenya, 161
Keywords, 70
Kickstarter, 163
Kleinrock, Leonard, 46
Kodak, 194
Kozmo.com, 66–67
Krakauer, Jon, 176
Kurzweil, Ray, 218n3

LastPass, 118
Latin America, 149, 159–160, 215n4
Law of unintended consequences, 137–140
Leasing, 125–126
Legal issues, 63
  Ashley Madison and, 109, 117
  class actions and, 4
  content blocking and, 132
  copyright and, 9
  digital divide and, 162
  intellectual property (IP) and, 9, 15, 34
  platforms and, 124, 132, 141
  privacy and, 85, 100–101
  search bias and, 141
  security and, 108, 111, 117
  Target and, 111, 117
  user agreements and, 89
  Yahoo! and, 17
Leibowitz, Jon, 141

Libertarian paternalism, 97
Licenses, 24, 34, 37, 58–59, 113, 124, 129, 143, 151, 157
LinkedIn, 97, 102, 176
Linux, 35, 206n33
Local area networks (LANs), 27–28, 33
Location data
  advertising and, 76, 79
  concept of online, 9
  hacking, 179
  privacy and, 4, 76, 84, 88, 90–92, 95, 97–98, 101–102, 136, 179, 184
  security and, 73
  telephones and, 43, 55, 73, 75–76, 90–91, 97–98, 102, 169, 184
  trust and, 179
Long-distance calls, 40, 44
Lotus, 102
Lucasfilm, 76
Lynch, Dan, 31

Ma, Jack, 171
Mac OS, 21, 38
MapQuest, 141
Market failure
  government and, 14–15, 43, 92–93, 99, 113, 115, 126, 139, 199
  Internet of Things (IoT) and, 219n15
  need for change and, 199
  negative externalities and, 116–119
  platforms and, 123, 126, 139
  prices and, 14, 43
  security and, 112–116, 118
  trust and, 185, 189
Market power, 20
  competition and, 42, 122–127, 133, 140, 143, 187, 197
  efficient outcomes and, 89, 126
  governance and, 16
  monopolies and, 41–43, 53, 123–126, 142–143, 151
  need for change and, 192–193, 195, 197, 199–200

Market power (cont.)
  paradox of, 199
  platforms and, 122–127, 133–134,
    140, 143–147
  prices and, 7, 42–43, 122–127, 140,
    143, 183
  trust and, 175, 183, 186–187
Márquez, Gabriel García, 83
Massachusetts Institute of Technology
    (MIT), 46, 108, 198
Mass production, 23
Medallion values, 129–130
Media Lab, 198
Mergers, 4, 19, 79, 126–127, 143, 195
Microsoft, 25, 38, 68, 98, 120, 127, 143,
    193–194
Mobile advertising, 75–77
Modems, 30, 49–54, 143
Monopolies, 41–43, 53, 123–126,
    142–143, 151
Moral issues, 109–110, 117
Mosaic, 5, 32
Mount Everest, 176
Mueller, Robert, 107
Multihoming, 26
Multistakeholder model, 18–19, 198–200
Multiuser dungeons (MUDs), 64
Music, 41
  advertising and, 67, 75, 79
  digital divide and, 153, 160
  digital rights management (DRM) and,
    68
  iTunes and, 9, 68–69
  Napster and, 65, 68
  platforms and, 128, 131
  privacy and, 94
  smartphones and, 57
  streaming, 36, 50, 58, 62, 68, 128
Mworia, Wilfred, 149, 171
Myspace, 144

Nader, Ralph, 107–108
Nairobi, 149, 160–161, 163

NASDAQ, 67
National Physical Laboratory (NPL), 46
National Science Foundation (NSF), 28
National Security Agency (NSA), 86
Natural monopolies, 43, 58, 123–125,
    143, 151
Natural resources, 4, 10
Need for change
  advertising and, 193
  algorithms and, 192
  Amazon and, 192, 194
  Apple and, 194
  competition and, 193, 197
  consumers and, 195, 197
  data breaches and, 192–196, 199–200
  do-no-harm approach and, 195–197
  economics and, 192–195, 198–200
  economies of scale and, 195
  entry barriers and, 199
  Google and, 194
  government and, 191–194, 198–200
  health issues and, 197
  innovation and, 195, 197–198
  market failure and, 199
  market power and, 192–192, 195, 197,
    199–200
  networks and, 195, 199
  personal data and, 194–195, 199
  prices and, 200
  privacy and, 192–193, 195, 197–199
  public good and, 197–198
  regulation and, 192–193, 198, 200
  retronyms and, 192–194
  revenue and, 194
  safety and, 196
  security and, 192–193, 195–196, 199
  smartphones and, 192
  social media and, 191–192
  standards and, 191, 193, 195, 198, 200
Negative externalities, 116–119
Netflix
  competition of, 69, 121, 128–129, 159,
    182

content-delivery networks (CDNs), 161

digital divide and, 159, 161, 163

privacy and, 94–95

recommendations and, 135

standards and, 31, 52

subscription model of, 68

Netscape, 35, 36

Network effects

digital divide and, 154, 163, 167

direct, 23–24

economies of scale and, 134, 141, 147–148, 167, 195

indirect, 23

large online providers and, 141

need for change and, 195

prices and, 135

privacy and, 94

standards and, 23–27, 37

switching costs and, 135

two-sided market and, 135

winner-takes-all markets and, 134–135, 144

Networks

advertising and, 64, 67, 74–75

broadband, 10, 15, 39, 42, 49, 51–59, 67, 94, 123–124, 150–156, 166–167, 170–171, 188

cable, 5, 8, 21, 28, 31, 40, 48, 52–53, 137, 150, 152, 156, 188

capacity and, 40–41, 46, 49–55, 59, 61, 133, 137, 150, 159, 162

digital divide and, 149–158, 161, 163, 166–168

economic benefits of, 5

end-to-end principle and, 30, 33

fiber-optic, 8, 28, 53, 57, 137, 150, 152, 162, 188

internetworking, 9, 27

local area networks (LANs), 27–28, 33

mobile, 8, 23, 28–31, 40, 53, 57–60, 75, 134, 149–152, 155–157, 168, 188, 199

natural monopolies and, 43, 58, 123–125, 143, 151

need for change and, 195, 199

permissionless innovation and, 29–31, 122

platforms and, 123–124, 128, 132–144, 147–148

prices and, 39–53, 56–62

privacy and, 87, 93–94

research, 6

security and, 108

size of, 7

standards and, 22–33, 35, 37

subscriptions and, 9, 24, 30, 40, 49, 51, 54, 55, 67–71, 75, 77–78, 147, 150, 152–153, 155, 158, 160

television and, 8, 23, 25, 30–31, 132

trust and, 188

universal coverage and, 150

utility, 14

virtual private (VPNs), 87

World Wide Web and, 8, 28–29, 32–33, 36, 93, 103, 159

Newspapers, 3, 17, 39, 63, 68, 77–78, 94, 129, 132, 199

New York Times, 70–71, 90, 129, 183

NSFNET, 28, 64–65, 108

Offloading, 150–151

Open Software Initiative, 35

Open-source software, 35–36, 108, 112–114, 120, 139, 206n33

OpenSSL, 36, 114

OpenStand, 33

Open Systems Interconnection (OSI), 26

Operating systems, 24–27, 35, 37–38, 110, 140

Orange, 197–198

Outside Magazine, 176

Packet switching, 44–48

Page, Larry, 171

PalmPilot, 66–67

Passwords
  easy, 97
  hackers and, 110–111, 118, 186
  managers for, 118
  security and, 72–73, 97, 102, 104,
    110–111, 118–120, 186
  social engineering and, 110
Patents
  digital rights management (DRM) and,
    68
  FRAND rates and, 34
  legal issues and, 34
  licenses and, 24, 34, 37, 58–59, 113,
    124, 129, 143, 151, 157
  platforms and, 124
  stacking, 34
  standards and, 31, 34, 36–37
Payment models, 93–96
Peering, 48, 216n14
Permissionless innovation, 29–31, 122
Personal data
  advertising and, 70, 76–79, 90, 139
  Ashley Madison and, 109, 112,
    115–117, 176
  California Computer Privacy Act and,
    103
  data breaches and, 86, 91, 97, 100,
    109–112, 117–120, 142, 176, 178,
    180, 185, 192–196, 199–200
  data sharing and, 145
  do-no-harm approach and, 195–197
  GDPR and, 100, 103, 139, 146, 183,
    187
  hackers and, 4, 62, 107–120, 179–181,
    185–186, 191
  identity theft and, 91, 111, 118
  location data and, 4, 76, 90–92, 95,
    97, 101–102, 136, 179, 184
  need for change and, 194–195, 199
  phishing and, 110–111
  platforms and, 139, 145–146
  privacy and, 6, 20, 62, 77, 85–88, 94,
    100, 102, 139, 145–146, 195, 199

  public good and, 197–198
  recommendation systems and, 94–95,
    135, 146, 181–182, 189
  Solid Pod and, 146
  targeted advertising and, 70, 76, 78–
    79, 90, 95–96
  trust and, 62
  user data vs. processed data, 145
  users' role in, 102–103
Personalized Privacy Assistant Project,
  184
Pew Research Center, 99
Phishing, 110–111
Photos, 73, 84, 97, 104, 109, 118, 144,
  179, 189
Pichai, Sundar, 183
Piracy, 65
Platforms
  advertising and, 122, 128, 131, 133,
    140, 143–144
  algorithms and, 137, 139–140,
    144–145
  Amazon, 121–122, 127, 129, 133–136,
    142, 144
  Android, 25–26, 35, 37, 42, 135, 140,
    164
  Apple, 127, 129
  apps and, 121–122, 128, 133–136
  business models and, 132, 144–145
  competition and, 122–148
  consumers and, 124–126, 130, 134–
    135, 141–142, 145, 147
  content, 131–133
  creative destruction and, 121–122,
    124, 128, 130, 143, 147–148
  data breaches and, 142
  digital divide and, 139–140
  economics and, 122–123, 126,
    130–138, 141, 143, 147–148
  email and, 139, 142
  entry barriers and, 122–128, 133–137,
    142, 144, 146
  Facebook, 121, 127, 133–134, 142, 144

fact-checking and, 138
Google, 121, 124, 127, 129, 133–145
government and, 6, 123, 125–126, 139
health issues and, 136
innovation and, 122, 124, 140–141,
    145, 147–148
legal issues and, 124, 132, 141
market failure and, 123, 126, 139
market power and, 122–127, 133–134,
    140, 143–147
music and, 128, 131
networks and, 123–124, 128, 132–144,
    147–148
patents and, 124
personal data and, 139, 145–146
prices and, 122–129, 134–135, 140–143,
    147
privacy and, 6–7, 84, 93–94, 98, 102,
    142, 145–147
regulation and, 121, 123–124, 130–133,
    139, 143
revenue and, 128, 131, 134, 137, 144
ridesharing, 121, 146, 197
search engines and, 124, 127, 134,
    140, 144
security and, 135, 140, 142, 146–147
size of, 6–7
social media and, 121, 127, 131,
    134–135, 142
standards and, 122, 128, 134, 141,
    146–147
subscriptions and, 147
sunk cost fallacy and, 137
telephony and, 128
television and, 128–129, 132, 135, 140
third parties and, 136, 144
trust and, 123, 125, 129–130, 136
Uber, 121, 129–131, 135, 146
user data vs. processed data, 145
videos and, 128–129, 131, 136, 138, 145
winner-takes-all markets and, 133–141,
    144
Podcasts, 131

Prices
apps and, 56–57, 61
broadband and, 51–56
competition and, 11, 40–44, 50–58,
    122–127, 141, 143, 147
consumers and, 41, 51, 55, 60
demand curve and, 11, 14, 126
developing countries and, 60
dial-up access and, 49–51
digital divide and, 156–162, 216n6
discrimination and, 42–44, 56, 125
efficient outcomes and, 89, 126
email and, 6
entry barriers and, 43, 50, 52
fair, 15
flat-rate, 51, 53
government and, 13, 15, 43, 61–62
Internet economics and, 10–16
Internet service providers (ISPs) and,
    8, 46–56
market failure and, 14, 43
market power and, 7, 42–43, 122–127,
    140, 143, 183
mobile technology and, 57–59
monopolies and, 41–43, 53
need for change and, 200
networks and, 39–53, 56–62, 135
open-source software and, 35–36, 108,
    112–114, 120, 139
packet switching and, 44–48
payment models and, 93–96
platforms and, 122–129, 134–135,
    140–143, 147
privacy and, 93–96
public goods and, 113
refills and, 42
regulation and, 43–44, 51–53, 58
setting, 41–44
smartphones and, 34, 37, 56–58, 60,
    206n24
smart speaker and, 5
smart TV and, 78–79
social media and, 61–62

Prices (cont.)
  stock market and, 66–67, 112, 117
  subscriptions and, 40, 49, 51, 54–55
  subsidies and, 44, 58, 61–62, 76, 157,
    162
  supply/demand and, 10–11, 60–61,
    126, 147, 152, 156, 166, 188
  taxicab medallion values and, 129–130
  technological effects upon, 39–40
  telephony and, 40–45, 49, 52–53, 55–58
  television and, 6, 12
  time-sharing and, 46
  trust and, 157–159, 183, 188
  usage-based, 42
  videos and, 52, 54–57, 60–61
Privacy
  advertising and, 70–71, 80, 90–91,
    94–96, 99, 102–103
  algorithms and, 95, 98
  Amazon and, 73
  analog world and, 83–84
  anonymity and, 70, 85, 87, 90, 94,
    189, 198
  Apple and, 76–77
  apps and, 3, 6, 84, 90–92, 97, 102,
    169, 184
  Ashley Madison and, 109–110, 112,
    115–117, 176
  assistants and, 184
  authentication and, 97
  banks and, 83, 88, 90, 99, 101
  business models and, 93–94, 98, 103,
    105
  California and, 103, 183
  consent and, 85
  consumers and, 88–89, 100, 104–105
  contact tracing apps and, 6
  cookies and, 4, 71–72, 91, 102, 184
  creep factor and, 91–92
  cyberattacks and, 5–6, 110, 116, 192
  data breaches and, 86, 91, 97, 100,
    109–112, 117–120, 142, 176, 178,
    180, 185, 192–196, 199–200

  data brokers and, 103–105
  data protection and, 62, 80, 100–102,
    105, 120, 142, 145, 195
  day care paradox and, 96
  by design, 97–99
  digital divide and, 155, 164, 169
  economics and, 83, 85, 88–93, 96–97,
    99, 103–105
  email and, 85, 88, 97, 101
  encryption and, 36, 76, 87, 97, 100,
    112, 120, 196
  Facebook and, 86, 88, 92–94, 98–99,
    103–104
  FTC and, 100
  GDPR and, 100, 103, 139, 146, 183,
    187
  Google and, 87, 95, 98
  government and, 83–86, 93, 99–105,
    183
  hackers and, 4, 62, 107–120, 179–181,
    185–186, 191
  health issues and, 87, 99
  human rights and, 83, 87
  Hush-a-Phone and, 29–30
  identity theft and, 91, 111, 118
  legal issues and, 85, 100–101
  libertarian paternalism and, 97
  location data and, 4, 76, 84, 88, 90–92,
    95, 97–98, 101–102, 136, 179, 184
  music and, 94
  need for change and, 192–193, 195,
    197–199
  networks and, 87, 93–94
  paradox of, 86–88, 96, 105, 176, 198–
    199, 209n7, 210n17
  passwords and, 72–73, 97, 102, 104,
    110–111, 118–120, 186
  payment models and, 93–96
  personal data and, 6, 20, 62, 77,
    85–88, 94, 100, 102, 139, 145–146,
    195, 199
  Personalized Privacy Assistant Project
    and, 184

platforms and, 6–7, 84, 93–94, 98, 102
public records and, 71
regulation and, 85, 93, 99–104
right to be forgotten and, 17
search engines and, 98
security and, 20, 80, 86, 91, 97, 101–102, 105, 120, 142, 146–147, 155, 164, 169, 175–177, 180, 183, 185, 188, 190, 192, 195, 199
smartphones and, 84, 86, 101
smart speaker and, 5
smart TVs and, 86
social media and, 86, 88, 102
solutions for, 93–103
standards and, 85, 99–100
statements of, 3–4
terms of use and, 3–4
third parties and, 4, 20, 86, 90–91, 99–101
trust and, 86, 94, 100–101, 175–177, 180, 183–185, 187–188, 190
Universal Declaration of Human Rights and, 83
user agreements and, 89
users' role in, 102–103
videos and, 88–89
virtual private networks (VPNs) and, 87
web beacons and, 4
Your Ad Preferences and, 99
Zuckerberg and, 183
Privacy deathstars, 103
Privacy fundamentalists, 87, 98
Privacy International, 103
Processed data, 145
Programmatic ads, 74–75
Project Loon, 157
ProtonMail, 101
Public good, 112–114, 120, 194, 197–198
Public records, 71
Punch cards, 125–126, 141, 179

Radio, 23, 27, 30, 52, 59, 63, 128
RAND Corporation, 46
Recommendation systems, 94–95, 135, 146, 181–182, 189
Regulation
advertising and, 72
cookies and, 72
digital divide and, 151, 165–169
FCC and, 5, 19, 30, 51–52, 58
FTC and, 100, 141
GDPR and, 100, 103, 139, 146, 183, 187
government and, 4 (see also Government)
International Telecommunications Union (ITU) and, 18–19, 153
need for change and, 192–193, 198, 200
platforms and, 121, 123–124, 130–133, 139, 143
prices and, 43–44, 51–53, 58
privacy and, 85, 93, 99–104
right to be forgotten and, 17
risks of, 16
standards and, 22, 30
trust and, 183
Request for Comment (RFC), 32
Response times, 136
Retronyms, 192–194
Revenue
ad blockers and, 77–78
advertising and, 65–70, 74–79, 94, 128, 131, 144, 164
digital divide and, 151, 157–158, 164, 168–169, 171
monopolies and, 41–43, 53, 123–126, 142–143, 151
need for change and, 194
platforms and, 128, 131, 134, 137, 144
search and, 69, 75, 88, 98, 144
supply/demand and, 10–11, 60–61, 126, 147, 152, 156, 166, 188
value of online services and, 88

Ridesharing, 121, 146, 197
Right to be forgotten, 17
Routers, 8, 21
Russian election interference, 5
Rwanda, 152

Safe Harbor agreements, 103
Safety
  automobile, 41, 93, 107–108, 115–120,
    186, 196
  bicycle, 101
  Facebook Safety Check and, 45
  hackers and, 180, 185–186
  need for change and, 196
  online, 101
  seat belts and, 93, 107–108, 196
  smart home and, 180
  trust and, 178, 180, 185–186
Samsung, 86
Sarkozy, Nicolas, 18
Saturday Night Live (TV show), 66
Scarcity, 3–4, 60
Schmidt, Eric, 87, 214n19
Schrems, Max, 102–103
Schumpeter, Joseph, 121–122
Search engines, 8
  advertising and, 69–71
  bias in, 141
  language and, 163, 217n21
  platforms and, 124, 127, 134, 140,
    144
  privacy and, 98
  public records and, 71
  ranking and, 70
  revenue and, 69, 75, 88, 98, 144
  security and, 113
Seat belts, 93, 107–108, 196
Secure Sockets Layer (SSL), 36
Security
  advertising and, 80, 109, 113
  apps and, 4
  Ashley Madison and, 109–110, 112,
    115–117, 176

asymmetric information and, 110,
    114–116, 120, 185
authentication and, 97
banks and, 108, 116–117
Clark on, 108
competition and, 114, 116, 119
consumers and, 111, 114–118
credit cards and, 4
cyberattacks and, 5–6, 110, 116, 192
data breaches and, 86, 91, 97, 100,
    109–112, 117–120, 142, 176, 178,
    180, 185, 192–196, 199–200
data protection and, 62, 80, 100–102,
    105, 120, 142, 145, 195
digital divide and, 155, 164, 169
economics and, 112, 114, 116–117
email and, 108–111
encryption and, 36, 76, 87, 97, 100,
    112, 120, 196
facial recognition and, 97, 181
GDPR and, 100, 103, 139, 146, 183,
    187
Google and, 114
government and, 109, 113, 115,
    117–118, 120
hackers and, 4, 62, 107–120, 179–181,
    185–186, 191
health issues and, 108–109, 119
home, 135
identity theft and, 91, 111, 118
Internet of Things (IoT) and, 185
legal issues and, 108, 111, 117
market failure and, 112–116, 118
National Security Agency (NSA) and,
    86
need for change and, 192–193,
    195–196, 199
negative externalities and, 116–119
networks and, 108
phishing and, 110–111
platforms and, 135, 140, 142, 145–147
privacy and, 20, 80, 86, 91, 97,
    101–102, 105, 120, 142, 146–147,

155, 164, 169, 175–177, 180, 183,
    185, 188, 190, 192, 195, 199
public goods and, 112–114
search engines and, 113
social engineering and, 110
standards and, 19, 38, 107–108,
    112–113, 115, 117, 120
third parties and, 111–112, 116–118,
    120
trust and, 108, 115, 119–120, 175–177,
    180–192
WannaCry and, 5
zero-day vulnerabilities and, 111–112
Self-driving cars, 120, 181, 185–189, 196
Sharkey, Noel, 75
ShowNet, 31
Silicon Valley, 143, 163
Singapore, 160
Siri, 169
Skype, 30, 55–56, 128
Sleeping Giants, 74
Small to medium enterprises (SMEs),
    168–169
Smart homes, 79, 180–182, 185, 193
Smartphones
  advertising and, 75–77
  Android, 35, 37, 42, 140, 164
  apps and, 37
  digital divide and, 150, 155, 169
  email and, 57
  Internet access and, 7
  iPhone, 26, 57–59, 66, 75–76, 91,
    97–98, 149, 171
  mobile networks and, 8, 23, 28–31,
    40, 53, 57–60, 75, 134, 149–152,
    155–157, 168, 188, 199
  music and, 57
  need for change and, 192
  patent stacking and, 34
  prices and, 34, 37, 56–58, 60, 206n24
  privacy and, 5, 84, 86, 101
  ride hailing and, 121
  standards and, 23, 34, 37–38, 42

subscriptions and, 9
  trust and, 188
SMS, 97, 128
Snowden, Edward, 102–103
Social engineering, 110
Social media
  Christchurch shooting and, 20
  digital divide and, 154, 158
  fact-checking and, 138
  need for change and, 191–192
  network size and, 7
  platforms and, 121, 127, 131, 134–135,
    142
  prices and, 61–62
  privacy and, 86, 88, 102
  real cost of, 78–79
  Russian meddling in, 62
  tax on, 158–159
Solid Pod, 146
Sony, 25
Sowell, Thomas, 3
Spam, 16, 62, 64, 139
Spectrum, 24–25, 41, 52, 58–59, 75, 91,
    151, 157
Spotify, 31, 69, 94, 128, 153, 163
Standard-essential patents (SEPs), 34
Standard Oil, 195
Standards
  agreement upon, 22
  Android and, 42
  Apple and, 25, 37, 42
  apps and, 23–24, 27, 37–38
  ARPANET and, 27–28, 64
  AT&T and, 24, 35
  Betamax and, 21, 25
  competition and, 24, 37
  converters and, 26
  cost of, 10
  DecNET, 26
  de facto vs. de jure, 25–26
  development of, 16, 20–38
  digital divide and, 149, 154
  economics and, 6, 23, 25

Standards (cont.)
 embedded, 6
 end-to-end principle and, 30, 33
 Ethernet, 8, 28, 33–34, 37, 66
 FCC and, 5, 30, 51–52, 58
 Google and, 25, 36–37
 government and, 25–27, 31
 IBM and, 24, 26, 31–32
 ICANN and, 9, 19, 154
 IETF and, 32–34, 72, 113, 154
 industrial revolution and, 23
 innovation and, 29–30, 37
 Internet service providers (ISPs) and,
  21, 29
 ISO, 26
 legal, 85
 need for change and, 191, 193, 195,
  198, 200
 networks and, 22–37
 NSFNET and, 28
 open, 22, 26–27, 31–38, 108, 112–114,
  120, 122, 139, 149, 191, 200
 OSI, 26
 passwords and, 72–73, 97, 102, 104,
  110–111, 118–120, 186
 patents and, 31, 34, 36–37
 PC vs. Mac, 21
 permissionless innovation and, 29–31,
  122
 platforms and, 122, 128, 134, 141,
  146–147
 prescriptive, 25–26
 privacy and, 85, 99–100
 public goods and, 113
 regulation and, 22, 30
 rough consensus and, 32
 security and, 19, 38, 107–108, 112–113,
  115, 117, 120
 setting, 22–27
 smartphones and, 23, 34, 37–38, 42
 subscriptions and, 24, 30
 TCP/IP, 22, 26–28, 31–33, 35, 143
 telephony and, 24, 28–31

 television and, 23, 25–26, 30–31
 trust and, 185–189
 VHS, 21, 25
 videos and, 25, 33, 36
 voluntary adoption of, 72
 W3C, 32–34, 113
 wars over, 25
 WebRTC, 32–33
 WGIG and, 18
 World Wide Web, 28–29, 32–33, 36
Standards-developing organizations
  (SDOs), 25–26
Starbucks, 3–4, 39, 62–63, 175, 199
Star Wars (film series), 76
Stock market, 66–67, 112, 117
Stop Enabling Sex Traffickers Act (SESTA),
  214n15
Strava, 73
Streaming
 audio, 36, 50, 62
 music, 36, 50, 58, 62, 68, 128
 videos, 4, 36, 52, 55, 68–69, 128–129,
  136, 159
Strowger, Almon Brown, 40
Subscriptions
 advertising and, 67–71, 75, 77–78
 AT&T and, 24
 digital divide and, 150, 152–153, 155,
  158, 160
 networks and, 9, 24, 30, 40, 49, 51,
  54–55, 67–71, 75, 77–78, 147, 150,
  152–153, 155, 158, 160
 platforms and, 147
 prices and, 40, 49, 51, 54–55
 smartphones and, 9
 standards and, 24, 30
 telephony and, 40
Subsidies, 44, 58, 61–62, 76, 157, 162
Sunk cost fallacy, 137
Super Bowl, 78–79
Supply and demand, 10–11, 60–61, 126,
  147, 152–156, 166, 188
Sutton, Willie, 108

Swahili, 163
Switchboard operators, 40
Switzerland, 12, 14, 44, 101, 113, 150
Systems Network Architecture (SNA), 26

Tablets, 7, 78, 168, 175
Tanzania, 151
Target, 95–96, 110–111, 117, 176
Targeted advertising, 70, 76, 78–79, 90,
    95–96
Tariffs, 53
TaskRabbit, 129
Taxis, 46, 61, 110, 117, 121, 129–131,
    158, 186–187
TCP/IP protocols, 22, 26–28, 31–33, 35,
    143
Telephony. *See also* Smartphones
  DSL and, 51–53
  exchanges and, 45
  location and, 43, 55, 73, 75–76, 90–91,
    97–98, 102, 169, 184
  long-distance calls and, 40, 44
  natural monopolies and, 151
  platforms and, 128
  prices and, 40–45, 49, 52–53, 55–58
  Skype and, 128
  standards and, 24, 28–31
  switchboard operators and, 40
  trunk lines and, 40
  volume limits of, 45
Television
  advertising and, 63, 78, 140
  airwave spectrum and, 52
  broadcast, 12, 52, 112–113, 128, 140
  cable, 8, 31, 52
  competition and, 128–129, 159
  DOCSIS and, 52
  networks and, 8, 23, 25, 30–31, 132
  physical world and, 9
  platforms and, 128–129, 132, 135, 140
  prices and, 6, 12
  privacy and, 86
  as public good, 112–113

smart TV and, 78–79, 86
  standards and, 23, 25–26, 30–31
Tencent, 133
Terms of use, 3–4
Tesla, 133, 196
Text messages, 30, 75, 97, 101, 128, 142,
    155, 159, 161
Third parties
  advertising and, 72, 76
  cookies and, 72
  government and, 14
  market failure and, 14
  negative externalities and, 116–118
  platforms and, 136, 144
  privacy and, 4, 20, 86, 90–91, 99–101
  security and, 111–112, 116–118, 120
Time-sharing systems, 46
Tomlinson, Ray, 29
Trump, Donald, 90, 97, 138
Trunk lines, 40
Trust
  algorithms and, 181–182, 187, 189
  Apple and, 183–184
  apps and, 179–180, 184, 188
  artificial intelligence (AI) and,
    181–183
  big data and, 178–179, 182, 187–189
  business models and, 183
  competition and, 187
  consumers and, 176, 186–187
  data breaches and, 176, 178, 180, 185
  digital divide and, 164, 188–189
  entry barriers and, 187
  Facebook and, 183–184
  future and, 175–190
  Google and, 179, 184
  government and, 179, 183, 188
  hackers and, 179–181, 185
  health issues and, 177, 180
  innovation and, 187
  Internet of Things (IoT) and, 180–182,
    185
  market failure and, 185, 189

Trust (cont.)
  market power and, 175, 183, 186–187
  networks and, 188
  paradox of, 176–178
  personal data and, 62
  platforms and, 123, 125, 129–130, 136
  prices and, 157–159, 183, 188
  privacy and, 86, 94, 100–101, 175–177,
    180, 183–188, 190
  regulation and, 183
  safety and, 178, 180, 185–186
  security and, 108, 115, 119–120,
    175–177, 180–192
  smartphones and, 188
  solutions for, 183–187
  standards and, 185–189
  violation of, 7
TrustArc, 100–101
T-shaped policy, 166–168
Twitter, 12, 97, 138

Uber, 164, 197, 212n1
  business model of, 129–131
  disruption of, 129–131
  platforms and, 121, 129–131, 135, 146
  privacy and, 100, 102
  trust and, 176, 186–188
Uganda, 158
UL (Underwriters Laboratories), 115
United Nations, 18, 83–84, 198
Universal Acceptance Steering Group
  (UASG), 154
Universal service fund (USF), 157–158
Unix, 26, 35, 37, 143
Unsafe at any Speed (Nader), 107–108
Urban Melting Pot, 104
US Communications Decency Act, 132,
  213n9
User 927 (play), 71
User agreements, 89

Venture capital, 66–67, 69, 164
Verizon, 45

Vertical mergers, 126
Vestager, Margrethe, 141
VHS, 21, 25
Videos
  advertising and, 68–69, 75, 78–79
  bandwidth and, 159
  calls with, 4, 33
  digital divide and, 159, 161–163
  ease of uploading, 9
  platforms and, 128–129, 131, 136,
    138, 145
  prices and, 52, 54–57, 60–61
  privacy and, 88–89
  standards and, 25, 33, 36
  streaming, 4, 36, 52, 55, 68–69,
    128–129, 136, 159
Virtual private networks (VPNs), 87
Vision 2020, 152
Voice recognition, 86, 135, 169–170, 188

W3C, 32–34, 113
Wainwright, John, 213n10
Walmart, 192–193
Wanamaker, John, 63–64, 78
WannaCry attack, 5
Watergate, 175
Web beacons, 4
WebRTC, 32–33
West, Kanye, 97
Westin, Alan, 209n8
WhatsApp, 30, 45, 128, 162, 165
Wikipedia, 35, 162–163
Windows, 38, 68, 120
Winner-takes-all markets
  economics of, 133–141, 144
  law of unintended consequences and,
    137–140
  network effects and, 134–135
  sunk cost fallacy and, 137
Working Group on Internet Governance
  (WGIG), 18
World Bank, 149, 155, 170
World Economic Forum, 198

World Health Organization (WHO), 18
World Intellectual Property Organiza-
    tion (WIPO), 18
World Summit on the Information
    Society, 18
World Trade Center, 44–45
World Trade Organization (WTO), 18
World Wide Web, 8, 28–29, 32–33, 36,
    93, 103, 159
World Wide Web Foundation, 93, 103

Xerox, 33

Yahoo!, 17, 116
Yassir, 164
YouTube, 6
  broadband and, 52
  Content ID and, 138–139, 145
  copyright and, 138–139
  platform power and, 131, 135,
    138–139, 145, 154, 161–162
  privacy and, 88
  standards and, 31

Zero-day vulnerabilities, 111–112
Zuckerberg, Mark, 93, 97, 171, 183